ENCHANTED

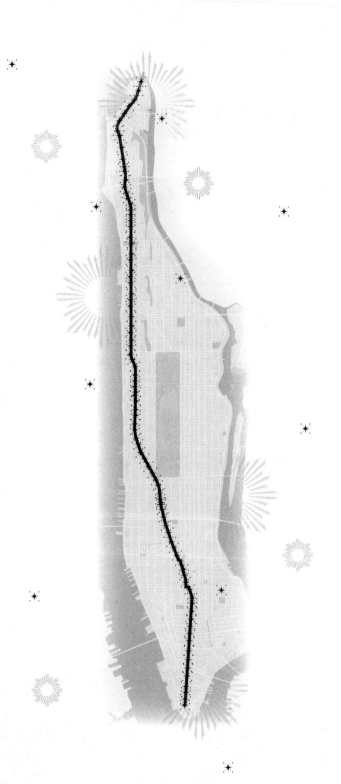

Enchanted New York

A JOURNEY ALONG BROADWAY
THROUGH MANHATTAN'S
MAGICAL PAST

Kevin Dann

WASHINGTON MEWS BOOKS

An Imprint of

NEW YORK UNIVERSITY PRESS

New York

WASHINGTON MEWS BOOKS
An Imprint of
NEW YORK UNIVERSITY PRESS
New York
www.nyupress.org

References to Internet websites (URLs) were accurate at the time of writing. Neither the author nor New York University Press is responsible for URLs that may have expired or changed since the manuscript was prepared.

Library of Congress Cataloging-in-Publication Data
Names: Dann, Kevin T., 1956– author.
Title: Enchanted New York : a journey along Broadway through Manhattan's magical past / Kevin Dann.
Other titles: Journey along Broadway through Manhattan's magical past
Description: New York : Washington Mews Books, an imprint of New York University, [2020] | Includes bibliographical references and index.
Identifiers: LCCN 2020005750 | ISBN 9781479860227 (cloth) | ISBN 9781479838264 (paperback) | ISBN 9781479828746 (ebook) | ISBN 9781479862061 (ebook)
Subjects: LCSH: Broadway (New York, N.Y.)—History—Anecdotes. | Magic—New York (State)—New York—History—Anecdotes. | Manhattan (New York, N.Y.)—History—Anecdotes. | New York (N.Y.)—History.
Classification: LCC F128.67.B7 D36 2020 | DDC 974.7/1—dc23
LC record available at https://lccn.loc.gov/2020005750

New York University Press books are printed on acid-free paper, and their binding materials are chosen for strength and durability. We strive to use environmentally responsible suppliers and materials to the greatest extent possible in publishing our books.

Book designed by Charles B. Hames. Typeset by Andrew Katz.

Manufactured in the United States of America

10 9 8 7 6 5 4 3 2 1

Also available as an ebook

For my father, Tyler Watts Dann,

my first guide on Broadway

CONTENTS

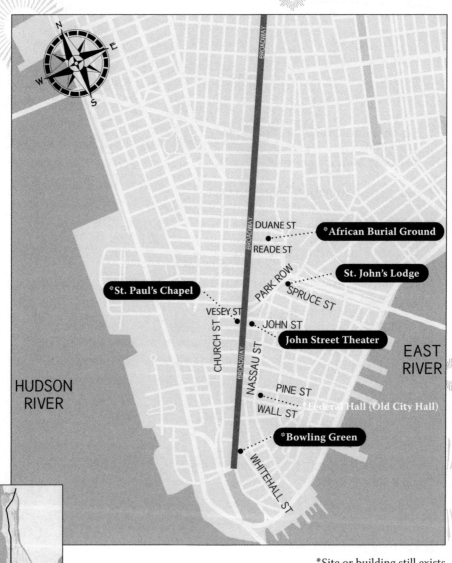

*St. Paul's Chapel

*African Burial Ground

St. John's Lodge

John Street Theater

Federal Hall (Old City Hall)

*Bowling Green

DUANE ST
READE ST
PARK ROW
SPRUCE ST
VESEY ST
CHURCH ST
JOHN ST
NASSAU ST
PINE ST
WALL ST
WHITEHALL ST
BROADWAY

HUDSON
RIVER

EAST
RIVER

*Site or building still exists

An Enchanted Inauguration

1789

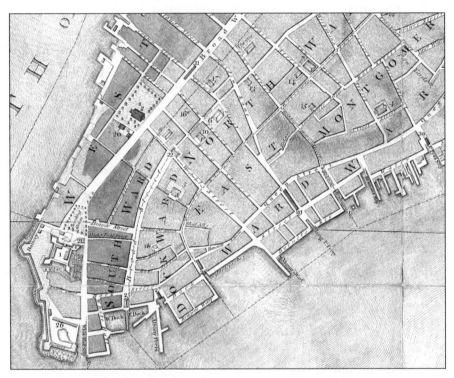

John McComb and Cornelius Tiebout's 1789 plan of the city of New York
(Library of Congress)

A T sunrise, the boom of artillery rang out from Broadway's southern terminus at old Fort George, across from Bowling Green. Almost as soon as the last cannon blast had sounded, men from all sections of the city began to gather before the mansion on Cherry Street that had only a week before become General George Washington's temporary home, in preparation for the military procession of five hundred men who would accompany their former commander in chief to the old City (now "Federal") Hall on Wall Street for his inauguration. Not since the British departure—and Washington and the Continental Army's triumphal procession down Broadway—in 1783 had the city seen such an enthusiastic throng of citizens fill the streets. At nine a.m., the bells of all the city's churches chimed for half an hour while congregants of every faith gathered to pray for heaven's blessing on their new government and for the favor and protection of their president-elect.

Outside City Hall, at the moment that Washington spoke the oath of office—his left hand over his heart, his right placed solemnly on a Bible supplied from the nearby St. John's Lodge of Freemasons— the crowd became silent. Washington then stooped to kiss the Bible, on which Jacob Morton, a local businessman and Grand Master of the St. John's Lodge serving as aide to the inauguration's marshal, stepped forward to mark the place Washington had placed his lips— Genesis 49 and 50, in which a dying Jacob reminds the Israelites that God had promised them a new land.

Stepping back inside to address Congress, Washington began by giving thanks for the "invisible hand" he esteemed to have brought forth the new nation. "Every step . . . by which the United States had come into being," Washington said, "seems to have been distinguished by some token of providential agency." As Washington walked up Broadway to St. Paul's Chapel for the prayer service after the inauguration, every man, woman, and child clamoring for a view of the great man would have held this as a blessed truth.

In the evening, there were fireworks surpassing any before seen in the city, and at the foot of Broadway between the Bowling Green and the Fort, there was a mammoth transparent painting depicting Washington overlighted by the allegorical figure of Fortitude. The facade of the John Street Theater was almost covered with magic-lantern illustrations, the chief one showing Fame as an angel from heaven, crowning Washington with the emblems of immortality. Broadway's grandest residences—the mansions of the French minister Count de Moustier and the Spanish minister Don Diego Gardoqi across from Bowling Green—also sported illuminated allegorical panoramas so striking that *Fenno's Gazette* declared them "a new, an animated, and enchanting spectacle."

As a byword for the events of April 30, 1789, "enchanting" hung between the older, magically charged meanings of "fascinating," "glamorous," or "bewitching" and the milder, post-Enlightenment sense of deeply entertaining. New Yorkers and others attending the inauguration of the country's first president were certainly "enchanted" by the tolling bells, the fireworks, the magic-lantern displays, and most of all, the charismatic presence of their beloved hero, Washington. Having suffered seven years of devastating war and occupation, then another half a dozen years of uncertainty about the fate of the new republic and their own city, New Yorkers were overcome by an awesome sense of relief, pride, and gratitude for their good fortune on this day.

Still, something more than secular enchantment was afoot in New York on inauguration day; George Washington's invocation of "Providence" signaled a magical, miraculous dimension to this auspicious occasion. Sharing with most Americans of his time the "Doctrine of Providence"—the belief that God acted directly in human affairs—he had throughout his life experienced this in a spectacular and widely acknowledged fashion. Washington's whole biography had seemed an act of magic, though he would never deign to use that word. New Yorkers loved to tell the story of Washington's extraordinarily fortunate Providence in August 1776, when a heavy fog suddenly dropped over the East River to hide the massive retreat of the Continental Army that he had ordered after the three-day-long Battle of Brooklyn. In July 1755, shortly after becoming one of Major General Edward Braddock's aide-de-camps, Washington was close by Braddock as a member of his force of fourteen hundred men as they forded the Monongahela River to attack the French and Indians at Fort Duquesne. As they were ambushed by whooping Ottawa and Potawatomi and surrounded by nine hundred French soldiers, the scene quickly devolved into a slaughterhouse. Sent by Braddock to retrieve two lost cannon and to direct a charge up a nearby hill, Washington was forced to ride all about the battlefield, where, despite having two horses shot out from under him, he miraculously escaped the rain of bullets—half a dozen of which ripped through his coat.

In letters, speeches, and conversations, Washington consistently employed "Providence" to describe the "inscrutable" workings of an "Omnipotent," "benign," and "beneficent" being that he alternately called the "Great Ruler of Human Events," "Supreme Ruler," "Author of the Universe," and—in the language of his brethren Freemasons—"Grand Architect." Washington amalgamated Freemasonic Deism with his homespun practical Stoicism to shape a much more liberal philosophy of life than the superstitious Providentialism of the United States' Puritan progenitors, who tended to see the working of the spiritual world for good and ill in even the most trivial of events. Along with Washington, all of the members of Congress, the governor and foreign ministers, judges, and other leaders who attended his inaugural address looked upon this earlier Providentialism as primitive superstition. Yet they themselves were hardly free of superstition and magical beliefs. Washington's kissing of the Bible, Jacob Morton's marking of the passages, and the widespread interpretation of the biblical text as prophetically affirming the United States' own providential destiny all subtly hint that beyond the popular belief in divine miracles, even the age's most enlightened acted in an "enchanted" manner, especially on ceremonial occasions.

In 1784, George Washington had learned from his close friend the Marquis de Lafayette of a more direct form of magical enchantment: *animal magnetism*, the Viennese physician Franz Anton Mesmer's term for a method of healing that he had discovered in 1779 and of which Lafayette—one of Mesmer's first students after his arrival in Paris—had himself become a devoted practitioner and proselytizer. Just before departing for America in June 1784, Lafayette had written to Washington to share his enthusiasm for Mesmer's great discovery: "I know as Much as Any Conjurer Ever did, Which Remind's me of our old friend's at Fiskills Enterview with the devil that Made us laugh So Much at His House, and Before I go, I will Get leave to let You into the Secret of Mesmer, which, you May depend Upon, is a Grand philosophical discovery." The "old friend at Fiskills" was Derrick Brinckerhoff, whose Fishkill mansion had served in 1777 as General Washington's headquarters and was where Lafayette had been nursed back to health in the fall of 1778. Lafayette's juxtaposition of "Conjurer" and the allusion to Brinckerhoff's supernatural tale places mesmerism in the context of magic, while his description of animal magnetism as a "Grand philosophical discovery" allies it with the rationalist, Enlightenment practice of science.

Revolutionary-era New York City was similarly poised between the intimate, animate, participatory, and sometimes magical consciousness of its colonial past and the instrumental, mechanistic, and antimagical consciousness of the nineteenth-century future. Most New Yorkers still trafficked in supernatural explanations and folklore, but a social and intellectual elite was fast making the city a crucible of the new natural philosophy that self-consciously aligned itself against all things "enchanted" that threatened to disturb and disrupt good civic order. Though New York's mayor had bestowed upon Lafayette the honorary title of Free Citizen during Lafayette's monthlong visit in September 1784, the city's physicians and other learned men had spurned his invitations to found in New York City a branch of the Societé de l'Harmonie Universelle—the Paris-based organ for the dissemination of mesmerism. At the American

Philosophical Society (APS) in Philadelphia, Lafayette had told members how, while aboard the *Courrier de New York* on his voyage from Paris to New York, he had used animal magnetism to revive a dying cabin boy who had fallen from the rigging. Warned already by their philosophical colleague APS founder Benjamin Franklin— who had led an investigation commissioned by the king of France— that mesmerism was a dangerous sham, the skeptical Philadelphians resisted Lafayette's proselytizing. By the time of his ten-day sojourn with Washington at Mount Vernon in November, Lafayette had found upstate among the Shakers at Niskayuna and the Oneida Indians gathered at Fort Stanwix in Rome to negotiate a peace treaty convincing evidence that Mesmer's animal magnetism was truly a universal principle. His efforts to promote mesmerism as a unifying, healing agent in the United States were largely foiled, however, by Benjamin Franklin's and Thomas Jefferson's sustained, strident efforts to discredit animal magnetism and its discoverer.

Lafayette brought to Mount Vernon a letter from Mesmer asking Washington to join the Society of Harmony. Appealing to the general as "the man who merited most of his fellow-men," Mesmer hoped that Washington would naturally take an interest in animal magnetism as a "revolution that might bring about the good of humanity." Washington very respectfully declined. Lafayette had told the American Philosophical Society members that he was not at liberty to disclose how mesmerism imparted its special powers to men but had promised to reveal just this to his bosom friend General Washington. Whether he ever did so remains a mystery, just as largely do the magical properties and potentials of Mesmer's discovery.

Mesmer, Lafayette, and Washington could speak openly about animal magnetism because it fell under the rubric of natural philosophy, no matter how strenuously it was opposed by what seemed to be the majority of scientific people. For every skeptical philosopher who used "wizard," "sorcerer," and "conjuror" as defamatory epithets, there was another who recognized Mesmer and his method as profoundly *magical* and employed these terms out of respect, curiosity, and admiration. The healing miracles, uncanny clairvoyance, and other hidden human powers revealed under the influence of animal magnetism truly did seem to be the harbingers of a *Novo Ordo Seclorum.*

* * *

Mesmer's and Lafayette's circumspection about the mechanics of their methods is characteristic of magical practice in all times and places. Dangerous at best, deadly and destructive at worst, the arcane art of magic is necessarily shrouded in protective secrecy because it is immensely powerful. Indeed, many "modern" sciences and technologies can best be recognized as (largely unconscious) magic because of the degree to which they are "occulted," that is, hidden from public view. If, in the past, magic was confusingly mercurial because of the secrecy that attended it, today it confounds largely because the materialistic worldview fails to come to terms with an art, science, and technology that, for all of its physical effects, always relies on invisible spiritual forces and beings to be effectual. Oblivious and opaque to these higher and subtler dimensions, our best science either ignores or actively rejects the magical realm.

Having originally employed magnets and then *baquets*—wooden tubs filled with iron filings, glass shards, and water—as electrostatic vectors for the universal fluid Mesmer believed to be the basis of animal magnetism's effects, he eventually abandoned these aids when he realized that it was the magnetizer's *will*, not any physical prostheses, that caused the healings and other effects. If the human will is the primary agent of magic, it would seem that all human activity is potentially magical—and so it is, and all organic and inorganic nature is potentially open to the working of the will. However, almost all human activity in modern times is routine, prosaic, unmagical, even if it is predicated on relatively arcane, specialized knowledge. What distinguishes *magical* will activity is its conscious aim to penetrate and utilize hidden powers of nature.

The rise of scientific anthropology and ethnology in the nineteenth century engendered the proliferation of conceptions of and definitions for magic predicated on the explicit and vehement rejection of it as real. To sidestep the terminological and theoretical tangle about magic, one can do no better than to listen to the words of the adoptive New Yorker and magical adept Helena Petrovna Blavatsky, who penned this magisterial descriptive survey of magic's underlying force from her Irving Place quarters in 1874:

> The Chaos of the ancients, the Zoroastrian sacred fire, or the *Atash-Behram* of the Pârsîs; the Hermes-fire, the Elmes-fire of the ancient Germans; the lightning of Cybele; the burning torch of Apollo; the flame on the altar of Pan; the inextinguishable fire in the temple on the Acropolis, and in that of Vesta; the fire-flame of Pluto's helm; the brilliant sparks on the caps of the Dioscuri, on the Gorgon's head, the helm of Pallas, and the staff of Mercury; the Egyptian *Ptah, Ra*; the Grecian *Zeus Kataibates* (the descending); the pentecostal tongues of fire; the burning bush of Moses; the pillar of fire of the *Exodus*, and the "burning lamp" of Abram; the eternal fire of the "bottomless pit"; the Delphic oracular vapors; the Sidereal Light of the Rosicrucians; the *Akâsa* of the Hindu Adepts; the Astral light of Éliphas Lévi; the nerve-aura and the fluid of the magnetists; the *Od* of Reichenbach; the fire-globe or meteor-*cat* of Babinet; the *Psychod* and "ectenic" force of Thury; the psychic force of Sergeant Cox and Mr. Crookes; and the atmospheric magnetism of some naturalists; galvanism; and finally, electricity—are but various names for many different manifestations or effects of the same mysterious, all-pervading Cause, the Greek *Archaeus*, or ἀρχαῖος.

Blavatsky accepted Mesmer's invisible magnetic fluid as the very same magical agent known throughout the ages. A natural-born magician as surely as was Franz Anton Mesmer, Madame Blavatsky recognized and celebrated Mesmer as the rediscoverer and rejuvenator of the essence of all these ancient magical doctrines. One must look to Blavatsky and other magicians, rather than Franklin and Jefferson and their Royal Commissions (and Mesmer, who was as poor an expositor of his science as he was nonpareil as practitioner) for any guidance through the maze that is magic. Most often, Blavatsky called Mesmer's magnetic fluid the "astral light," deeming it "the same as the *sidereal* light of Paracelsus and other Hermetic philosophers, . . . the ether of modern science, . . . the *anima mundi* of Nature and all the cosmos." As many as there are different names given to this veiled universal aspect of nature, humanity has devised rites, rituals, and techniques to actively work with it. History is also universally marked by episodes when this powerful "fluid" is active in human affairs but goes unrecognized by all but a small circle of initiates into magical knowledge. New York City since the American Revolution has been a place where, at each step of its prodigious biography, both witting and unwitting actors have engaged in magic, often with enormous historical consequences rippling out far beyond Manhattan's shores.

* * *

Mesmer's healing magic also shared a great deal with contemporary folk magical practices—whether in Germany, France, or across the Atlantic in America. Indeed, while urban elites mocked Mesmer and his students, rural people understood his magical role and methods as clearly akin to their communities' traditions of cunning men and women who possessed supernatural powers. Beyond lower Broadway's fashionable and glamorous mansions, in the shipyards and markets, in taverns and tan yards, and on most Manhattan farms, there was little "science" (it would be decades before the word entered the vernacular) and much cosmological, alchemical, and astrological mother wit and wisdom, mixed with the enchanted inner landscape of "Wonders" and "Providences," full of more than merely natural portent and power. Though not by any means the enchanted isle of Shakespeare's *The Tempest*, Manhattan in 1789 had its fair share of Prosperos who sought by way of sorcery and spirits to increase harvests, protect ships and sailors from harm, and heal illness. Folk magic was common enough that the New York State Legislature, the year before the inauguration, had included "all jugglers, and all persons pretending to have skill in physiognomy, palmistry, or like crafty science, or pretending to tell fortunes, or to discover where lost goods may be found" in a new statute "for apprehending and punishing disorderly Persons."

A considerable number of New Yorkers at the time of Washington's inauguration were not so much enchanted as *enchained*. Every fifth person living in the city in 1789 was a slave; George and Martha Washington had as members of their Broadway mansion household in 1790 seven African slaves: William Lee, Christopher Sheels, Giles, Paris, Austin, Moll, and Oney Judge. Regarded as property, not citizens, African slave laborers largely built Broadway and its buildings (including the original Trinity Church, in 1697), but no Liberty Pole was erected for them. At the time of the Revolution, New York had the highest number of enslaved Africans of any English colony and the highest ratio of slaves to Europeans of any northern settlement.

New York City's Africans practiced a highly syncretic form of indigenous magic metamorphosed through its contact with the Creole cultures of both the Caribbean and New York City itself. Archeological finds from the "Negroes Burial Ground" (today the African Burial Ground National Monument at Broadway and Duane) give us some inkling of the magical dimension of eighteenth-century black New Yorkers. Conjuring bundles of iron spheres, quartz, and round disks were placed inside the coffins; one older woman wore around her waist a string of blue and gold beads and cowrie shells, and there was an unused clay pipe—tobacco still in that age holding much of its ceremonial aspect of sending thoughts and prayers to heaven—beneath her. Archeologists believe that some of the beads found with the dead were manufactured in Ghana and other parts of Africa. The cowrie shells alone conjure cosmologies and cosmic conflict, as they were the preferred material for the dice tossed in *owó mérindinlógun*—"sixteen cowries"—the principal Yoruba divination technique.

New York's series of slave insurrections—imagined or real—suggest that the city was in that "enlightened" eighteenth century never free from the same sort of mortal fear that drove the Salem witch hysteria. In 1712—the year the African Burial Ground is thought to have opened, perhaps to bury the executed dead from the revolt—twenty-three enslaved Africans killed nine whites and injured six others. Seventy Africans were arrested. Of twenty-seven who were put on trial, seven were executed, one by breaking on a wheel—a form of punishment outlawed for whites at the time. Six of those arrested were reported to have committed suicide. Magical practices are most intensively cultivated when there is an imbalance of power; in the 1712 slave uprising, the conspirators bound themselves to secrecy by sucking the blood of each other's hands and were given even greater spiritual aid by a free black sorcerer who gave out a powder that, when rubbed on their clothing, made them invulnerable to harm from their oppressors.

No accounts have been found that give a picture of the ceremonial dimension of this sacred ground, but there is one place where the burial ground's memory is decisively and suggestively mapped and that must be reckoned with as another important aspect of magic: the black-magical psychological effects of torture, murder, and terror. In 1813, seventy-six-year-old David Grim created from memory a map entitled *A Plan of the City and Environs of New York as They Were in the Years 1742, 1743 and 1744* that does not directly label the African Burial Ground but marks it off as an event: the "Negro Plot of 1741," a purported slave insurrection that coincided with a series of thirteen large fires in Manhattan. Of the two hundred people arrested, seventy-two men had been deported to Newfoundland, the West Indies, and the Madeiras. How many people were burned, hanged, or gibbeted is unknown; the bodies of two supposed ringleaders were left to rot in public view for weeks.

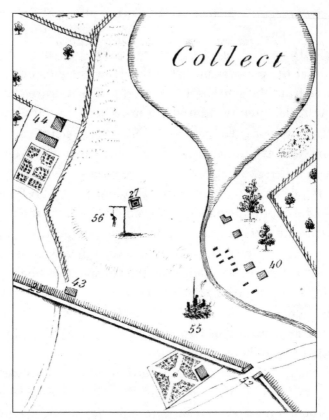

Detail from *A Plan of the City and Environs of New York as
They Were in the Years 1742, 1743 and 1744*
(New York Public Library Digital Collection)

Grim drew two silhouetted images of black figures on his map,
one hanging from a gibbet (or gallows), the other burning at the stake
(marked by 56 and 55, respectively, on the map). Four years old when
the insurrection occurred, he had like most of the city's children been
taken to view the executions. "I have," Grim wrote, "a perfect idea of
seeing the Negroes chained to a stake, and there burned to death."
This was exactly the purpose of these brutal public executions—to
dramatically demonstrate to all that there were deadly consequences
for contravening established authority. Seventy-two years after Grim

witnessed the gruesome spectacle, he engraved his own inner terror on his map. Even in the most modern societies, torture, murder, and terror *haunt*, by way of their psychological grip on witnesses. Perhaps no island on Earth has experienced this more deeply, and with more devastating social, political, and spiritual consequences, than Manhattan.

As surely as compassion, friendship, and sympathy are magically charged blessings, antipathy—hostility, enmity, violence, terror—is far more than a metaphorical curse; it has magical effects. The lesson from the Franklin commission's debunking of Mesmer's healing powers was not that magic is not real but that one cannot divorce magic from morality. Mesmer, Lafayette, and Washington were powerful magicians because of their profound love and sympathy for the highest human ideals. The Freemasonry to which Franklin, Washington, Lafayette, and so many of their Enlightenment brethren belonged was meant to be a path of moral development, ensuring the benevolent, *philanthropic*—that is, imbued with the love of humanity—working of their will. Absent true philanthropy, magic will always become sorcery. We moderns often act as willful magicians, perilously lacking any of the traditional spiritual safeguards.

The events of April 30, 1789, in lower Manhattan truly were an enchanted inauguration, ritually encompassing all the philanthropic potentials of that moment. Even the very word "inauguration" has magical roots, for the Latin *inauguratio* meant "consecration," in the sense of "installment under good omens." Uniquely favored by the gods, George Washington, New Yorkers, and the American people simultaneously received and summoned divine favor on that day, by the exercise of faithful and sincere powers of hope and gratitude.

* * *

"Magic" to most modern ears now means sleight-of-hand stage illusion. Emerging within Western culture, the term has historically often had pejorative connotations, with things labeled magical perceived as being socially unacceptable, primitive, or foreign. Indeed, globally, societies have largely defined themselves as modern by the degree to which they have banished magical practice. Modernity means many things but at its foundation implies the rejection of the reality of the spiritual world and, with that rejection, a conscious and sustained dismissal of magic. Modern magical episodes have tended to be erased from orthodox histories, in a manner parallel to how certain natural phenomena drop from scientific sight, consigned to the "paranormal." This book seeks to uncover these histories in the United States' premier perennially magical city.

New York's story has always been the United States' story; this is true equally in "the magician's land" as in music, theater, and art. The city has incubated, generation after generation, a suite of strange and preternatural productions that can only be described as magical. Walking up New York's central thoroughfare, Broadway, this Promethean avenue, we are afforded an alternative history of the United States, one that feels more like Neil Gaiman's *American Gods* than your college American history textbook. Mapping these sites and stories as a journey through time up Broadway, this guidebook to magical Manhattan offers a history hidden from your *Lonely Planet* or *Fodor's* guide. The historical avenue traced here clearly shows that—paraphrasing what the historian and sociologist of science Bruno Latour has said about our mistaken claim to a universal procession toward modernity—"we have never been disenchanted."

Magic is the putting into practice of the principle that the *subtle always and everywhere rules the dense.* "Mind over matter" is not just a prosaic truism; it is the foundation of magical practice. Subtler than matter, spirit is the superior agent, so all activity that works directly with spiritual forces and beings is inherently magical. Psychic phenomena, anomalous natural events, precognition, psychokinesis, clairvoyance, near-death experiences, astral travel, and those who experience them or make serious study of them have all been marginalized from scholarly historical work. These borderland phenomena—which hold such a powerful fascination in modern popular culture—and their histories invite exploration because they subvert and disrupt our conventional wisdom and offer new insights about how and what we hold to be true about the world.

In former ages when belief in magic was universal, a small group of skilled practitioners mastered their culture's techniques to divine future events; bring about changes in nature, like making rain or augmenting agricultural harvests; and communicate directly with higher spiritual beings through mediumship. Magicians the world over followed strictly prescribed ritual formulas to heal, to divine, and to otherwise intervene in the visible physical world by spiritual, invisible means. Given the principle of the subtle ruling the dense, the "hardware" of magic has always been rudimentary and easily accessible to all, while the "software"—the elaborate symbolic systems to enact magic—universally requires intense personal preparation, strict soul hygiene, and prodigious study of arcane texts and images.

Enchanted New York illuminates that at every stage of New York City's history, there have been individuals and communities dedicated to using magic for both practical, short-term goals and lofty, often utopian ends. Following the trail of tales in this book, one might even say that Manhattan has long been the site of a protracted magical battle, one whose outcome still remains uncertain. A disenchanted age necessarily mistakes the causes and consequences of magical events both as they happen and, retrospectively, when it comes to consider them as history. Though the histories of Freemasonry, mesmerism, Spiritualism, Fortean phenomena, parapsychology, and twentieth-century Faustian science and technology have been the subject of much scholarly and popular attention, they are almost never considered from a magical point of view. The Gotham stories narrated here are meant to be both familiar and representative of the United States as a whole but also uniquely illustrative of a peculiarly magical place—in the sense of both its psychological effect on its people and its uninterrupted stream of magical explorers and practitioners. My magical map of Manhattan is new and surprising to the degree that it seeks to make sense of the island's thaumaturgical landscape from a magician's point of view.

Comprehensive histories of magic must always come to terms with the forces and institutions that reject and discredit the magical. Since the Enlightenment, materialist science has waged a sustained war against magic, all the while pushing deeper and deeper into the very realms that are the basis of magical power. Pioneers of medicine, psychology, chemistry, physics, and engineering have long practiced their arts along Broadway, where for over two centuries have also been found the financial and ideological supports to sustain them. Manhattan is a modern imperial city in both its cultural power and its financial power, and like all past empires, the United States continues to wage forms of magic from here, even as it continues to marginalize magic. The modern history of scientific and technological magic is largely a history of unintended consequences, from Faust to eugenics to the atom bomb. For all of Prospero's good white-magic intentions, he eventually breaks his wand and drowns his book, seeing what chaos his art of enchantment can engender. Gotham's tempestuous past uncannily parallels Prospero's fate.

I was born on this magic isle, the Western island and the city that arguably above all others can truly be called *modern*. Unlike Paris, London, Berlin, Rome, and Mexico City, New York has no ancient monuments to mark its magical adolescence. We have here embedded in the landscape no local memory of celebrated witches, warlocks, gods, or goddesses, no myths of magical metamorphoses. New York is the only world city whose entire life history has played out *after* the birth of the modern economic human.

In 2018, Manhattan was host to one stream of "magical" activity that has been more celebrated and disseminated than any other in the modern era. Not Harry Houdini or David Copperfield or David Blaine could grab the headline marquee that the young wizard Harry Potter garnered that year: in April 2018, *Harry Potter and the Cursed Child* opened to sold-out houses at the Lyric Theater on Times Square; in October, the British Library's *Harry Potter: A History of Magic* came to the New-York Historical Society; a few weeks later, the second *Fantastic Beasts and Where to Find Them* film opened.

In this sequel, the action shifts from 1926 Manhattan to Paris, but the Woolworth Building on Broadway is still the glittering home of the fascist, no-magic "New Salem Society."

You and your children or friends may have read all seven Harry Potter novels, seen the films, attended the two-part Broadway show, the New York Public Library exhibit, and maybe even the *Fantastic Beasts* film, but have you ever stopped to consider why it is that the United States continues to look across the pond for magical inspiration, or at least for *stories* of magic? Could it be that we have neglected to explore our own indigenous history of magic, for clues about what our future magical activity might look like?

I wrote this book because I am convinced that Manhattan's and the United States' magical destiny needs careful comprehension, contemplation, and conversation. Here I aim to offer a comprehensive overview of my natal city's magical past, through site-specific stories of witches, warlocks, wizards, fairies, stage magicians, and the modern will-imbued magics of science and technology. Organized as a geographic and chronological progression up Broadway from Battery Park to Inwood, the chapters all provide a surprising picture of a city whose ever-changing fortunes have always been founded on magical activity.

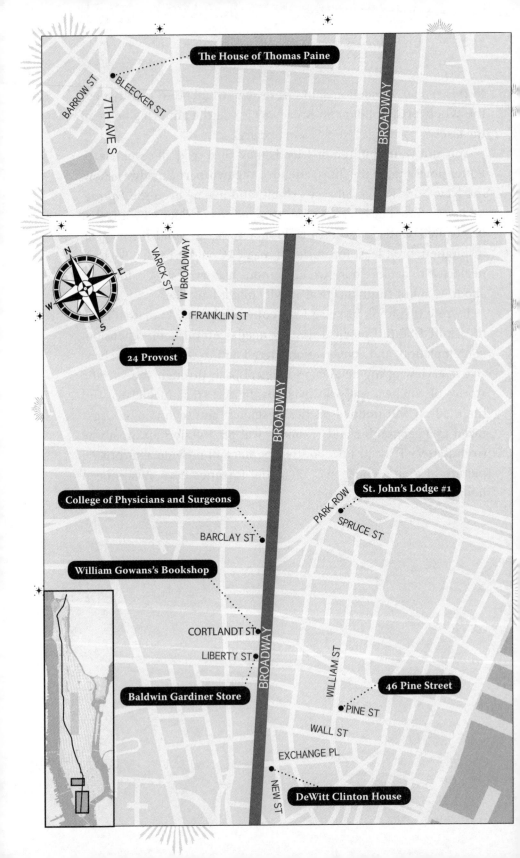

The House of Thomas Paine

BARROW ST
BLEECKER ST
7TH AVE S
BROADWAY

N
E
W
S

VARICK ST
W BROADWAY
FRANKLIN ST

24 Provost

BROADWAY

St. John's Lodge #1
PARK ROW
SPRUCE ST

College of Physicians and Surgeons
BARCLAY ST

William Gowans's Bookshop

CORTLANDT ST
LIBERTY ST

Baldwin Gardiner Store

WILLIAM ST

46 Pine Street
PINE ST
WALL ST
EXCHANGE PL

NEW ST

DeWitt Clinton House

2

Masonic Manhattan

1798–1835

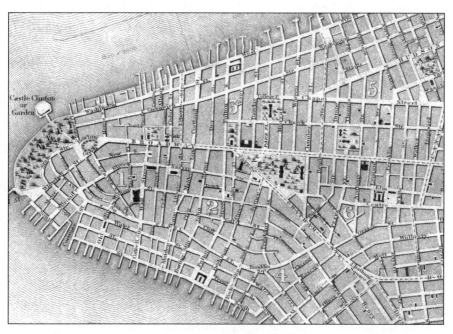

City and County of New-York
(J. H. Colton, 1836)

Most citizens of the fledgling republic—save, understandably, former Tories—shared their new president's Providential perspective. Without the assistance of a host of invisible helping hands, how ever could the upstart nation have succeeded in overthrowing the world's most powerful empire? Along Broadway and every Main Street in the towns and villages of the former thirteen colonies, wonderful tales were told of death-defying local militia heroics, of the dastardly deeds of the British, and of the transformative power of liberty on a people. Yet, for all the triumphal bluster, there was a steady strain of anxious talk in America following the Revolution. No sooner had the Union Jack been pulled down from the Battery flagpole—the last act as the British quit their seven-year occupation of New York—than social and political squabbles, factionalism, and yellow-fever epidemics (in 1795, 1796, 1802, 1803) unnerved the confidence of New Yorkers.

One expression of that anxiety was a vigorous condemnation of anyone who professed allegiance to magic. Jeffersonian- and Jacksonian-era New Yorkers made a philosophical inquiry into the nature of magic and the supernatural a prominent part of their politics. For the time being, witch hunts might be over, but unsettling questions about special human powers lingered. In the city's rural hinterland, out beyond the African Burial Ground, itinerant jugglers and fortunetellers prompted the state legislature to outlaw all "*pretended* knowledge of magic, palmistry, conjuration, etc." Meanwhile, Freemasonic power, while anything but magical, gained by virtue of its secret rites and rituals a terrifyingly supernatural and numinous aura, leading to an epic national political crisis.

Though the history of Freemasonry is complicated by various pseudohistories fostered by its own membership, its roots lie in an authentic tradition and practice of magical spiritual initiation. Freemasonry had undergone rapid secularization in Great Britain and the Continent over the course of the seventeenth century, and its

American variants accelerated the attenuation and eventual loss of magical practices while continuing to promise initiates specialized esoteric knowledge—and thus power. Hyperalert to the threat of a homegrown political and social aristocracy, post-Revolutionary America felt deeply threatened not by any residual magical power but by Freemasonry's fraternal economic and political allegiances.

Thwarted by Franklin, Jefferson, and their skeptical colleagues, mesmerism in America disappeared from view, but other magical currents surfaced occasionally. "Supernaturalism," according to the New England poet John Greenleaf Whittier, was "the unearthly and superhuman bursting up through the thin crust of convention and common-place existence." It is indeed a universal rule that in those places and times where materialism has its tightest stranglehold on the human soul, there will spring up from every direction *magical* manifestations. Prodigies, wonders, and miracles will forever give the lie to those who would deny that the Earth, the Cosmos, and the human being are shot through and through with magical forces and potentialities. The early nineteenth century saw New York physicians and natural scientists increase their determination to disenchant and debunk the supernatural at every turn.

Site #1: St. John's Lodge #1, Frankfort Street and Park Row, June 3, 1803

In 1803, the St. John's Lodge of Ancient York Masons brothers—the same lodge that had provided the Bible for Washington's inauguration—laid the cornerstone of the first building in New York City ever consecrated for strictly Freemasonic purposes. The Masonic brothers chose June 3 instead of Saint John the Baptist's feast day—June 24—for the consecration of their new lodge, since New York in that era was still a fervently anti-Catholic place. They held a procession on this June day and marched all over lower Manhattan—through Williams, Wall, Broad, Nassau, and Trinity Streets—while two marching bands provided the meter.

Entered Apprentice degree ritual
(*Initiation eines Suchenden in die Freimaurerei*, 1805)

Given such ostentatious ritual displays, how in the world is it that this most public of New York City and American institutions—Freemasonry—has come to be regarded as a Bohemian Grove of secrecy and subterfuge? The brethren of St. John's Lodge were in every instance the most public of men, carrying on in the most public manner. Though a measure of secrecy prevailed inside the lodge rooms, in order to more effectively shock candidates for initiation, even there the secrecy was more apparent than real. For a generation, New York's Masons had met in all the city's leading public houses. By convening inside their own building, they were afforded a certain privacy, but they were altogether expecting public approval and admiration. St. John's Lodge fronted on City Hall and its park, the most prominent parade ground of the little metropolis. The main motivation for building the lodge was to be able to elaborate the ritual aspect, the baroque trimmings beyond compass and square, level and plumb rule, and trowel. Apace with Manhattan's theaters, St. John's Lodge would innovate strategies to dazzle and amaze its audience, in a sustained, concerted attempt to create intense emotional bonds between the leading men of the city.

Freemasonry imagined itself the modern legacy of ancient Egypt's most mysterious rites, including the "faculty of ABRAC"—the titillating title for Egyptian magic—but its entire enterprise by 1800 was truly one of *disenchantment* rather than enchantment. Rituals became more theatrical, more emotionally charged, but the "Ancient Mysteries" were not promulgated or penetrated. Obscured and profaned, the original *esoteric* rites of Freemasonry, magical operations designed to initiate the candidate safely into the spiritual world, were stripped of their transformational potential, becoming merely "mysterious," as in "secret" or "obscure." Freemasonry became simply a tool to fulfill political, not *spiritual*, goals.

The rituals were unmistakably oriented to the symbolic death and rebirth of the individual. As candidates for initiation into the First Degree of Entered Apprentice entered the Preparing Room, they were stripped of all material possessions, especially all metal objects—jewelry, coins, and so on. Understood by the candidate as a symbol that he was thereby freed from values other than those imparted by his own inner being, this critical step was originally a wholly *magical* action, taken to ensure that the metal would not interfere with the intended activation of subtle energies. The Deacon tied a handkerchief or hoodwink over the kneeling candidate's eyes, placed a slipper on his right foot, and afterward put a rope, called a cable-tow, once around his neck, letting it drag behind. An elaborate series of movements, gestures, and oaths followed, after which the "Worshipful Master" stripped off the hoodwink and noose from the still kneeling candidate.

The lengthy, rarified, and highly poetic suite of gestures and words rang with grave solemnity in antebellum ears. The candidate was finally led to stand with his feet forming a right angle at the northeast corner of the lodge, where he was asked, "How did Entered Apprentices serve their Master in ancient times, and how should they in modern?"

"With freedom, fervency, and zeal," the candidate proclaimed.

Asked, "How were they represented?" he answered, "By Chalk, Charcoal, and Clay."

Then slowly, pausing in full consideration of this extraordinary cascade of oaths and images, the candidate faces the final question: "Why were they said to represent them?" In reply, the candidate made this wholly alchemical declaration: "Because it was said there was nothing more free than Chalk, which, under the slightest touch, leaves a trace behind; nothing more fervent than Charcoal to melt—when well lit, the most obdurate metals will yield; nothing more zealous than Clay, or our mother earth, to bring forth."

Like the pillars of Jachin and Boaz, the square, level, and plumb, and even the checkered mosaic floor of King Solomon's Temple, chalk, charcoal, and clay—alchemical terms for steps in spiritual transformation—had in all American lodges lost their magical meaning and effect. At the same moment that these Freemasonic oaths, ceremonies, and symbols were becoming routinized and stripped of their magical effect within the city's ten lodges, Freemasonry as a whole was coming under intense criticism for these very same magical systems. In 1803, two of the best-selling books at both the anti-Jacobin bookseller John Ward Fenno's shop at 141 Broadway and the fervent revolutionary Hoquet Caritat's store and circulating library (boasting thirty thousand volumes) a few doors up at the City Hotel did a brisk trade in the former English Mason John Robison's *Proofs of a Conspiracy* (1797) and the Jesuit priest Abbé Augustin Barruel's *Memoirs Illustrating the History of Jacobinism* (1798–1799). (The first American editions of both these books came—in 1798 and 1799—from New York City printers and publishers.) Both works maintained that the French Revolution had been fomented by Freemasonic secret societies dedicated to Theosophical and Rosicrucian magic, in order to overthrow not just Christianity and the monarchies but civilization itself. The higher degrees of Freemasonry particularly excited Barruel's imagination: "We comprehend under the designation of Occult Lodges, or the higher degrees of Masonry, all Free-Masons, in general, who after having past the first three degrees of *Apprentice, Fellow-Craft,* and *Master,* show sufficient zeal to be admitted into the higher degrees, where the veil is rent asunder, where emblematical and allegorical figures are thrown aside, and where the principle of Liberty and Equality is unequivocally explained by *war against Christ and his Altars!*" Robison, Barruel, and their readers suspected that the high ideals of brotherhood, liberty, and equality were but convenient and deceptive masks to disguise their diabolical plot to overthrow society by magical and mystical means. The rituals and hermetic symbols, the talk of all-powerful mysterious Rosicrucians, alchemists, and Cabalists, and the descriptions of "the triangles, the table, the urns, and the magic mirrors—in a word, all the science of the Cabalistic Rosicrucian"— were as titillating as they were threatening. Many people bought these exposés because they deeply desired a glimpse into the occult world of magic.

Barruel and Robison drew their critiques less from their hours inside the lodge than from half a century of widely available literature describing the arcana of Freemasonry. The few New Yorkers who had some acquaintance with Rosicrucianism would have recognized these ritual objects as identical with the treasures inside Christian Rosenkreutz's crypt, as described in the 1614 anonymous Rosicrucian manifesto, the *Fama Fraternitatas.* Like that work, the Christian Cabalism of the Freemasonic lodge was a deeply esoteric system of symbols whose meaning was only open to those who had experienced initiation. Absent that initiatory knowledge, the Christian Hermeticism at the heart of Freemasonry was practically guaranteed in both pre-Revolutionary and post-Revolutionary America to be misunderstood, even as it fascinated those both inside the lodge and without.

Site #2: The House of Thomas Paine, 293 Bleecker Street, June 8, 1809

The archradical Thomas Paine published the first part of *The Rights of Man* in London in March 1791, and by 1792, when he wrote the second part, it had sold about a million copies—to fellow freethinkers from religious dissidents to craftspersons to skilled factory hands. Government agents followed Paine around London, instigating mobs to hang him in effigy. While in prison, expecting to be taken to the guillotine, Paine wrote the first part of *The Age of Reason*, whose subtitle—*Being an Investigation of True and Fabulous Theology*—gives it away as a major text in the history of "disenchantment," the steady march toward modern denial of the subtle forces of nature. Shortly after part 1 was published in London in 1794, the printer John Fellows at 131 Water Street—one of the forty-seven printers, twenty-three booksellers, and fourteen bookbinders who plied their trade just a block from the East River docks—brought out the first American edition. Fellows and Paine—and the bookseller Hoquet Caritat—became close friends after Paine moved to New York.

Published in three parts in 1794, 1795, and 1807, Paine's *Age of Reason* became a best-seller in the United States, and one can without too much exaggeration claim Paine as the great-granddaddy of generation after generation of Manhattan-dwelling archskeptics. *The Rights of Man* did not just reject the Book of Revelation and Christ's miracles; Paine took satirical potshots at the very nature of wonder and mystery itself, in order to advance the cause of human freedom. In his zeal to debunk the Bible, Paine drew on the example of Parisian *phantasmagoristes*—sleight-of-hand artists using the latest magic lanterns to create the illusion of specters and ghosts. His wit was rapier sharp, so cutting as to make believers in even the smallest of everyday "miracles" ashamed of themselves: "The most extraordinary of all things called miracles, related in the New Testament, is that of the devil flying away with Jesus Christ, and carrying him to the top of a high mountain; and to the top of the highest pinnacle of

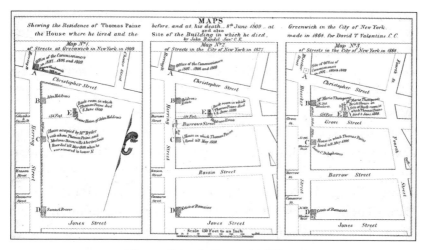

Thomas Paine in Greenwich Village
(New York Public Library Digital Collections)

the temple, and showing him and promising to him all the kingdoms of the world. How happened it that he did not discover America; or is it only with kingdoms that his sooty highness has any interest?" At the end of part 2, Paine calls "mystery, miracle, and prophecy" the "three friends" whom he sorely detests, thinking them anything but friendly to man.

There is no miracle, no mystery, no prophecy without something very like *magic*. Absent the "three friends" in Manhattan's post-Revolutionary Freemasonic lodges, in the churches, or abroad in the streets, where might a man or woman find the faculty of ABRAC? Despite Paine's protestations about Reason's enemies, those who were allied with magic were in hasty retreat at the outset of the nineteenth century. Already, up and down Broadway, a Gothamite might find on each block vociferous champions of reason and nary a one defender of magic.

Sick and old when released from prison in 1802, Paine sailed to New York and boarded with Mr. and Mrs. Ryder at 293 Herring (now Bleecker) Street. On June 8, 1809, he died in the brick house around the corner on Grove Street. Paine's Greenwich Village convalescence saw him largely housebound at his writing desk, not afoot on Broadway. But in 1827, G. N. Devries, from his print shop at the corner of Vesey Street and Broadway, brought out an edition containing both sections of *The Age of Reason*. In 1833, when there were more than a dozen booksellers on Broadway between the Bowling Green and Washington Square, it was still a local best-seller.

By 1930, when the house at 293 Bleecker was torn down, Tom Paine was long forgotten, and Greenwich Village had already become so gentrified that the first twentieth-century Bohemians—Mabel Dodge, Eugene O'Neill, Edna St. Vincent Millay, Djuna Barnes, Dylan Thomas—many of them devotees of the sort of mystical and magical currents that Paine abhorred, had moved out of the city.

Site #3: "Does It Not Seem like Magic?!": DeWitt Clinton House, 52 Broadway, July 4, 1810

Far from the mansion of New York City Mayor DeWitt Clinton at 52 Broadway, way upstate in the little burgh of Schenectady in July 1810, the mayor (who served as Grand Master of the Grand Lodge of New York from 1806 to 1819) and three other Erie Canal commissioners prepared for an exploratory expedition of the canal's entire route. Commissioner Thomas Eddy had forgotten to arrange for boats, so Mr. Walton, the local undertaker, scrambled to get them a pair of *bateaux*—one for the men and a second for their baggage. The boats had to be caulked and painted, delaying their departure until a fortuitous date—the thirty-fourth anniversary of American independence.

Doubly fortunately, while stopping overnight in Albany on the way north, Mayor Clinton had purchased a pair of recently published books: Frederick Henry Quitman's *A Treatise on Magic; or, On the Intercourse between Spirits and Men* (1810) and David Low Dodge's *A Religious Conference, in Four Dialogues, between Lorenzo and Evander* (1808). Clinton added these to the boat's "library"—a trunk in whose charge the commissioners placed a young gentleman acting as their waterborne liveryman. Though Walton warned the

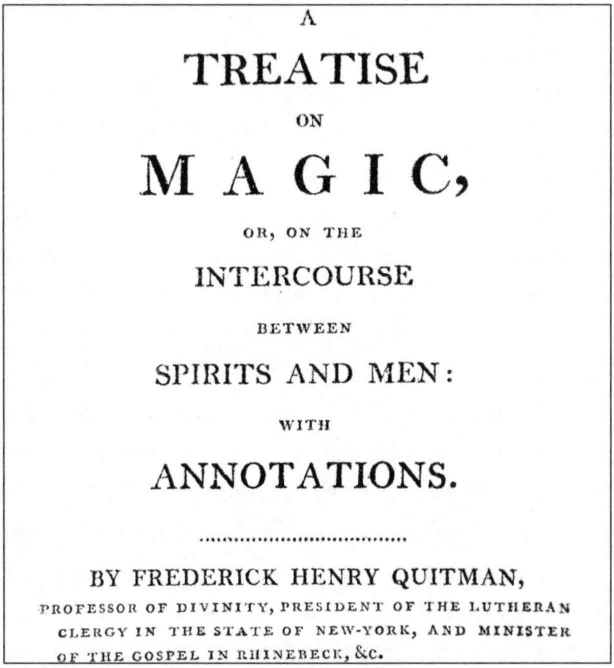

A

TREATISE

ON

M A G I C,

OR, ON THE

INTERCOURSE

BETWEEN

SPIRITS AND MEN:

WITH

ANNOTATIONS.

....

BY FREDERICK HENRY QUITMAN,
PROFESSOR OF DIVINITY, PRESIDENT OF THE LUTHERAN
CLERGY IN THE STATE OF NEW-YORK, AND MINISTER
OF THE GOSPEL IN RHINEBECK, &C.

Frederick Henry Quitman's *A Treatise on Magic*, 1810
(author photo)

New York City men that they would never get off on the fourth, on account of the holiday revelry, Clinton and his companions managed to shove off upstream toward Utica, motivated largely by their dread of passing the fourth in such a drab and dreary place as Schenectady. Clinton, an avid historian, was most impressed by the historic associations of the places they passed as they ascended the Mohawk River; passage after passage in his diary waxes eloquent about the Mohawk Indians' superiority over their savage neighboring tribes.

Clinton's fellow commissioner and close friend Gouverneur Morris's exclamation a decade before, upon hearing the first rumblings of the great canal plan—"Does it not seem like magic?!"—expressed best the attitude of the age. "The proudest empire in Europe," Morris declared, "is but a bauble compared to what America *will* be and *must* be, in the course of two centuries, perhaps of one." Even before completion of the Erie Canal in 1825, the marvel of engineering (one historian has called it "a combination of Disneyland, the Grand Canyon, and a high-tech laboratory in Silicon Valley") drew sophisticated sightseers like William Cullen Bryant, Edward Everett Hale, Nathaniel Hawthorne, and the British actress Fanny Kemble.

The footlocker library of the *Eddy* (the humble name chosen for the commissioners' canal boat) concisely held the consensus on the battle between Magic and Skepticism. The Manhattan millinery storeowner and city measurer David Low Dodge's *Religious Conference* argued for the reality of past miracles and the possibility of their continuation even into this era of calculated materialist enterprise. Quitman's *Treatise on Magic*—motivated by the author's experience of a stone-throwing poltergeist haunting a Rhinebeck farm family in 1808—was anything but. It was instead a prosaic compendium of the most quotidian materialist "common sense" about supernatural phenomena. A young woman bewitched near Poughkeepsie; the Shaker-style dancing frenzy at Tarrytown; the mania for Captain Kidd's treasure; or the turning of a quarter of Rhinebeck upside down by the raucous shenanigans of mischievous spectral imps—Reverend Quitman was quickly quit of them all, not through compelling argument but by ad hominem attack.

A professor of divinity, president of the Lutheran clergy in New York State, and minister of the Gospel in the prosperous Hudson River town of Rhinebeck, Reverend Quitman begins his treatise with an altogether sensible definition of magic: "the art of producing supernatural effects, by the agency of spirits." But like most of the skeptical tracts of his day, Reverend Quitman's survey of Egyptian sorcerers, the Witch of Endor, Simon Magus, Theosophy, and astrology takes them all to have been *supposed* "intercourse between spirits and men." His annotations on magical topics ranging from talismans, amulets, and charms to Cabala and Cagliostro are characteristically superficial. He even admits to his own ignorance; under "Rosicrusian order," Reverend Quitman notes that Robert Fludd "has published many works on the wonders of alchymies and the mysticism of the Rosicrucians, but they are profoundly obscure."

A reviewer of *A Treatise on Magic* writing to the *Medical Repository* in 1811 complained that folk magical beliefs persisted in the face of the forces of disenchantment. "In this enlightened age and country there are, even at this day, many traces of magical delusion," he lamented, pointing to the fact that an "esteemed" New York almanac still annually displayed the zodiacal Man of the Signs as its frontispiece. Like Quitman, Clinton, and his Freemasonic confrères, the reviewer wholly approved of a newly passed special statute of New York, prohibiting palmistry, fortune telling, and "such like crafty arts." That the statute prescribed sixty days of hard labor for such a crime suggests a certain urgency to maintain order in those precarious years following the Revolution.

With each spade full of good New York soil tossed up to make the Erie Canal towpath, with each "improvement" in the metropolis or its suburbs, the microcosm was sundered from the Macrocosm. Urbanization in America and worldwide almost invariably engendered rationalization and the concomitant delegitimization of magical activity, and the Erie Canal was antebellum America's premier agent of rationalization of the rural landscape, as it inexorably drew the far-flung rural hinterland toward New York City's urban core.

Site #4: Devotional Somnium, 24 Provost (Now Franklin) Street, February 9, 1815

On the streets of lower Manhattan in the early nineteenth century, the "Nestor of American science," Dr. Samuel Latham Mitchill (1764–1831) was the commonest of sights, going about in his blue coat, buff-colored vest, and buckled shoes. Though a conspicuously local figure, Dr. Mitchill was equally cosmopolitan. After the British occupied New York City, he had left his medical practice to study at the University of Edinburgh, where he rubbed elbows with such notables as Sir James Mackintosh, who became a preeminent

Dr. Samuel Latham Mitchill

Scottish jurist; the physician and anatomist Caspar Wistar; and Thomas Addis Emmet, the Irish revolutionary and later American lawyer and politician. He was also a colleague of the leading philosophes of London and Paris. As Dr. Mitchill perambulated the streets of Gotham, his voracious curiosity treated his native city as inquisitively as if he were on a pioneering scientific expedition abroad.

"Pioneering" is in no way too strong a word for Dr. Mitchill, whose entire biography seemed to play out along the frontier of science and technology. An early advocate of the new Lavoisierian system of chemistry, his 1797 mineralogical survey of New York included an analysis of the Saratoga mineral waters. Sir Humphry Davy's conception that acids were substances that contained replaceable hydrogen was aided by Dr. Mitchill's research on septic acid; his 1795 reflections on the anesthetic state produced by nitrous-oxide inhalation preceded Davy's celebrated research by five years and was the inspiration for Davy's discoveries. He exchanged observations and speculations on American climate, geology, paleontology, and ethnology with Thomas Jefferson; brought out the first American edition of Cuvier's *Essay on the Theory of the Earth* (1818); and then improved it considerably for his American audience by his detailed narrative of the bedrock landscapes of "Fredonia" (the alternative name he proposed, and long cherished, for the United States of America), especially the New York City region. With Joseph Priestley, he penetrated phlogiston, that mysterious substance transcending the alchemists' four classical elements; with Thomas Jefferson and Charles Willson Peale, he probed the "American *incognitum*"—the mastodon. In the words of a late nineteenth-century biographer, "He wrote largely to Percival on noxious agents. He cheered Fulton when dejected; encouraged Livingston in appropriation; awakened new zeal in Wilson the ornithologist, when the Governor, Tompkins, had nigh paralyzed him by his frigid and unfeeling reception; and, with Pintard and Colden, was a zealous promoter of that system of internal improvement which has stamped immortality on the name of Clinton."

It is little wonder, then, that when upstate doctors were baffled by the case of Rachel Baker, they should seek out Dr. Mitchill. Brought to New York City from the Onondaga County hamlet of Marcellus, twenty-year-old Rachel Baker had for the previous three years been subject to nightly trances in which she uttered hour-long Christian exhortations, all while fast asleep. Her trance-state sermons were delivered in vocabulary and fluency completely absent in her waking life. By the time of her trip to New York City—a three-hundred-mile carriage journey meant to provoke a cure by way of the novelties of a crowded, bustling city or its humid, saline atmosphere—dozens of people were regularly coming to the Baker home to hear Rachel's "sleep preaching."

In February 1815, Rachel's strange altered state was observed at the home office of Dr. John Douglass by a small circle of Douglass's colleagues, including Dr. Mitchill, who soon published his report on the case: *Devotional Somnium; or, A Collection of Prayers and Exhortations, Uttered by Miss Rachel Baker, in the City of New-York, in the Winter of 1815, during Her Abstracted and Unconscious State; To Which Pious and Unprecedented Exercises Is Prefixed, an Account of Her Life, with the Manner in Which She Became Powerful in Praise to God and Addresses to Man; Together with a View of That Faculty of the Human Mind Which Is Intermediate between Sleeping and Waking; the Facts, Attested by the Most Respectable Divines, Physicians, and Literary Gentlemen; and the Discourses, Correctly Noted by Clerical Stenographers. Devotional Somnium*—Mitchill's term for the state between waking and sleeping—was America's first attempt at a phenomenology and theory of the dream state. It was also a calculated attack on popular magical or miraculous explanations of Rachel Baker; in the preface to the work, Dr. Douglass explicitly voiced its intent, asking "by what means [shall] these seraphic visions be dissipated, and their organ reduced to the ordinary level of womankind?"

Dr. Mitchill divided somnium into two types: "Symptomatic," a passive state engendered by indigestion, "Nightmare" (thought by Mitchill to arise from blockage of blood to the heart and lungs), water in the chest, fever, fainting, nitrous-oxide inhalation, and narcotic or alcohol use; and "Idiopathic," a more active state, which included reverie, lunacy, "somniloquism" (sleep-talking), somnambulism (sleep-walking), somnium with invention (literary or musical composition during the dream state), hallucination, and "somnium with the ability to pray and preach"—that is, the faculty exhibited by Rachel Baker. The "remarkable" and "extraordinary" abilities of the young Somniloquist thus were separated from such magical powers as prophetic clairvoyance ("foretelling lugubrious events by a sort of SECOND SIGHT") and seership ("where visual impressions are so strong, that the dreamers are called SEERS").

Mitchill pioneered for the obscure mysteries of the human mind the same sort of compelling taxonomy that he crafted for disease states, for Fredonia's mineral wealth, or for the fishes of New York Harbor, using—like his scientific hero, Erasmus Darwin—flowery prose and even poetry in a highly self-conscious democratic campaign to dispel darkness about every corner of Dame Nature. This taxonomy often ran to both rhetorical and theoretical excess; *Somnium* was of a piece with Mitchill's theories about infectious diseases. He and his friend Dr. Elihu Hubbard Smith had founded *Medical Repository*—the nation's first medical journal—in 1799 explicitly to address the public terror caused by New York's deadly yellow-fever epidemics in 1795 and 1797. Mitchill proposed as the cause of the disease "the gaseous oxyd of azote," which he also called "septon." Despite the scientific-sounding name, Mitchill's septon was hardly distinct from the lay public's "contagion," or Mesmer's invisible fluid. That Mitchill frequently referred to septon as a "pestilential fluid" shows that he had only partially removed disease theory from the arena of the magical.

The key to the gradual process of disenchanting all earlier natural magic explanations of nature and the human being was linguistic and psychological. Little by little, the wide public for whom Mitchill crafted his treatises adopted bits and pieces of his rhetoric and thus his worldview. Mitchill largely concurred with Dr. Benjamin Rush of Philadelphia that "somnambulism is nothing but a lighter grade of delirium," a "transient paroxysm of madness and illusion." By these two words—"nothing but"—materialist science would over the next two centuries dismiss thousands of years of veridical accounts of more than just dreams. Ever perceived as a threat to authority, magic was largely banished by an infinite regression of "nothing buts."

Mitchill's ability to disenchant Rachel Baker's otherworldly productions drew on his earlier success arguing for septon and sanitary practices on the city's streets. Mitchill's natural history was dense, specific, and altogether recognizable to his fellow New Yorkers. Laying out the prescriptions for ameliorating the urban environmental conditions that promoted the spread of yellow fever, Mitchill pointed out how the city's shorelines were being extended by unsanitary construction materials—bones, oyster shells, wood shavings, street scrapings, offals. There was a kind of Gothic tenor to Mitchill's writing, akin to the very language that his Friendly Club friend Charles Brockden Brown would employ in *Wieland; or, The Transformation* and *Memoirs of Carwin the Ventriloquist*. Brown's novels—America's first Gothic tales—occupied themselves with the same sort of psychological mysteries that drew the attention of Mitchill and his fellow physics. By way of cunning word craft, both art and science at the opening of the nineteenth century were inevitably, inexorably drawn right back into the magical realm.

That this highly social and political epistemological project that Drs. Mitchill and Douglass were advancing still faced opposition from the public is suggested by Mitchill's preface to the 1818 volume of the *Medical Repository*. Mitchill complained, "There are, accordingly, *root* doctors, who direct vegetable simples; *witch* doctors, who chase away evil spirits by exorcism; *cancer* doctors, who treat the worst of ulcers and sores; *stroking* doctors, who affect to drive away distempers by the power of animal magnetism; *indian* doctors, deeply versed in all the remedies of the savages; *obi* doctors, who dispel the incantation or expel the poison that works upon the body, under African magic; with a variety of other modes and forms, the offspring of weakness and superstition."

The word "symbol" appeared not once in Mitchill's treatise on Rachel Baker. Like the clairvoyant aspects of somnambulism, symbols held no interest for early nineteenth-century savants intent on rationalizing the soul. Only half a century before, Freemasonry had stewarded the most essential knowledge about the esoteric physiology of sleep and dream. The magical adepts—Cagliostro and the Count of St. Germain principal among them—who had founded Egyptian Freemasonry in the eighteenth century knew that human beings' nervous system, brain, and all sensory organs were but the outer, material expressions of an invisible "body," the etheric body, that assembled and maintained the physical form. This etheric body was the foundation of Mesmer's healing magic and of most systems of magical healing on the planet, but it was also possible to heal by way of the astral body—the invisible constitution of instincts, passions, desires, and feelings. The series of degrees of Freemasonic initiation were a sort of stepwise recapitulation of the evolution of human consciousness, employing these earlier states as a method for candidates to directly *experience* the meaning of the arcane symbols, out of the clairvoyance cultivated in their astral bodies. The rituals in the lodge were carefully designed to separate the etheric and astral bodies—as well as the upper member of the human constitution, the "I"—from the physical body, thus permitting entry into the spiritual world.

True Freemasonic—and other magical—initiates understood that all humanity had once possessed a dream consciousness, in which the spiritual world was as real as the physical world. The world's myths—especially the Temple Legend that was the basis of Freemasonic symbolism and ritual—preserved knowledge of that "dream time" of the collective human soul. Magical adepts understood that while ordinary dreams gave simple, mostly chaotic symbolic expression to the activity of the etheric body, highly symbolic, dramatic dreams represented the encounter of the individual astral body with the cosmic astral of all nature. Only through such mystery knowledge might the magical phenomena of somnambulism be understood.

Site #5: Gabriel Furman's Magical Quest: William Gowans's Bookshop, 169 Broadway, 1827–1835

Born in 1765 in the house across the street from the Fulton Ferry landing in Brooklyn, Gabriel Furman became Brooklyn's first historian, the first dedicated American antiquarian, and New York's foremost collector of books on magic. Serving as Brooklyn Municipal Court judge from 1827 to 1830 and in the New York State Senate from 1839 to 1842, he became an inveterate collector of local

La Très Sainte Trinosophie, Section V panel

folklore. Browsing his sixteen volumes of manuscript notebooks at the Brooklyn Historical Society, what is most striking is how many of these tales have some magical or supernatural dimension. It is almost as if Judge Furman were inventing his own catholic salvage ethnology, sensing that these folkways would soon recede before the onslaught of aggressive rationalism.

His favorite recreation was to take the ferry across to Manhattan to haunt the Broadway bookshops, hunting for treasures. New York City's premier bookseller and bibliophile, William Gowans, said that Furman was the only man in New York interested in Americana, crediting his own expertise in American books to Furman's friendship and encouragement. Furman would lend his books to anyone who asked, including loaning out even the rarest treasures. He owned copies of books that would fetch hundreds of thousands of dollars today, such as Agrippa's *Three Books of Occult Philosophy*, Bodin's *Demonology*, and one of the only two copies of *La Très Sainte Trinosophie*, thought to have been composed by Europe's most spectacular wizard, the Count of St. Germain. Gowans said that Gabriel Furman also had the finest library of astrology of anyone in the United States.

Judge Furman's leather-bound notebooks are a joy to behold, chock-full of the most illuminating juxtapositions of everyday reports and a veritable Cabinet of Curiosities, Wonders, and Mysteries. From his own neighbors, he gathered a treasury of "love charms": young women would use the crooked bone between the breastbone and the neck of a chicken—called by them the "merry thought"—and pull on it like a wishbone to determine who would be the first to be wed. There were elaborate rituals involving apple seeds and the names of potential husbands and the practice of paring an apple while standing in front of a mirror, tossing the unbroken skin over the right shoulder, and then divining the first letter of a suitor's name from the shape it made when it landed. Judge Furman recalled the strange disappearance of Colonel Henry Livingston of the state senate; one summer evening, he stepped out from the City Hotel on Broadway to make the five-minute walk to visit friends who lived in one of the marble homes opposite the Bowling Green, and he was never heard from again. In Judge Furman's estimation, all such stories pointed to the unseen forces lying behind nature and history.

The good judge came to a terrible end, for having taken opium to alleviate his pain during the cholera epidemic in 1832, he became addicted to it; and it gradually drove him insane. He ended up in a rooming house on Frankfort Street next to where the Bridge Café now stands. He had gone missing for some time until his old friend Alden Spooner, who published the *Long Island Star*, tracked him down and brought him and his books and papers—depositing them for a while in the Ferry House—back to Brooklyn, but he died shortly thereafter.

The mystery of death was something quite close and omnipresent in diseased-ravaged Masonic-era Manhattan, not just in the mock death and resurrection pantomime of the lodge initiations. Gabriel Furman's notebooks are filled with tales of ghosts, goblins, and violent and sudden death, as well as the occasional miraculous story of overcoming death. By the 1830s, one personality had achieved worldwide fame for cheating death: the Count of St. Germain (1712–1784), the purported author of the very same alchemical treatise, *La Très Sainte Trinosophie*, that Furman had obtained in his magical grimoire quest. Voltaire, in a 1758 letter to King Frederick of Prussia, had called St. Germain "a man who does not die, and who knows everything"; at courts and in cafés throughout Europe, St. Germain famously recounted history's most important events as if he had been an eyewitness to all of them. The origins of St. Germain—alchemist, diplomat, adventurer, painter, composer, and inventor—were and remain totally unknown to outer history, but to a few initiates both in his own time and later, he was known to be identical with Christian Rosenkreutz (1378–1484), understood to be the reincarnation of Hiram Abiff, whose story formed the central ritual of Egyptian Freemasonry. This individual's most significant incarnation was as Lazarus/John, the "disciple whom Jesus loved," author of both the Gospel of John and Revelation.

When Christ raised Lazarus from the dead (the true meaning of "loved" in the above phrase), he had imparted a copy of his etheric body to Lazarus, which both endowed him with extraordinary powers of healing, longevity, and memory and also made it possible for Lazarus/John to overcome physical death. The rumor of St. Germain's immortality stemmed from this unique karmic biography; since the time of John's initiation by Christ, he had incarnated in every single century, always as a supreme friend and helper of humanity. Some of these incarnations were as individuals unknown to history, but many were significant and celebrated: Charibert von

Laon (Charlemagne's grandfather, born ca. 690 AD, died after 747 AD), Prester John (son of Feirefis, the brother of Parzifal in the ninth century), and William the Silent (1533–1584). Lazarus/John had been the first person on Earth to *experience* the magical secret of the Philosopher's Stone—the overcoming of physical death through his direct resurrection by Christ—and in each of his later incarnations worked within the culture of his time to share this secret with his fellow human beings. As the individuals at the fount of modern Freemasonry before its corruption into political intrigue and mere secular fraternal fellowship, Christian Rosenkreutz and St. Germain (with his close ally and magical adept Count Cagliostro) brought the mystery of the Philosopher's Stone right up to the threshold of the modern era. In 1790, five years after St. Germain's supposed death, he wrote to a friend to say, "Exactly in eighty-five years will people again set eyes on me."

Gabriel Furman's notebooks record no observations or speculations about *La Très Sainte Trinosophie*, but it is almost certain that both the manuscript's text (a gloomy, subterranean voyage that suddenly ends when the narrator, striking the sun with a sword, hears a voice cry out, "The work is accomplished!") and its arcane symbols (among them the altar, bird, and torch of the panel shown in the accompanying illustration) would have baffled him. In exactly eighty-five years, however, another magical adept would appear in New York who would understand both these symbols and the mysterious count who painted them.

Site #6: Martin Harris Seeks Out Dr. Samuel Latham Mitchill: College of Physicians and Surgeons, 3 Barclay Street, Spring 1828

A decade before Mormonism firmly took root in the city in 1838, the Palmyra, New York, farmer Martin Harris arrived at the College of Physicians and Surgeons, seeking out Dr. Samuel Latham Mitchill to show Mitchill several manuscripts given him by the Prophet Joseph

Smith. According to the journalist James Gordon Bennett, who interviewed Harris in 1831, he carried for Mitchill's inspection transcripts of engravings on a pair of mysterious golden plates unearthed by Smith. After receiving Harris "purlitely" (Bennett's use of upstate dialect intended to render Harris a bit of a country bumpkin), Dr. Mitchill compared the engravings with the hieroglyphics discovered by Champollion in Egypt and pronounced them as the language of some now-extinct people in the East. Both Joseph Smith and Charles Anthon—Mitchill's colleague and a classical philologist, whom Harris also visited for translation help—gave a number of conflicting accounts of this episode over the years, a commonplace of all events in early Mormon history.

As with Salem witchcraft, Spiritualism, and dozens of other events in American history, the story of Smith's Golden Plates suffers from the absence of any understanding of this as a *magical* episode. In recent decades, scholars have come to understand the founding of the Mormon religion by Joseph Smith as an outgrowth of his family's sustained practice of folk magic. This scholarship ultimately discounts magical efficacy, but the appearance to Smith of the "Angel Moroni" is clearly an episode of magical evocation. The whole "affair Mormon" is from beginning to end an object lesson in the dangers of practicing magic without the protection of spiritual purification. Neighbors from the Palmyra area knew Joseph Smith and his family as money diggers and necromancers. Having met while treasure-hunting on September 21, 1823, just the sort of amoral, mischievous elemental guardian "gnome" warned against by all traditions of folk magic, young Smith fell under its spell, obeying its magical instructions for a full four years before—in a somnambulic trance state, employing "seer stones"—he "translated" the "golden plates" that he had seen in an altered state of consciousness. Dr. Mitchill and Professor Anthon never heard from Martin Harris about the manuscript's origins in grave robbing, animal sacrifice, and demonic invocation.

After the *Book of Mormon* was published in 1830, Smith and his magic-working confederates never spoke about the treasure-

Portion of Anthon transcript of *Book of Mormon*

guarding toad who transformed himself into the Angel Moroni. No one seemed to notice that "Moorman" was the Scottish term for someone in charge of cattle in waste ground or that "Mormo" was an archaic name for a spirit who terrified children (antebellum dictionaries gave "Mormo" as "bug bear; false terror"). In the early years after Smith's encounter at Hill Cumorah, he referred to the angel messenger interchangeably as both "Moroni" and "Nephe"—the latter meant "departed spirits called out by Magicians and Necromancers." The intellectual elite of New York lacked the requisite spiritual and magical knowledge to comprehend either Smith's somnambulic state or the sort of beings who might invade the somnambulist's consciousness. This very incomprehension would soon unleash an epidemic of "Mormos" after somnambulic Spiritualist mediums were given carte blanche to do their own conjuring.

Site #7: The Kingdom of Matthias: Baldwin Gardiner Store, 149 Broadway, 1832

Historians of antebellum America love to study, diagnose, and occasionally—as did sophisticated urban editors of the early nineteenth century—lampoon the "burned-over district" of western New York State. For every frenzied revival, apocalyptic prophet, and millennial epidemic up north, there were two or three happening along Broadway. Given Manhattan's dynamism, these episodes have just been buried under the palimpsest of other events and now are forgotten.

Take, for example, Elijah Pierson, one of New York's best-known religious reformers, an ally of the Free Church movement, and a tireless activist in missions to blacks, Jews, and prostitutes. One day in 1831, going down Broadway in an omnibus, God spoke to him: "Thou art Elijah the Tishbite! Gather unto me all the members of Israel at the foot of Mount Carmel." Up on Bowery Hill with his wife, Sarah, and a flock of converts, Elijah the Tishbite instructed his followers to intensify their visions by fasting—which led to Sarah Pierson's death. Convinced that his wife would immediately rise from the dead, Elijah spent days waiting beside her open casket.

While practicing the laying on of hands and other miracle working, Elijah then was told by the Lord that he might do whatever he could: "Nothing should be impossible to me." He expected 144,000 converts: "as many as I would." By the spring of 1831, as his own fanatical star was descending, the star of one of his flock—Robert Matthews, aka "Matthias"—was rising. While Elijah's eccentricities ran toward Old Testament desert asceticism, Matthias loved fancy clothing—long green coats of the finest cloth, with white or pink silk linings, and gold braid and fancy brass buttons; ruffles at his wrists; a black cravat; a fine silk vest; a crimson sash; Wellington boots—and he often visited Broadway's most fashionable drapers and mercers.

On a visit to Baldwin Gardiner's silverware emporium, Matthias began one of his flighty orations, boasting of his supernatural powers and of his dominion to save or destroy. His favorite conceit was that he could destroy all the flies in the world as easily as *that*— whereupon he would rap his fingers on a nearby box. In the kingdom over which he would soon rule, Matthias promised, all houses would be so clean that no flies would be able to live in them. By summer's end, Elijah was sent to the Bloomingdale Lunatic Asylum, Matthias

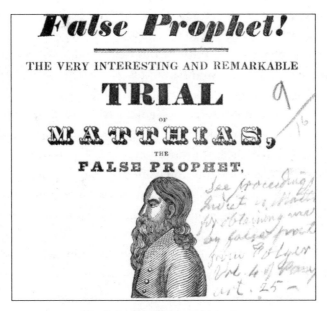

The *False Prophet!* pamphlet, 1835

to an apartment for the insane poor at Bellevue. While under reha-
bilitation at Bloomingdale, Elijah became convinced that Matthias
was actually the devil.

In an earlier era, say 1692, and under Cotton Mather's most considered scrutiny, the cases of both Pierson and Matthews would
have been understood as episodes of possession by demonic—or
at least devilishly mischievous—lesser spiritual beings, known by
Paracelsus, Agrippa, Trithemius, and other early modern mages as
"elementals." In classic fashion, the elemental beings playing havoc
with the two men—and, by succession, all their followers, family,
and friends—chose some authoritative biblical persona as a deceptive mask, guaranteeing them respectable cover while they went
about their ridiculous, usually destructive, antics. Joseph Smith's
toad-*cum*-angel Moroni was an elemental being as well, whose pretensions of grandeur were so sincerely believed that they led to a
worldwide religion.

Ultimately, these elementals were just like actors; they craved attention, wishing to be worshiped, just as they had been in ancient times, by peoples with an entirely different mode of consciousness than nineteenth-century Manhattanites. Before the arrival of Europeans, *all* of nature received supplication and devotion. In the mad modern commercial city, objects—gold, silver, glass, silk, crinoline, silk—were the gods, and thus they enraged with jealousy the forgotten hosts of elementals. It was not Matthias who craved silver; it was the possessing being who thus intensified by magical means the worship by physical beings—modern, "reasonable" men and women—of altogether invisible hobgoblins. Whether in upstate rural hamlets or the most fashionable Manhattan neighborhoods, such beings were sustained by the intensity of human longing, and when emotions were sufficiently kindled by desire, both individuals and crowds were susceptible to being swept up in the most uncanny madness.

Site #8: Colonel Stone on Masonry and Anti-Masonry, 46 Pine Street, 1832

In the ritual for the Third Degree of Freemasonry, candidates for initiation enacted the role of one of the conspirators who had brutally murdered Hiram Abiff, revered as the builder of Solomon's Temple and Grand Master of all Freemasonry. "Conspiracy" was a word often on the lips of Americans in the 1830s, particularly in the partisan political world of New York City. In the wake of the Freemason William Morgan's abduction and murder in 1826 and the minimal sentence given to his kidnapers, the Anti-Masonry Party had formed to counter what was widely perceived as the antidemocratic, conspiratorial machinations of Masonic elites. As a Seventh Degree Grand Arch Mason, "Colonel" William Leete Stone, publisher and editor of the *Commercial Advertiser*, was in a unique position to defend the institution—or condemn it, should there have been cause. He offered his thoughts on the subject in 1832 in *Letters on Masonry and Anti-Masonry*—a collection of forty-nine letters written to former president John Quincy Adams, who in retirement had allied himself with the Anti-Masonic movement.

When, in 1815, the twenty-three-year-old Stone had been initiated as an Entered Apprentice, he had done so out of an intense curiosity about the potential mystery knowledge that he might gain as a Freemason. He told President Adams that he had never expected any truly sublime secret to be revealed, but he still believed there would be *something*: "I resolved to proceed to the end, and, if there *were* any secret, to *find* it—if any mystery to *solve* it." By the time that he took the seventh degree of initiation, the Royal Arch degree, fellow Masons promised that it would be the "summit and perfection" of initiations, "indescribably more august, sublime, and important, than all which precede it."

Stone described the ceremony opening with members kneeling reverentially around the altar, their hands joined, while the high priest read a benediction from Saint Paul. There followed the recitation of the Temple Legend—the journey to rebuild Solomon's Temple and a band of Freemasons' discovery of a secret gold-lined vault bearing the Ark of the Covenant, the pot of manna, and Aaron's magical rod. Admitting that the richly colored curtains of the lodge room, the prayers and lectures recited, and the robes and jewels of the high priest made for a very attractive pageant, Stone dismissed it all as a fantastic legend with no grounding in historical fact. The only danger that he could see was that some impressionable men with little historical or scriptural knowledge would take it as a rendering of actual events. Stone's—and the modern world's—error was his failure to discern the symbolic dimension of the Temple Legend. Magical practice always and everywhere relies on the power of symbolism, and Masonic-era Manhattan—despite being replete with erudite Masonic scholarship—was wholly uninformed about the esoteric spiritual realities standing behind the symbols.

As a young man, Stone had read the alarming conspiracist works of Abbé Barruel and John Robison about the illicit powers wielded by Freemasons and was affected by them enough that it was only after a trusted friend invited him to Freemasonic membership that he had done so. Now, after a dozen years of membership in the Masonic brotherhood, reflecting in a letter to President Adams on the charges that Adam Weishaupt's semisecret society the Bavarian Illuminati had instigated the terrors of the French Revolution and that there had been Illuminists among the Founding Fathers, he found these ideas absurd.

As to Freemasonic secrets—the initial lure for Stone as a young man—he found not a single one. "The essential secrets of Masonry consisted in nothing more than the signs, grips, pass-words and tokens, essential to the preservation of the society from the inroads of impostors." He noted that special handshakes and passwords were common to the much less mysterious Tammany Society, Phi Beta Kappa, and other fraternal orders and that the symbolic emblems and arcane language were strictly to permit Freemasons to converse intelligibly with each other.

The terrible prescriptive oaths uttered in the initiations Stone found to be merely in bad taste, not dangerous. Still, since Freemasonry's pretensions to antiquity were a fraud, its rites and ceremonies frivolous, its symbols and allegories backward, its oaths perhaps illegal, the whole business being "a great waste of time," in the end, this formerly loyal Royal Arch Mason emphatically told Adams that "THE ORDER OF FREEMASONRY OUGHT FOREVER TO BE RELINQUISHED."

But in reality, the oaths and passwords and handshakes were potentially dangerous, rooted as they were in deep magical principles. All magical activity is based on the correspondence between the Macrocosm and the microcosm; as the "little world" that contains within all of the powers and potential of the Cosmos, the human physical body is the template on which much magical action depends. Mesmer and his disciples had demonstrated the magical power of the hands; many witnesses had actually seen silver, gray, and bluish rays emanating from the hands of the magnetic healers. The fingers and fingertips are especially charged, and hence in

Freemasonic ritual, with its roots in the ancient mysteries, hand-clasps played an important magical role. Signs, words, and even the special garments—such as the famed Freemasonic apron—activated certain astral and etheric currents. Designed by magical adepts both to heal and to awaken the invisible organs of the astral body, by the time that Stone was initiated, all of these magical gestures had degenerated into awkward, often annoying playacting.

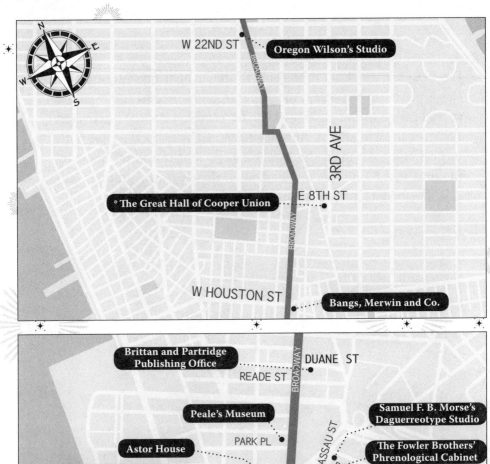

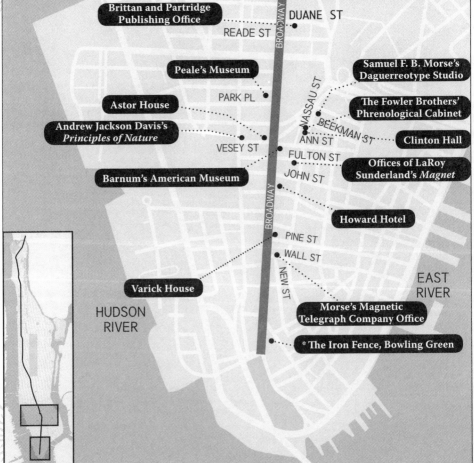

Magnetic Manhattan

1836–1874

Map of the City of New York Extending Northward to Fiftieth St.
(Surveyed and drawn by John F. Harrison C.E., published by M. Dripps, 1852)

L ower Manhattan harbors the history of the very beginnings of scientific inquiry in New York City, and it is the birthplace of technological developments that would change all America and the world. In the early decades of the nineteenth century, this neighborhood also became a prodigious *psychological* laboratory—in that era's sense of the plumbing of the depths of the soul, via the mysterious phenomena of animal magnetism. By 1850, the area between the Battery and City Hall Park was a hotbed of spiritual, psychological, and thus *magical* experimentation.

It was not until the 1830s that the word "science" even entered the American vernacular, and so the subjects of study that made up scientific inquiry may seem oddly eccentric. But the "Magnetic" era was when mesmerism, machines, and monsters all cohabited a common noetic space, before Romantic wonder yielded to reductionist rationalism. Many of these subjects seem, even now, positively *magical*.

Taken in hand at Bowling Green by the mesmerized Loraina Brackett and her mesmerist Colonel Stone, we will waft up to Broadway's stretch on the other side of City Hall Park, then jump way north to 945 Broadway, up by Madison Square. In between, we will take in antebellum New York's premier places of scientific demonstration, which were equally showplaces of pure *wonder*: Varick House, Peale's Museum, the Fowler Brothers' Phrenological "Cabinet," Astor House, P. T. Barnum's American Museum, the Howard Hotel, Clinton Hall, and the Great Hall of Cooper Union. In the antebellum era, these were Samuel Morse's streets, abuzz with the promise of telegraphy and the daguerreotype.

That the magical "action" of Manhattan still largely lay in Broadway's lower reaches in these decades of explosive economic, social, and cultural growth suggests a kind of lingering magical power contained within lower Manhattan. Indeed, those blocks from no. 1 to no. 900 constitute a veritable *battery* of magical forces.

Site #1: The Iron Fence (Still Standing), Bowling Green, August 1836

With all of the frantic activity—hurried commuters emerging from the Bowling Green subway station, school groups queueing up at the foot of the Custom House steps to see the Museum of the American Indian, the hordes of Instagraming tourists encircling the Bull—it is easy to overlook the shiny, black-enamel iron fence protecting the perimeter of the Bowling Green. But this humble enclosure holds an extraordinary history and is the only artifact about that dates to the colonial era. Approach it from the Custom House steps, enter the south gate, and be sure to touch the tops of the posts—which once bore hospitality-signaling iron pineapples but were knocked off by Liberty Boys intent on the overthrow of George III, whose equestrian statue once occupied the oval's center.

On August 26, 1836, the writer and editor William Leete Stone took the seventeen-year-old Loraina Brackett—then of Providence, Rhode Island—on a sightseeing stroll up Broadway. Beginning at the Battery, they stopped at the footbridge to Castle Garden, which Miss Brackett did not care to cross. She pointed out the odd costume of a member of the Castle Garden Boat Club, whose boathouse stood at the far end of the footbridge. Across from Bowling Green, she admired the bronzed lions flanking the entrance to a grand home on Broadway. In front of Trinity Church, Miss Brackett was disturbed by the jostling of the crowd. At the newly opened Astor House, after Colonel Stone narrated John Jacob Astor's rags-to-riches tale, Miss Brackett asked if they might go in but then shrank back at the sight of the crowd of men on the stairs.

Passing the American Hotel, they were about to turn left down Park Place, toward Colonel Stone's home, when Miss Brackett stopped to examine the sculpture—*Charity Tending to Orphan Children*—that adorned the cornice of Mechanics' Hall across the street. When they reached the Columbia College Green, Miss Brackett was disappointed that no one was about. Colonel Stone

The Bowling Green fence
(New York Public Library Digital Collections)

explained that the college was on vacation and then entertained his young guest with a brief history of Columbia since the time of the Revolution. When he asked her how she liked the trees on the Green, she answered that one of them was badly decayed and should be removed.

Miss Brackett's remark took Colonel Stone by surprise. He had not been aware of this injured tree when he had left home a few days before, to travel to Providence for an audience with Miss Brackett and her physician, Dr. George Capron. For, in fact, this pleasant stroll from the Battery to Mr. Stone's home on the Columbia College Green was actually taking place *in Providence*. It had begun when Stone asked Miss Brackett if she would like to see New York and proposed to travel there by steamboat. The adventurous teenager proposed that they fly instead; taking hold of both of Colonel Stone's hands and making him promise not to let her fall, away they went.

Miss Brackett had been left totally blind after an iron weight had fallen on her head, nearly killing her. After fifteen months of recuperation, her health was restored, but with no hope of recovering her sight, her family planned to take her to Dr. Samuel Gridley Howe's Asylum for the Blind in Boston, to see if she might be trained as a teacher for the blind. Stopping in Providence to visit friends who had Dr. Capron as their physician, Capron learned of Miss Brackett's condition and proposed to treat her blindness by way of animal magnetism, with which he had recently become acquainted after the visit of the pioneer French mesmerist Charles Poyen. Dr. Capron's magnetic treatments had improved Miss Brackett's sight so that she could distinguish light from darkness, but they had—like so many other mesmeric cures—also led her to spectacular experiences of clairvoyance. This is why William Leete Stone had come to Providence—to test this faculty of clairvoyance by inviting Miss Brackett, who had been placed by Dr. Capron in a mesmeric trance, to New York City.

Before Colonel Stone's trip to Providence, he had been "not only an unbeliever, but a satirist" of animal magnetism. He believed that the German healer Franz Anton Mesmer was an impostor and that his followers were deluded. But Stone was by nature both inquisitive and fair. Along with his editorial work, he had won distinction and acclaim for a wide variety of other initiatives. He had drafted the plan for slave emancipation recommended to Congress by the Baltimore Anti-Slavery Convention of 1825. He had advocated for Greek independence and had written, as we have seen, an even-handed examination of Freemasonry and Anti-Masonry in the wake of the sensational William Morgan murder, as well as a level-headed report on the "impostures" of the apocalyptic Prophet Matthias, an exposé of the falsehoods of Maria Monk's claims of having been sexually assaulted by Montreal priests, and a superb biography of the Mohawk military and political leader Joseph Brant. Stone had a passion for truth, a warm interest in human beings, and an empiricist's eye for descriptive detail—all of which made him the ideal candidate to bring to Gotham's attention and discernment this fantastic new power of seeing far-off places without the use of physical eyes.

Stone's "walk" with Loraina Brackett—particularly incidents like her pointing out the injured tree (upon his return to New York, Stone found a partially debarked tree near his home, wrapped in a tar-covered canvas bandage)—had completely convinced him of Miss Brackett's ability to leave her body and travel to witness a foreign landscape as if she were indeed walking there. He was an avid art collector, and the balance of his Providence experiment consisted of walking around his Manhattan home examining paintings and prints. Miss Brackett described a painting of Christ in agony with a crown of thorns, a copy of Guido Reni's *Ecco Homo* that Stone had just purchased; a portrait of an Indian chief with a shaved head and topknot, a copy made by George Catlin of the last portrait done of Chief Joseph Brant, commissioned by Stone for his forthcoming biography of the Mohawk leader; and another picture of Chief Brant that Brant's daughter had lent to Stone for reproduction in the biography. Most spectacular for Stone, however, was Miss Brackett's description—"three Indians sitting in a hollow tree filled with marks"—of a landscape by the New York artist Stansbury Hoxie. Stone knew both the painting and the actual location—an enormous sycamore in Montezuma, New York—and that visitors seldom noticed the native hieroglyphs carved into the trunk. "And yet," Stone exclaimed, "this blind lady, with bandaged eyes, who had never been in New York, nor heard a whisper of the existence of this picture, had discovered them!"

Before their tour ended, Stone asked Miss Brackett if she had heard of Wall Street and the great fire of 1835 and proposed that they walk down to see the rebuilding of the new Stock Exchange. Stepping into Trinity Church along the way, Miss Brackett complained that the pews were ugly and inconvenient, that the pulpit needed new drapery, and that the cushion upon which the Bible lay was threadbare. Upon Stone's return, he paid a visit to Trinity and found all of this to be true.

At last—after about four hours—Colonel Stone proposed that they return to Providence, clasped the young clairvoyant's hands, and away they flew, Miss Brackett exclaiming, "Oh how beautiful it is to look down upon the city! How vast! How grand!" William Leete Stone's lengthy letter to his friend Dr. Amariah Brigham, published in his own *Commercial Advertiser* newspaper and then as a pamphlet, excited considerable attention in New York. For the historian, the lover of old maps, and the lover of New York City, there is something altogether irresistible about this late-August 1836 stroll of the erudite editor Colonel Stone and his impressionable ingénue guest Miss Loraina Brackett. It is not that Colonel Stone's account is very likely the first American report of an out-of-body experience. It is not that the walk they took together—one in his imagination, out of his power of memory; the other in "real time" with her astral body— should have been up the most celebrated road in America, the *Breede weg*, Broadway. It is not even the special satisfaction that one receives when, Dripp's 1852 map in one hand, Doggett's 1842 *New York City Directory* in the other, one locates the people and places from Stone's account—including the very same iron fence around the Bowling Green that stood here on the day of their walk—almost feeling oneself flying above lower Manhattan, much like Loraina Brackett did in 1836.

The deepest delight of this admittedly minor event in the annals of this great metropolis is that the entire episode unfolded so innocently. A cosmopolitan New York City gentleman takes it upon himself to travel two hundred miles to present himself to a total stranger, a blind teenage girl, who hesitates for not one second to take up the stranger's hand and "fly" with him—no *carte de visite*, no elaborate introductions. The instant intimacy they enjoy we enjoy too. It is the bond forged when one shares the things—people, place, objects— one loves most deeply with another. Miss Brackett *loved* seeing New York, from Castle Garden to the hieroglyphs on that sycamore tree. And the blind girl in Providence even saw things that had escaped the observant gentleman's attention, right in his own backyard.

Not all that many years later, students of the mysteries of mesmerism wondered how it was that the earliest subjects—unlike those who came later—so often exhibited such spectacular feats of clairvoyance. A heavy fog of skepticism and cynicism would soon enshroud investigators and end the atmosphere of *sympathy* (a keyword for Americans in these midcentury decades) that prevailed when magnetic clairvoyant states were first being promulgated and explored. Along this very avenue, America and New York would in just a few years conjure the man—P. T. Barnum—whose productions often elicited cries of "Humbug!" in the face of mystery and wonder. But at least for a brief moment, destiny brought together an earnest seeker of truth and an eager young sightseer and allowed them to witness to each other, affording us a glimpse of their sympathetic clairvoyant resonance on a truly transcendental walk along Broadway.

Site #2: The Arcana of Animal Magnetism: Charles Ferson Durant's "Experiment" at Varick House, 108 Broadway, August 13, 1837

From our distant vantage point of the present, it is difficult to tease apart the tightly woven fabric making up mesmerism. Equal parts serious scientific experimentation and theatrical spectacle, the "performance" of mesmeric study demanded an audience and thus theatrical spaces. It was a commonplace of the era that hotels, museums, and libraries were used to display the latest technological wonders, and mesmerism was very much seen as a kind of human technology. The popular hotel Varick House was just one of dozens that lined Broadway. These establishments were long ago replaced by the gargantuan towers of the financial industry, and the best way to get a feel for them now is perhaps to visit the plush lobby bar of the Beekman Hotel on Beekman Street at Park Row. The brightly lit atrium space, surrounded by glass-covered bookshelves, its walls decorated with the very personalities—Edgar Allan Poe, Ralph Waldo Emerson,

Experiment in animal magnetism
(C. F. Durant, *Exposition; or, A New Theory of Animal Magnetism*, 1837)

Henry David Thoreau—who walked these streets in the mesmeric era, is the perfect picture of these vanished venues.

No sooner had Colonel Stone's report on his astral adventure with Loraina Brackett appeared in the local press than "skeptical philosophers" set out to debunk and ridicule this fantastic episode. One of the city's practical mechanics, Charles Ferson Durant, as a printer, had his own press at his disposal to try to refute Colonel Stone's report in his *Exposition; or, A New Theory of Animal Magnetism, with a Key to the Mysteries: Demonstrated by the Most Celebrated Somnambulists in America* (1837). Over twenty-two chapters, Durant purports to give "conclusive and overwhelming" evidence that animal magnetism is "a deception so simple and wicked, that reason must brand with *weakness, infatuation, and idiocy* the men who will hereafter believe in it." Durant's ad hominem attacks on Colonel Stone took for granted that "'*charms*,' '*fortune-telling*,' and '*astrology*'" were all magical practices assumed to have been disposed of by the glorious Enlightenment.

While Durant and his fellow skeptics hoodwinked themselves, the magnetic revelations continued apace up and down Broadway.

It was as if Miss Bracket's astral flight had left a trail of fairy dust over the magic isle below.

Site #3: Samuel F. B. Morse's Daguerreotype Studio, 142 Nassau Street, May 1838

A horse-drawn carriage rounded the corner of Rector Street onto Broadway on November 16, 1832. It conveyed brothers Richard, Sidney, and Samuel Finley Breese Morse, along with a large burlap-wrapped package that "Finley" believed would both elevate the artistic tastes of New Yorkers and make his fame and fortune. The brothers had just fetched Finley and his parcel from the pier on the Hudson, after his long transatlantic crossing. Morse's *Gallery of the Louvre*—whose six-by-nine-foot canvas reproduced in miniature copies of masterpieces by Leonardo, Titian, Raphael, Rembrandt, and others—would go on exhibit within the year in a gallery above Carvill & Company's bookstore on Broadway and Pine Street. Critics were charmed; the public—admitted at twenty-five cents each—was not. Their disinterest in Morse's painting only confirmed his conviction that "Every man is driving at one object—the making of money—not the spending of it."

In mid-May 1838, Samuel Morse boarded a steamboat to Europe, this time not as an aspiring painter but as the inventor and hopeful promoter of the "American Electro-Magnetic Telegraph." In March 1839, just before he left Paris for Liverpool and his voyage back to New York, he arranged to visit with stage designer Louis Daguerre at his celebrated Diorama, where Daguerre made spectacular theatrical magic with sound and lighting effects to animate enormous panoramic landscape paintings. With his partner, Daguerre had discovered a process that could chemically fix an image in a camera obscura—a device and process that Morse had experimented with over fifteen years before. Morse was amazed by what he saw: "No painting or engraving ever approached it." The next day, Daguerre came to Morse's room for a demonstration of the telegraph; while

Samuel F. B. Morse
(Library of Congress)

there, a fire broke out at the Diorama, destroying the paintings. Neighbors rescued the daguerreotype apparatus, however.

"It is one of the most beautiful discoveries of the age," Morse declared to his brothers in a long letter that they published in the May 18 issue of the *Observer*—the first eyewitness account of photography to appear in America. Shortly after Morse arrived home, he went across Nassau Street to the workshop of the scientific-instrument maker George W. Prosch, and together they devised a rudimentary camera. Morse made his first daguerreotype from the doorway of Prosch's workshop. It showed City Hall and the park, complete with a "coachman stepping on his box." Morse's publisher brother Sidney's *Observer* offices were now across the street at 142 Nassau; by October, Morse moved in to a studio on the building's roof, where he made what may be the very first urban cityscape photographs in America. When Albert Sands Southworth went to Morse for training a few months later, he reported that "very clear, distinct views of Brooklyn in the distance and roofs in the foreground, taken from the tops of the buildings in Nassau Street, were upon his table."

After Morse and his fellow University of the City of New York professor John William Draper perfected their technique for making daguerreotype portraits, Morse quickly became the most prolific instructor in the new art; among his early trainees were Edward and Henry Anthony, whose studio just south of St. Paul's, at the junction of Fulton and Broadway, was the principal anchor point of "Photographers' Row." The city's first daguerreotype district included the Meade Brothers' gallery—the largest in New York City—on the second floor of the Astor House, and Matthew Brady's studio and gallery, directly across Broadway, next to Barnum's American Museum. This tightly circumscribed confluence of America's leading practitioners of the new image-making alchemy, conjunct with the confluence of Gotham's centers of politics, journalism, religion, commerce, leisure entertainment, and education, meant that the street life of these few city blocks was the most commonly captured image in America for the first couple of decades of daguerreotyping. The concentration of engravers in the area along lower Broadway, close to Printer's Row, meant that this area also saw the most rapid application and adaptation of the daguerreotype to newspaper and book publishing. The entire history of the gradual process by which the word became supplanted by the photograph could be written by studying the history of a four- or five-block stretch of Broadway with St. Paul's at its center. The stately stone chapel, with its spire reaching toward heaven and its enveloping gravestones and greenery, provided a reassuring sense of permanence amid the maelstrom of innovation swirling about the neighboring streets.

Far from Broadway, in every colonized corner of the globe, many people of traditional societies saw photography as a powerful form of sorcery. Even rural Americans mixed their admiration of the camera with a bit of awe-filled fear, and the native peoples being driven from their green ancestral homes to deserts out west beyond the Mississippi universally condemned cameras as "soul-stealers." Though the exotic technology quickly lost its magical luster, enough so that once-fearful people came to cherish photographs as dearly as New Yorkers did, and though thanks to social media there is an ironic ring of truth to that old superstition of cameras stealing souls, there is to this day something distinctly uncanny about the photograph's effect on our psyche.

Site #4: Mesmerism at Peale's Museum, 252 Broadway, February 1841

Whatever the lecture, demonstration, or visual spectacle taking place at the New York Museum of Natural History and Science (popularly known as "Peale's Museum"), proprietor Rubens Peale always advertised the venue as "across from the Park." "The Park" in those days meant City Hall Park, the hub of all New Yorkers' daily social commerce. The little four-story structure directly across Broadway from City Hall was then the epitome of bourgeois culture, where art and science and spectacle all freely mixed promiscuously—but altogether *properly.*

Colonel Stone's pamphlet describing his journey with Loraina Brackett and other mesmeric experiments went quickly through several editions, leading Dr. David Reese to call animal magnetism the "reigning humbug in the United States" but particularly popular (and pernicious!) in New York City: "Should any reader inquire why we select the city of New York as the scene of our strictures, he may be reminded that it is the theater of humbugs, the chosen arena of itinerating mountebanks. . . . Here is found a motley population, multitudes of whom spend their time in nothing else, but in searching after some new thing."

It is not surprising that in New York City mesmerism early on left the parlor for the stage. On February 8, 1841, Rubens Peale presented

Rubens Peale
(National Gallery of Art)

at his museum the Englishman Robert Collyer, who mesmerized a young woman and then blindfolded her and stood behind her. Whatever gesture Collyer made, the young woman repeated. When Peale pulled a hair from Collyer's head, she instantly felt as if he were pulling on her hair. Peale held up a series of objects—all of which she named. When he held out his pocket watch, she told him the time to the exact minute.

P. T. Barnum soon lured Collyer down Broadway to the American Museum, and Peale—who, like Colonel Stone, had been a complete skeptic about animal magnetism—undertook the role of mesmerizer himself, charging twenty-five-cent admission to his demonstrations. His subject was Miss Mary Mattock, an inmate at the Institution for the Blind who had been blind since birth. At first, he followed a routine similar to Collyer's, until that summer, when a doctor in the audience suggested he might awaken individual organs of the brain. Unfamiliar with phrenology, Peale turned for help to the Reverend LaRoy Sunderland, a Methodist minister with an interest in phrenology. As Mary sat playing the piano, Peale passed his fingers upward over her "organ of music," and suddenly she could no longer play. Reversing the direction of his fingers over her head, she began instantly where she left off. Sunderland pointed out the "organ of hunger"; Peale passed his fingers over it, and instantly Mary asked for something to eat.

On September 8, 1841, Peale called together some forty physicians, clergymen, and others for a rigorous test of this "sympathetic clairvoyance." Once again, "Blind Mary" was the subject, and this time the invited scientific gentlemen were permitted to carry out their own investigations. Individuals' names and addresses, letter and numbers written on cards, and a wide variety of objects, from a phrenological almanac to a vial of vinegar—Mary promptly identified them all while entranced. They also repeated the experiment at the piano, with the same results.

One of the guests was Orson Squire Fowler, who, with his brother Lorenzo was the main American promoter of phrenology. He devised a most elaborate experiment: with both Peale and Mary blindfolded, Fowler took hold of Peale's hand and passed it over one organ area after another—the phrenological organs of "Combativeness," "Pity," "Self-Esteem," "Reverence," and so on—atop Mary's head, following a list written down by a committee of the spectators. They had invented "Phreno-Mesmerism." The *New York Tribune* editor Horace Greeley was especially impressed with the demonstrations and endorsed them in February 1842.

"Invention" was a double-edged epithet in this era; Collyer is a perfect expression of this. The gifted magnetist had in 1851 gained a patent for a new method of crushing quartz. In 1852, he invented a new amalgamating apparatus. Along with improving the breech-loading cannon in 1854, he secured patents for a quartz pulverizer and gold amalgamator. In 1859, he devised a new type of coating for the hulls of iron ships. When skeptics accused Collyer and other animal magnetists of "invention," they were quite right.

Site #5: The Fowler Brothers' Phrenological Cabinet, 131 Nassau Street, 1842

The intersection of Nassau and Beekman Streets was at midcentury a veritable crossroads of modern cultural currents and, as such, a fitting home for two of the era's most prominent mesmeric practitioners, brothers Orson Squire and Lorenzo Niles Fowler, to open up their Phrenological Cabinet in 1842. Like so many of the neighboring establishments, the "Cabinet"—they simply scaled up the term for a collection of curiosities to denote the whole enterprise—was part parlor, part sales floor, part hostelry. Anyone who stepped through the Fowler Brothers' door knew they would come into contact with the very latest knowledge about the twinned sciences of mesmerism and phrenology.

None of Magnetic Manhattan's "pseudosciences" have come in for as much ridicule as phrenology, the study of human character and mental abilities as expressed in the shape and size of the cranium. The Fowlers boasted "Busts and Casts from the heads of the most distinguished men that ever lived; Skulls—human and animal—from all quarters of the Globe—including Egyptian Mummies, Pirates, Robbers, Murderers, and Thieves," all free to visitors. They offered at the Cabinet professional phrenological examinations, reading their subjects' bumps and lumps to prescribe the most suitable occupations, selection of business and romantic partners, and other useful insights, along with a written description of one's character. "These mental portraits," the Fowlers observed, "are becoming almost as common and indispensable as a Daguerreotype of the outer man."

Sometime just before July 1855, Ralph Waldo Emerson made a brief entry in his journal:

The new professions—
The phrenologist
The railroad man
The landscape gardener
The lecturer
The sorcerer, rapper, mesmeriser, medium
The daguerreotypist

Emerson was himself acting as a kind of phrenologist in compiling this vocational roster, for it gave a characterological reading of American culture at midcentury. The "railroad man" was the easy choice, as by 1855 rail lines penetrated every corner of the country and had transformed the social and economic lives of many Americans. Emerson's other choices hardly composed a nested set, but they all were professions that burst quickly on the scene and then, perhaps with the exception of the landscape gardener, went extinct. Phrenology was already by 1855 losing its former cachet, displaced by other "sciences of the mind"; the wet developing process, which dramatically reduced the exposure time for making photographic images, came into its own this year; the lyceum movement had peaked, and though Emerson went on lecturing until 1870, lecturing as a profession was certainly on the wane; the mesmerizer had been largely replaced by Spiritualist mediums, who saw their commercial opportunities contract as spirit rapping became a hobby for millions.

Phrenology, landscape architecture, professional public speaking, Spiritualist and mesmeric performance, and daguerreotype portraiture were united by something other than their meteoric rise to obsolescence; they were all "physiognomic" pursuits, seeking to reveal or enhance hidden inner qualities. The phrenologist was the direct descendant of Franz Joseph Gall and Johann Spurzheim, who in the late eighteenth century developed a science of physiognomy. Landscape architects and the gardeners who executed their plans sought to discover the inner quality of a place and then to sculpt the soil and plants to best express that quality. Lecturers like Emerson

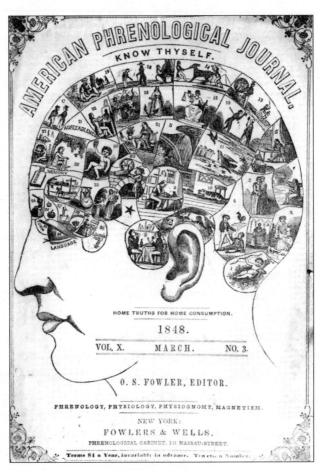

The Fowler brothers
(*Phrenological Journal*)

and his protégé Henry David Thoreau read the physiognomy of their fellow citizens and then suggested through their rhetoric how their audiences might better shape their ideas and actions to the pursuit of goodness, truth, and beauty. Sorcerers of all stripes— from the stage magician to the professional or amateur mediums and mesmerizers—used theatrical technique and prescribed physical gestures to lead their subjects and audiences into another world.

The daguerreotypist was antebellum America's supreme recorder of gestures, to whom everyone rushed to immortalize their countenances before their facial physiognomy began to fail and fade away. Like other midcentury vocations, all aspired to scientific objectivity; in their pre-Enlightenment forms, all of these professions would have been "arts," while in 1855, each one claimed for itself the mantle of science.

There is at the heart of phrenology a magical principle that must be kept in mind if we are not to perennially fall back into old magics rather than step forth into the destined new ones. Tea leaves, dice, cards, scapulas, Ouija boards, and irises—*anything* can be used for augury and divination. That antebellum America saw the skull become a favorite site of physiognomic divination is completely characteristic, since Reason—believed to be seated in the physical brain—was becoming the great idol. Those phrenologists who could accurately—sometimes as uncannily as the Tarot reader or magnetic clairvoyant—read one's fate from the top of the head were employing the same sympathetic, *magnetic* forces as were everywhere swirling about this magic isle in the 1830s and '40s. Phrenology *could have* become a science and remains as pseudoscience only because our divinatory faculties remain asleep.

Site #6: Astor House, Corner of Vesey and Broadway, Fall 1842

Standing just across Vesey Street from the venerable St. Paul's Chapel, the Astor House was for half a century North America's premier hotel, a meeting ground of the titans of commerce, politics, science, literature, and art, as storied as the street on which it fronted. The 1915 edifice that replaced it (home to a Staples store at ground level) bears a faint echo of the old hotel's Greek Revival lines. It is worth recalling that the men and women who enthused over the "dark sciences" of the antebellum era were all schooled in classical education; they probably knew a little Greek and Latin, read Homer, and could quote Aristotle or Plato nearly as readily as they could quote Barnum and Dickens.

Along with the concentration of mainstream Christian sects in lower Manhattan, there emerged in the 1830s and 1840s a variety of "eccentric" faiths, new churches founded to explore Swedenborgianism, Spiritualism, and other visionary streams that embraced science as a way of knowing that was superior to divine revelation. On these streets and sidewalks (New York's very first sidewalk was constructed along Broadway between Fulton Street and Park Place) walked not just the orthodox parishioners of Trinity, St. Paul's, St. Peter's (Roman Catholic), Brick (Presbyterian), and Dutch Reformed Churches; there were also the heterodox followers and practitioners of mesmeric healing, phrenology, and Swedenborgian astronomy. In fact, lower Manhattan was in the antebellum period perhaps the most intense region of visionary seeking in America, denser and more fervent in its desire for spiritual clairvoyance than the famed "burned-over district" of evangelically enthusiastic rural western New York State.

Because this area was at midcentury the heart of New York's publishing industry, the neighborhood was full of influential writers and artists who took an interest in clairvoyant communication equal to their fascination for the new communications technologies of photography and telegraphy. One prominent mesmeric circle included the famed painter Henry Inman, his younger brother Charles, the poet Frederick G. Tuckerman, and the editor and author Charles Fenno Hoffman. The cabinetmaker Charles Inman proved to be an excellent mesmeric subject and came to the attention of Dr. Joseph Rodes Buchanan, who in the fall of 1842 performed a series of experiments with Inman at his room in the Astor House. Presenting to Inman letters from correspondents, he found that Inman was able, just by merely touching the letters, to give a detailed description of the emotional state of the letter writer. Through the mysterious faculty of "sympathy," Inman would become so immersed in the writers' views and feelings that he was able to also describe their

Astor House, 1854
(New-York Historical Society Digital Collections)

relationships to each other. Holding one pair of letters from two men who were bitter opponents, he asked Buchanan to stop the experiment, for he felt their antagonism as his own inner state.

Buchanan gave to his new clairvoyant science the name "psychometry" (i.e., "mind measurement") and drew immediately on the authority of the daguerreotype to suggest psychometry's possibilities. "In this first psychometric experiment . . . I was fully satisfied that, by this process, we might obtain *a mental daguerreotype* of any one whose autograph we obtain, as perfect as the physical daguerreotype of the features, obtained by the agency of solar light."

Buchanan's next experiments consisted of giving Inman a set of letters from John Adams, George Washington, Lafayette, and other great men of the early republic; the results convinced him of the new science's efficacy as a practical means of judging human character. In advance of the presidential election of 1848, Buchanan submitted a set of autographs of General Zachary Taylor, General Lewis Cass, Martin Van Buren, and Gerritt Smith, certain that a psychometric analysis would provide voters with the requisite information about their respective characters that they would choose the most worthy man for president.

Buchanan and those who followed him into this exploration of the past through psychic means, were sure that they now possessed the Rosetta Stone for deciphering *all* the secrets of history, which they imagined locked in an invisible fluid, just as early paleontologists had penetrated ancient strata to depict ancient antediluvian scenes populated with fossil monsters. "The Past is entombed in the Present!" proclaimed Buchanan, who inspired a Boston geologist named William Denton to take up this psychometric research program, giving specimens of fossiliferous rock to his wife for clairvoyant examination. "Aye," said Buchanan, "the mental telescope is now discovered, which may pierce the depths of the past and bring us in full view of all the grand and tragic passages of ancient history!" This tenacious faith in the accuracy of the representations mirrored the faith in the daguerreotype's absolute fidelity to nature. All that was required to write a complete history of civilization, the psychometrists believed, was a sufficient set of physical artifacts; Buchanan longed for a set from Julius Caesar, Cicero, Plutarch, Pericles, Plato, Solon, Alfred the Great, Confucius, and Mohammed. One cannot overstate that these clairvoyant aspirations and expectation were absolutely *normal* for Buchanan's contemporaries, *fact*, not fiction. That such aspirations—and phenomena—have widely resurfaced in our own time should give us pause about the materialist suppositions of twenty-first-century science.

Site #7: Barnum's American Museum, Broadway and Ann Street, Fall 1842

If you take a seat in St. Paul's Chapel, looking east across Broadway through either the north or south Broadway entrances, you are looking straight at the site that once held America's most celebrated phantasmagorium: Mr. Phineas T. Barnum's American Museum.

Barnum's American Museum, 1853
(New-York Historical Society Digital Collections)

"Ladies and Gentlemen! Step right up! Don't be bashful now! All you need to do is squint your right eye closed, and you'll see it! Convivial home to the Feejee Mermaid and Tom Thumb; to Chang and Eng, the Siamese Twins; Grizzly Adams's trained bears; a flea circus; an oyster bar; rifle range; wax museum; freak shows; and general phantasmagoria. If your taste should run to entertainments more educational, be sure to visit the Dioramas, Panoramas, and Cycloramas. Perhaps if it is your lucky day, you may meet Mr. Barnum himself!"

For nearly half a century, until P. T. Barnum's American Museum burned down in one of the city's most spectacular fires, on July 13, 1865, the clergy at St. Paul's had to compete for the attention of their congregation with New York's greatest attraction, located directly across the street at the corner of Ann Street and Broadway. St. Paul's churchyard—whose soil, every spring, heaves forth a crop of late eighteenth- and early nineteenth-century crockery, china, and clam shells—is a perfect place to contemplate this jarring juxtaposition of antebellum cultural institutions. Along with inheriting the flotsam and jetsam of John Scudder's and Rubens Peale's carnivalesque collections, Barnum took on the role of scientific cultural broker, interpreting the world's wonders for the wide public—for just twenty-five-cent admission.

Neither philosopher nor physician—rather, gonzo *pataphysician*— Barnum surely held a higher place in Gotham's scientific pantheon than all the MDs and PhDs put together. "Imagination," he declared, "is a gift, it is the incredible elixir of life." Barnum gave New Yorkers ample fodder for the imagination, often to the great dismay of the city's tastemakers. Cultural historians have found in Barnum *the* representative man of antebellum America, the independent, irreverent, audacious New Man of the new upstart nation. He played the part of impresario in the three-ring circus of nineteenth-century America's democratization of knowledge; by parading objects of dubious authenticity, Barnum taught America to make up its own mind. His lifelong sleight-of-hand worked because he knew that in nature—as in narrative—truth is stranger than fiction. His motto, "Wonderful, because mysterious," invites us to take Barnum out of the wax museum's Hall of Confidence Men and set his bronze bust erect in the Hall of Scientific Men, next to both well-respected members of the Lyceum of Natural History and Rev. LaRoy Sunderland and the serious investigators of the new magical phenomena bursting asunder along Broadway.

Though Barnum played down his knowledge of natural history, saying that he did not know a clam from a codfish, he exchanged specimens and correspondence with leading naturalists, museum curators, and animal dealers who respected his considerable curiosity and expertise about animals and their habits. In among all the hype and humbug of playbills and posters advertising Barnum's museum, there was always a deferential and serious nod to natural history's educational value. Still, in the 1840s, the clean categories of zoology did not yet exist in full, and even the most outrageous of Barnum's contrived category violations helped to create public conversations about the chain of being. Edwin Chapin, a Universalist minister who preached from his pulpit up Broadway near Spring Street, in 1843 told his congregation that "it is not only an arrogant but a shallow philosophy that says 'the existence of this or that is impossible, it is contrary to the laws of nature.'" As American natural science became increasingly rationalized, Barnum's menageries presented a perennially renewable source of wonder, while at the same time teaching a wide American public to think independently and critically about the marvelous in nature. For all of his "humbugging," we might think of Barnum as this magic isle's most marvelous magician, keeping wonder alive in an era of pronounced disenchantment.

THE FEEJEE MERMAID AND MAGIZOOLOGY

Though from the safe perch of the present, we know she was nothing more than a mummified monkey's torso with a fish's tail sewed on it, Barnum's Feejee Mermaid titillated the public like no authentic animal ever could. Cries of "Impossible!" were far more often raised in reaction to real animals than to hoaxes like the Feejee Mermaid. Authentic "ambiguous" animals—such as sea anemones, given their odd combination of qualities of plant and animal; or butterflies, whose patterns perfectly imitated each other or their environment—seemed too marked by artifice to be real. The wide range of illusions that marked mid-nineteenth-century popular culture—stage magic, ventriloquism, trompe l'oeil paintings, and Barnumesque frauds—sometimes caused folk to utter "Humbug!" when it was not necessary.

J. K. Rowling may have coined the term "Magizoologist" for her character Newt Scamander, but it is a completely apt moniker for P. T. Barnum, as well as for most of his fellow antebellum collectors of flora and fauna, for natural history at that pre-Darwinian

EGYPTIAN MUMMIES,
and ancient Sarcophagi, 3000 Years old ; and an entire
Family of Peruvian Mummies ;
the DUCK-BILLED PLATYPUS, the connecting link between
the BIRD and BEAST, being evidently half each ;—the curious
half-fish, half-human

FEJEE MERMAID,
which was exhibited in most of the principal cities of America,
in the years 1840, '41, and '42, to the wonder and astonishment
of thousands of naturalists and other scientific persons, whose
previous doubts of the existence of such an astonishing creation
were entirely removed ;

P. T. Barnum's Feejee Mermaid, 1842

time still shimmered with the erotic anticipation of the fantastic. In Rowling and Newt's world, there are *Acromantulas, Basilisks, Chimaeras, Dragons, Manticores, Wampus Cats,* and *Werewolves.* These CGI monsters are wan imitations of Barnum's Feejee Mermaid or of the sea serpent—the real ones that in Barnum's day haunted the American imagination so palpably that they generated intense scientific discussion and controversy. Monsters—demons, hybrid animals, and misshapen humans—had been a constant production of ancient magic, but they frequently appeared in the new nineteenth-century magics of magnetically or somnambulistically altered states. Rachel Baker, in her first trance fits, before she began to preach in her sleep, had seen such demons. Dismissed by science as "hallucinations," these monsters would not go away but would actually take on more puzzling—and sometimes terrifying— physical form over the century to come.

"THE SEA SERPENT CAUGHT AT LAST!"

In February 1858, the *New York Tribune* published a Melville-worthy tale of a crew member aboard the *Monongahela* spying a sea serpent, which was then shortly after harpooned and brought back to shore. The compelling account of the chase and killing concluded with exact measurements (103 feet, 7 inches long; 19 feet, 11 inches around at the neck) and a description of the animal's stomach contents (squid and blackfish). Only after the story was picked up by newspapers in London (including the *Zoologist*), Rome, and Berlin was it exposed as a hoax.

Newspapers around the world had been publishing actual accounts of sea serpents for half a century, and for the eyewitnesses, it was heartily hoped that natural science would get to the bottom of the creature's life history and habits. Dr. Samuel Latham Mitchill read a paper on the sea serpent to the New York Lyceum in 1828; the *American Journal of Science* printed the report in 1829. It included an account of a conversation at a hotel on Broadway between William Warburton and Sir Isaak Coffin. Warburton—along with "Miss Magee, daughter of a New York merchant"—had seen the sea serpent on a vessel bound from New York to Boston; two days later, it was reported off Cape Cod.

The monster continued to be sighted occasionally right into the 1850s, and certain peak years stirred scientific interest once again. In 1835, the *American Journal of Science*, reporting on another Massachusetts sighting, concluded, "We must therefore consider this case as settling the question of the real existence of a Sea Serpent. The absence of paddles or arms forbids us from supposing that this was a swimming saurian." This equivocation suggests that at least in 1835, there was still—as with the existence of the unicorn—some scientific hesitancy to unilaterally declare the nonexistence of the sea serpent. But by 1850, a number of sophisticated hoaxes had been executed, which in this age of humbug served to quickly provide an

The sea serpent seen in 1826

easy excuse for those who wished to banish the anomalous creature from any serious consideration. The dozens of explanations provided by debunkers (almost all of whom never came anywhere near the places where the spectral animal had been seen) do not alter the fact that there were thousands of eyewitnesses, among them the most trusted men of their age: sea captains. Upon hearing of a sighting from Captain Thomas Perkins in 1817, Edward Everett, a brilliant scholar and statesman, had made a special study and concluded that Perkins and the other witnesses (including Daniel Webster!) had indeed seen a serpent. The *American Journal of Science* editor Benjamin Silliman and the British Royal Society scientists Joseph Banks and Joseph Hooker were all convinced of the creature's existence, and as late as 1847, the *Zoologist* editor Edward Newman opened up the pages of his scientific journal to an open-minded discussion of the topic. "It has been the fashion for . . . many years to deride all records of this very celebrated monster," his editorial stated. He chided critics for a priori approaches that ignored "fact and observation" on the grounds that the sea serpent "ought not to be." "Fact-naturalists," he said, "take a different road to knowledge, they enquire whether such things are, and whether such things are not."

The following year, the most famous sea-serpent report of all time took place. It occurred on the afternoon of August 6, 1848, and the witnesses were the captain and crew of the frigate *Daedalus*, on their way back to England from the Cape of Good Hope. Soon after the frigate's arrival at Plymouth, England, on October 4, several newspapers reported rumors of a spectacular twenty-minute sea-serpent sighting, and the Admiralty asked the captain to supply a report either denying or detailing the incident. The captain fully verified the report, which was reprinted widely in newspapers and was even noticed in *Scientific American*.

There was something altogether uncanny about the sea serpent, and "fact-naturalists" the world over all suffered from a like disadvantage in their attempts to place the creature in their Cabinets—both the wooden ones bearing specimens and the one inside their minds. Though a very small minority of the sightings were hoaxes or honest observational errors, the vast majority were honest eyewitness reports made by trustworthy citizens. The sea serpent and other "magical animals" (today they are called "cryptids") are epistemological bellwethers, dramatic indicators of the inability of modern materialism to understand that spiritual beings—especially those conjured by the intense, emotionally charged thoughts of the masses—can, under certain conditions, become *physically* manifest. Such appearances were truly "gossamer" in their ephemerality, their mercurial essence once upon a time known to each and every culture on the planet.

These sea serpents, despite having all the physical attributes that would make them a powerful adversary of humanity, never attacked anyone. They seemed more like the sylphs and salamanders and gnomes and undines, in that they were relatively shy and quite ephemeral, even if they made repeated appearances in an area.

Site #8: Offices of LaRoy Sunderland's *Magnet*, 138 Fulton Street, October 1842

By December 1841, Rubens Peale had sold his museum to P. T. Barnum, and he soon left New York City, though he continued to practice mesmeric healing until his death in 1865. Meanwhile, the Methodist minister turned mesmeric physician LaRoy Sunderland continued these experiments in 1842 in his home and at the offices of his new periodical, the *Magnet*, which became the principal organ for explaining the magnetic/mesmeric state to an American audience. The mesmeric trance he participated in with Peale had contributed to his abandonment of the ministry; during his years as a minister, Sunderland's observation that so many people when entranced had experiences identical with religious ecstasy caused him to turn from religion to science as a path toward the spiritual world. The lengthy title of Sunderland's book—*Pathetism; With Practical Instructions. Demonstrating the Falsity of the Hitherto Prevalent Assumption in Regard to "Mesmerism" and "Neurology," and Illustrating Those Laws Which Induce Somnambulism, Second Sight, Sleep, Dreaming, Trance, and Clairvoyance, with Numerous Facts Tending to Show the Pathology of Monomania, Insanity, Witchcraft, and Various Other Mental or Nervous Phenomena* (1843)—summarized his mesmeric observations and experiments. It suggests that "pathetism"—his term for the magnetic state—held the key to an enormous range of psychological and spiritual mysteries.

Beginning his research in his offices at 138 Fulton Street, then at a variety of venues throughout New York City and the Northeast, over a period of almost twenty years, Sunderland estimated that he "pathetized" thousands of individuals and that his demonstrations were witnessed by hundreds of thousands. Often he brought a seasoned somnambulist along with him, but he never failed to find equally capable subjects among his audiences; his trademark demonstration—pathetizing a single person, who then sympathetically transmitted actions and thoughts to numerous others on the stage—relied to a certain extent on the existing relations between members of his audience.

The characteristic of the magnetic state of most interest to Sunderland was *clairvoyance*; people of all ages, backgrounds, religious beliefs, and perceptual abilities, when placed into a state of "magnetic sleep," exhibited an extraordinary range of extrasensory perceptions. Brooklyn housewives left their bodies to report on domestic scenes in homes across the East River; well-respected merchants, physicians, and scientists calmly gave forth medical prescriptions for their own and others' illnesses, witnessed clairvoyantly; by the mere contact of one's hand with an anonymous lock of hair, a mesmerized subject might give a detailed summary of that person's character and personality, diet and health, habits and idiosyncrasies; the subject might even narrate in great visual detail some incident or incidents that were to occur in the future.

Sunderland matter-of-factly discussed his personal observations of scores of cases of somnambulant trances, second sight, presentiment, prophetic dreams, and transposition of the external senses to the stomach, palms of the hand, and soles of the feet. Wholly sensitive to the need for experimental proof, after a litany of stunning historical and contemporary cases of clairvoyance, Sunderland admitted their seeming extravagance, "as if they asserted the actual resurrection of the dead."

Press reports from Sunderland's demonstrations unanimously puzzle over his capacities to effect wondrous results. These noted especially how Sunderland could entrance dozens of people in a hall, without a single gesture or pronouncement. He would walk to the front of a lecture hall, step onto the stage, display a white handkerchief or his cane, and ask the audience to gaze upon it, and instantly people would drift up toward the stage, already in trance. Sunderland's pathetizing powers were so formidable that some people arrived at the venue *already* in a state of trance. By merely visualizing scenes or objects, he could create impressions in the minds of his subjects. Needing no magnets, rods, "tractors," or even motions of his fingers or hands to produce deep trance states in others, Sunderland was in a unique position to argue against all the materialist explanations of "magnetic fluid," "nervaura," and other concepts then prevailing.

Along with his repertoire of healing—from painless tooth extraction to curing nervous tics and fits—and his ability to induce second sight and other forms of clairvoyance in both the blind and sighted, Sunderland's philosophical and experimental bent produced extremely helpful new insights into the mesmeric state. By simple experiments such as blindfolding a dozen subjects, telling them he was passing a magnet down their backs, but instead holding a piece of chalk or nothing at all, Sunderland demonstrated that the will of the operator—not magnets or other devices—was the effective agent in mesmerism/pathetism.

Sunderland stressed that results varied depending on the expectations of both operator and subject. He extended this notion to solve the riddle of the variety of charismatic or ecstatic religious experiences; Methodist, Swedenborgian, Shaker, Baptist, and Mormon revivals differed according to both their doctrines and, more immediately, were influenced by the personality of the preachers. There were extraordinary implications in Sunderland's capacities, echoing these massive outbreaks of religious fervor: "If I have one clairvoyant in a company of 10 or 10,000 entranced, who are not clairvoyant, of course I can control them simultaneously, as one person, because they are all in sympathetic communication with the one who is clairvoyant of my will, and knows what my wishes are."

Sunderland was a gifted scientist as well as mesmerist, combining a knack for deft experimentation with a philosopher's wider ken. In 1853, he published a report on his continuing research in *Book of Psychology: Pathetism, Historical, Philosophical, Practical; Giving the Rationale of Every Possible Form of Nervous or Mental Phenomena.* Anyone seeking a full understanding of lower Manhattan and America's explosion of id in the antebellum era can do no better than to peruse this book. By some uncanny avenue of destiny, the lapsed Methodist minister arrived by virtue of his own curiosity at the *Method*, a truly Hermetic grasp of his era's magnetic manifestations. Coming to the "Philosophical" section of *Book of Psychology*, one reads that the theory of pathetism rests fundamentally on the following:

1. The triune of all things, in Essence, Form and Use.
2. The philosophy of Spheres, Natural, Human, and Divine. The qualities of things, the sources whence originate all Sympathies, Antipathies, Apathies, Attractions (love) and Repulsions (hatred).
3. The doctrine of Relations, Correspondencies, Associations, whence originates Power, physical, and moral.

It is almost as if Hermeticism's fabled founder, Hermes Trimegistus, is speaking to us from out of 138 Fulton Street, which was in 1853 the geographic center of the American periodical-publishing industry. Sunderland's *Magnet* shared that address only with the *New York Watchman*, but their neighbors on Fulton Street included the *Sun*, the *Herald*, and a dozen lesser publications, from *Ladies Companion* to *Youth's Cabinet* to the *New York Lancet*, the *New York Evangelist*, and the *New York Sabbath School Monitor*. Around the corner on Broadway were the offices of *McIntire's Bank Note List*, the *New York Commercial Gazette*, and the *Penny Magazine and Cyclopedia*.

Use the digital magic of Google Books and find a yellowing old copy of the first volume of the *Magnet* or simply the cover page of *Book of Psychology*. The subtitle is there in black and white: *Known under the Technics of Amulets, Charms, Enchantment, Spells, Fascination, Incantation, Magic, Mesmerism, Philters, Talismans, Relics, Witchcraft, Ecstacy, Hallucination, Spectres, Trance, Illusions, Apparitions, Clairvoyance, Somnambulism, Miracles, Sympathy, etc.*

LaRoy Sunderland—who began his Hermetic career when he realized that something downright magical was happening under his nose as he watched parishioners at revival meetings fall into trance—had ended up writing a modern *grimoire* for the uninitiated.

Like the ouroboros adorning the old alchemical tracts, history had reached right around to swallow its tail, as Enlightenment science slept through it, while nineteenth-century moderns played in plain sight with the very forces that occultists had kept secret for a thousand years.

Book of Psychology has one more section to its laughably long triptych title: *Showing How These Results May Be Induced, the Theory of Mind Which They Demonstrate, and the Benevolent Uses to Which This Knowledge Should Be Applied.* Herein lies the key to the mystery of Magnetic Manhattan, one that Sunderland himself was most suited to discover and explicate. All of the phenomena of magnetism expressed *the moral qualities of the magnetist!* LaRoy Sunderland—like Mesmer, Lafayette, and many others—was a *philanthropist*, literally, a lover of his fellow human beings. He was a healer who labored tirelessly for the good, the true, and the beautiful, and his capacious heart brought him a seemingly endless stream of magical discoveries and brought to others blessings now long forgotten.

Site #9: Andrew Jackson Davis's *Principles of Nature*, 24 Vesey Street, January 1846

Directly north of St. Paul's churchyard, earthy repository of many a pre-antebellum actor on the Broadway "stage"—the very street and its adjacent enterprises—the block that was then the south face of the Astor House is today lined with twentieth-century edifices. But if one stands in the graveyard proper, looking under the broad canopy of the London plane trees, one can slip back in time a bit, to consider the man who was a mesmeric wunderkind—a kind of antebellum conglomerate version of Eckhart Tolle, Deepak Chopra, and even Malcolm Gladwell.

On January 19, 1846, drawn by a recent notice in the *New York Tribune*, two men with a keen interest in the clairvoyant possibilities of the mesmeric state arrived at 24 Vesey Street, to attend the trance lectures of the "Poughkeepsie Seer"—nineteen-year-old

Andrew Jackson Davis
(New-York Historical Society Digital Collections)

Andrew Jackson Davis. With the short stories "A Tale of the Ragged Mountains," "Mesmeric Relations," and "The Facts in the Case of M. Valdemar," Edgar Allan Poe had already done much to publicize and sensationalize the mysteries of mesmerism. He was also quite dubious of Davis's claims of clairvoyant travel to other planets and mountaintop chats with the spirits of Swedenborg and Galen.

Not so the other visitor, George Bush, former professor of Hebraic literature at New York University and American's most zealous Swedenborgian. Observing Davis's trance lectures, Bush felt that there was no limit to Davis's "power of imparting light on any theme of human inquiry." In November, after news of the discovery of Neptune was published, Bush wrote to the *Tribune* to attest that he had been present at the Vesey Street lectures where Davis had spoken of a yet-to-be-discovered eighth planet.

The lectures that Poe and Bush heard continued intermittently for over a year, becoming part of the eight-hundred-page tome published in 1847 as *The Principles of Nature, Her Divine Revelations, and a Voice to Mankind*. Davis focused the debate about clairvoyance in a dramatic new way, for he made sweeping scriptural, theological, and cosmological claims—all dictated to him by disembodied "spirits." Davis's spirits laid out an elaborate cosmology, a history of the Earth, and a lengthy analysis of human society. Antinomian in the extreme, *Principles of Nature* dismissed the Bible, offering a grossly materialist worldview, but it had instant appeal for Americans looking for new gospels that emphasized science over revealed religion; the book sold nine hundred copies the first week and went through thirty-four editions in the next thirty years.

When the book appeared, Professor Bush rethought his former enthusiasm for the young clairvoyant, declaring that the revelations in *Principles of Nature* were not Davis's but of some "obsessing spirit." Poe put his thinly veiled critique of Davis in his lengthy prose-poem *Eureka*, which parodied both the pompous rhetorical style and content of *Principles* and other trance literature. Davis's tome opened: "IN THE BEGINNING the one boundless, undefinable, and unimaginable ocean of LIQUID FIRE! . . . It was without parts; for it was a Whole. Particles did not exist; but the Whole was as one Particle." Poe's *Eureka* answered and satirically echoed, "What God originally created—that that Matter which, by dint of His Volition, He first made from His Spirit, or from Nihility, could have been nothing but Matter in its utmost conceivable state of—what?—of Simplicity."

LaRoy Sunderland was equally dismayed by Davis's "revelations." Saying that he had been observing the trance state for over thirty years, he pointed out that trance speakers' "descriptions of 'heaven & hell,' the 'planets,' their visits to the moon, and their assumed conversations with the dead," never agreed with each other but did typically agree with the individual views the speakers held while awake.

Sunderland went further than Bush, who criticized Davis by comparing him unfavorably to the Swedish seer Emmanuel Swedenborg, arguing that both of the supposed seers were susceptible to "disease, error, and death."

Tucked in among the more spectacular revelations made by Davis in *The Principles of Nature* was his statement that the truth of a world of spirits would "ere long present itself in the form of a living demonstration. And the world will hail with delight the ushering-in of that era when the interiors of men will be opened, and the spiritual communion will be established." While Davis gave no exact date for the arrival of the event, Shaker somnambulists in the 1830s had made a similar prediction for the year 1848 and also prophesied that America would see an extraordinary discovery of material wealth to accompany the spiritual wealth. The discovery of gold at Sutter's Mill came only two months before Kate Fox taught Mr. Splitfoot to speak in raps. (See Site #10 in this chapter.)

Davis's *Principles of Nature* presented a muddy, grandiose-sounding cosmogony in its first section, a damning review of the Old Testament and a rejection of the divinity of Christ in the second, and a program for a Fourierist-style socialism in the third. Some of Davis's cosmic pronouncements seemed to come from a true clairvoyance: in advance of the discovery of Neptune and Pluto, he spoke of eighth and ninth planets, and his descriptions of Uranus's composition accorded with later findings. He also seemed to know about the Galactic Center long before its discovery. But the bulk of his book delivered wild descriptions of inhabited planets, pop versions of Swedenborg's otherworldly visions. Saturn he described as inhabited by a more advanced race of humanity, while on Venus and Mars, the inhabitants were more primitive than on Earth.

Like nearly all clairvoyants, Davis often erred in interpreting what he beheld in vision. He was clearly what we know today as an "empath," and this condition was often a burden to him. Passing certain individuals in the street, he would feel "a flash of electric pain"—an intense impression of a stranger's unhappiness: "If a person is very poor, or very sick, or mentally out of balance, I seem to know it all instantly, whether I touch him or not; and ofttimes I am thus overpowered by the conditions of unknown individuals when I pass the dwellings in which they live. It is becoming painful, yes, almost intolerable, to walk through some of the side streets, and even in Broadway, where wealth, rank, education, and luxury abound." Andrew Jackson Davis was clearly a "prodigy," both in his youth when he became such a celebrity and also as a kind of harbinger of the confused clairvoyant currents that were yet to emerge fully in the late nineteenth and early twentieth centuries. That the upstate boy became a literary and cultural sensation of his era owes entirely to his arrival on this street, with its enormous power to magnify and broadcast virtually anything and anybody on whom it trained its gaze.

Site #10: Morse's Magnetic Telegraph Company Office, 10 Wall Street, January 26, 1846

In 1832, during the five-week passage from Havre to New York on the packet ship *Sully*, Samuel Morse had been busy sketching a subject much more plebeian than the Louvre masterworks—the world's first "electric telegraph." A few days before landing at the Rector Street wharf, Morse had declared to Captain William Pell, "Well, Captain, should you hear of the telegraph one of these days, as the wonder of the world, remember the discovery was made on board the good ship *Sully*." Captain Pell's memory of Morse's declaration was duly recorded as one of the innumerable documents entered into court records as Morse and his partners contested adversaries' claims to priority for the invention. Indeed, as with Fulton's steamboat, the telegraph had been around in many forms for decades before Morse secured his patent in 1847.

One of the first bird's-eye views of New York City, published in 1847, was of the brand-new Trinity Church, its 246-foot spire looming over the western end of Wall Street. In the lower-right-hand

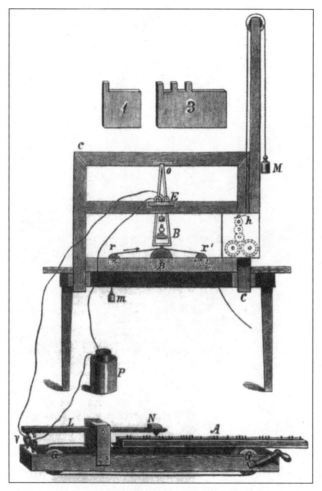

Samuel Morse's telegraph

corner of the image, one sees a tiny pole standing at the northeast corner of Broadway and Wall Street. The three thin wires it bears were the Morse telegraph lines to Washington, Boston, and Buffalo. The building just visible beside it is 10 Wall Street, where, in the offices of expressmen John J. Butterfield and Theodore S. Faxton, Morse established the nation's first telegraph office. Today this is the site of the Bankers Trust Building (1912), celebrated for

Trinity Church, 1847
(Metropolitan Museum)

its ziggurat-shaped apex. It is but a single block from where *Gallery of the Louvre* had its disappointing unveiling. Instead of a gallery of the great European masters, Morse gave America dots and dashes engraved on strips of paper by a pulsing electromagnet. Dr. Mitchill and his paleontologically curious Lyceum brethren were just scratching the surface of time; Morse had already burst the limits of space, starting a technological juggernaut that would soon circle the globe. For anyone with a bird's-eye view of human history, it is quite clear that at the very moment when a host of new clairvoyant human faculties were opening up, they were being supplanted in parallel by mechanical simulacra of clairaudience, clairvoyance, clairsentience.

These were on both hands "magical" faculties, for they were expanding human consciousness at a rate and distance never before seen in human history. The question remains as to whether the triumph of the mechanical simulacra has come at the permanent expense of our innate, destined spiritual capacities.

Site #11: Fox Sisters at Barnum's Howard Hotel, 176 Broadway, June 1850

From about the last week of May through mid-July 1850, a steady stream of visitors made their way to a parlor in Barnum's Hotel on Broadway. On the door of the room, they found a notice giving the rules for guests: the admission fee (one dollar per person), seating arrangement, and instructions to act as if in a solemn religious gathering. Visitors then took a seat at a long table that sat up to thirty people, to put questions about their deceased loved ones, or general questions about the afterlife, to "the spirits," courtesy of Maggie and Kate Fox, teenage sisters from a small village upstate whose Morse code–like communication with a disembodied being had received wide attention after a demonstration in November 1849 at Corinthian Hall in Rochester.

The sisters had begun their "spiritual telegraph" innocently enough, playing with a household poltergeist as if with a cat, but this cat had a voracious appetite and began to devour the unsuspecting girls and any who would follow them. The story of the Fox sisters and the birth of Spiritualism has been told many times: on April Fool's Eve in 1848, two sisters aged ten and fourteen—having grown up in a house reputed to be haunted—play at speaking with the ghost by way of a rapped code; the invisible entity tells the girls lurid tales about a murdered peddler; the girls' older sister exhibits them as having the ability to speak with the dead, giving birth to the many-colored movement known as Spiritualism. To get at the truth of this seemingly eccentric episode of American history requires a certain sideways glance.

The Fox sisters, 1852
(Library of Congress)

At the very same moment when the Fox sisters arrived in Manhattan, another poltergeist was grabbing headlines across America. On Sunday, March 10, the Reverend Eliakim Phelps of Stratford, Connecticut, returned with his family from church to their sprawling mansion on Elm Street to find all the doors and windows open. Inside, they found the furniture knocked over, dishes smashed, books, papers, and clothing scattered all over. They had not been robbed; Reverend Phelps found his gold watch, silver heirlooms, and even loose cash undisturbed. In an upstairs bedroom, a sheet was spread over a bed, and Mrs. Phelps's nightgown was laid out on it. At the bottom, a pair of stockings were stretched out, and the arms of the gown were folded across the chest, like a corpse.

Later, while the rest of the family returned to church for the afternoon service, Reverend Phelps hid in his study with a pistol, hoping to catch the intruders should they return. After some time, he went downstairs and, entering the dining room, found a circle of eleven effigies of women, kneeling or standing in prayer, some holding Bibles. Articles of the family's clothing had been stuffed with rags and other materials from around the house to create the dummies, which had been put in place during the brief period while Phelps was standing guard. Over the next few months, twenty more mock women would appear out of the blue. They would be joined by leaping umbrellas, silverware, books, and other household objects; bedding sailing off beds; food and clothing dropping out of nowhere onto the breakfast table while the family ate. Friends and other visitors to the house watched as these objects fell at impossibly slow speeds or changed course in midair. By the end of April, the disturbances had turned quite nasty: screams and odd sounds were heard each night; silverware was mangled; windows were broken; the children's limbs were jerked about violently; and welts appeared on their skin. Reverend Phelps's son was hit with a barrage of small stones. Later, in front of a dozen witnesses, the boy vanished and was later found tied up and suspended from a tree in the yard.

As the most famous authority on Spiritualism in the nation, Andrew Jackson Davis made a visit to Stratford to investigate. Davis lent his authority to the genuineness of the activity and stated that the outbreak was caused by "vital radiations" from the Phelps children, whose "magnetism" caused objects to be attracted to or repelled from them. As with eyewitness reporters in Hydesville, Davis chose "spirits of the dead" as the rubric for understanding the disturbances, rather than the more common interpretation given them by local rural people—these were lowly tommyknockers, house hobbies, mischievous fairies tweaking the noses of a minister of the Gospel's family. Both Davis and all the other commentators somehow missed the "telegraphic" aspect of the Stratford knockings. A week before the odd visitation, Reverend Phelps and a friend had been discussing Spiritualism and decided to hold a séance, at which they produced knocking and rapping sounds, just as the Fox sisters had in Hydesville. Following their lead, Phelps decided to try communicating with the spirit by a system of telegraphic raps, and he soon ascertained that his resident poltergeist was a tormented soul in hell. When Phelps asked how he might help, the spirit asked Phelps to bring him a piece of pumpkin pie. Asking again, the invisible trickster asked instead for a glass of gin. When the exasperated minister finally asked why the spirit was making such mischief, it replied, "For fun." It went on to give an elaborate tale of having been a law clerk in Philadelphia who had been convicted and jailed for fraud. Like the Hydesville "spirit," who claimed to have been a peddler murdered by previous occupants of the Fox house, the Stratford spirit's information was frequently false, and yet all were puzzled as to how the disembodied intelligence could exist at all.

Both the Hydesville and the Stratford specters, and thousands of others who manifested themselves throughout America, claimed and were believed to be spirits of the dead, and despite the rude, lewd, and downright demonic nature of much of their communications, they became venerated by millions of people eager for proof of life after death. The faithful turned a blind eye to the fact that Kate Fox's first words to the pioneer poltergeist at Hydesville were "Do as I do, Mr. Splitfoot!" (i.e., the devil) or that that first manifestation had commenced on the eve of the most favorable day of the year for elfin activity. Clergymen who suggested that the spirits were devils in disguise were ignored or ridiculed. Their congregations—and often they themselves—had long since ceased believing in the active presence of nonhuman spiritual beings within the spiritual world. They reasoned that these phantasmic folk must be spirits of the dead, and the more physical their manifestations—moving tables, playing musical instruments, oozing ectoplasmic limbs, producing bouquets of flowers, and other such corny parlor tricks—the more credence they were given.

The year 1850 was surely the most important year in the growth of American Spiritualism, for the publicity generated by the Hydesville and Stratford poltergeists caused an explosion of mediumistic phenomena from coast to coast. "Experimental" Spiritualist circles formed in Boston (where there was estimated to be over a thousand mediums by 1850), Philadelphia, Providence, all the major cities in New York State, all the New England states, Cincinnati, Memphis, St. Louis, California, Oregon, Texas. All the way into Spiritualism's resurgence in the 1920s, New York City would play a major role in the elucidation and dissemination of its credo.

In America, every day of the year became April Fool's Day for the liberated sprites and poltergeists. The Stratford shenanigans were just a small sampling of their kaleidoscopic circus of tomfoolery. Puritanical matrons manipulating Ouija boards were made to utter the foulest of oaths. Greedy fortune hunters were promised gold and silver in a thousand secret locales. Would-be prophets were tantalized with authentic tidbits of advantageous foreknowledge, then sucker-punched with ersatz revelations guaranteed to be passed on to the multitudes. Earnest seekers of spiritual truths were hoodwinked with bizarre celestial untruths; the planetary fantasies of Andrew Jackson Davis were repeated in a hundred varieties by unsuspecting Spiritualist mediums. Masquerading elementals donned the personas of every historical celebrity imaginable, from George Washington to Alexander the Great, proclaiming all sorts of twaddle as the most sacred scripture. The Frankenstein monster of Spiritualist manifestations was a dubious bargain made by the United States just at the moment when the country's own national science was maturing into a daylight endeavor capable of penetrating nature with new power.

The electric telegraph worked by a kind of "contagion." A cascade of electrons set in motion was constrained within a thin wire, conducted to just those places where its operators wished it to go. In borrowing the metaphor of the telegraph, Spiritualists glibly believed that their new communication device ran directly between heaven and Earth. Lacking any proper magical education, they failed to realize that electricity was a *subearthly* force, not heavenly, and that, as such, it trafficked with subearthly *beings*. They also were oblivious to magnetism's *wireless* nature. Any single person sitting at a séance became a "carrier" of the invisible subearthly entities, distributing them far and wide from the epicenter Spiritualist circle. In hindsight, we can easily track the progression of the possessing entities as they gain an increasing hold on the consciousness of the host human. Strange rapping noises, a ringing doorbell, scraping on an upstairs floor—these get the attention of the occupants, and the more fear and curiosity the specters evoke, the more power they are given. Think of the ugly toad whom Joseph Smith first met on Palmyra's Hill Cumorah; after promising the eager treasure seeker great riches when he returned, the toad had become the Angel Moroni!

"Test the spirits," said the Apostle John, but the entire history of Spiritualism demonstrates that far too few followed his sage advice.

Site #12: Thomas Lake Harris's *Epic of the Starry Heavens*: Brittan and Partridge Publishing Office, 300 Broadway, January 1854

Spiritualism had made enough inroads in America in the two years following the Fox sisters' sojourn at Barnum's Hotel that in 1852, a pair of leading New York Spiritualists, Samuel Brittan and Charles Partridge, founded their *Spiritual Telegraph*, the first national Spiritualist periodical. In January 1854, they brought out from their publishing office at 300 Broadway a block north of A. T. Stewart's sprawling white-marble department store *An Epic of the Starry Heaven*, by Thomas Lake Harris. "Epic" was indeed an apt title for this tour of the celestial spheres in verse form—which had become the specialty of the trance medium Thomas Lake Harris. Brittan— who with his partner Partridge had been a witness at many of the twelve sessions in November and early December 1853—estimated that Harris had produced the two-hundred-page poem in twenty-six hours and sixteen minutes.

Conducted by an "angel," Harris had made a tour of the "electric oceans" in proximity to the seven celestial spheres—from Earth upward to Saturn. Along the way, he both met companies of angels and was given visions of humanity's coming tribulations and triumphs. Though Harris was hailed by Brittan, Partridge, and their wide Spiritualist circles as a modern Dante, his poetry was saccharine and overblown, save for occasional passages of lucidity and lyricism.

> And a spiral winds from the worlds to the suns,
> And every star that shines
> In the path of degrees forever runs,
> And the spiral octave climbs;
> And a seven-fold heaven round every one
> In the spiral order twines.

This verse's perception of the spiral or vortical nature of planetary and starry spheres hints that there was beneath all the poetic hot air some authentic clairvoyance, for in just a few brief decades, the earliest photographs of space would discover just these spirals.

Though the poem's prophecies are very vaguely phrased, truth appears in some of them as well:

> Man is the true Republic. Earth shall see
> A New Democracy,
> A New Theocracy,
> The Priesthood of the Free

Before that utopian republic might arise, however, there would be a "Babylon of Slavery" and an apocalyptic conflagration. These were common millennial images in the years leading up to the Civil War, but Harris's subsequent career, through some four-dozen books—he soon moved from poetry to prose, and these are as "epic" productions, running to four hundred to five hundred pages—demonstrates that he was possessed of a certain elemental clairvoyance.

"Elemental" and "clairvoyance" are key, but double-edged, terms in coming to grips with Thomas Lake Harris. One of his books reports on an interview Brittan conducted with Harris's inspiring "angel" at Charles Partridge's 26 West Fifteenth Street home, the day after Harris's trance production had ceased. The being described how it was that spirit beings could visit and essentially replace the ego of a person in trance and went on to report that these beings had given a "sun-stone" to Harris, an "occult"—in the sense of being invisible—talisman by which he was kept in magnetic *rapport* with these beings, who were from the Mercury sphere.

Harris would soon leave New York City for greener pastures, establishing industrious farming communities both upstate, in Brocton, on the shores of Lake Erie, and then in Santa Rosa, California. His vineyards were esteemed enough that for some time in the late nineteenth century, one could purchase "Fountain Grove Winery" vintages at a retail outlet in Manhattan. But even before he left New York, he began to unfold the most extravagant portrait of nature, as filled to the brim with "fays"—fairies—who both could be seen by certain people (especially children; Harris correctly reported that much of the time, when we see infants reaching into the air, they are playing with the invisible beings) and who could under certain circumstances come to *dwell within people, especially poets and other creative individuals.* In time, Harris would come to develop a vision of restored human society that depended on a wholesale "demagnetization" of the existing demonic elemental beings, the "infernal fays." In his 1878 poem "Demagnetise," he advises,

> If you, dear friends, would hold your States
> With Fairies wise, with Fairies wise,
> When joy within the heart abates,
> Demagnetise, demagnetise!

If you would overcome disease,
With Fairies wise, with Fairies wise,
Call Virtue through you like the seas:
Demagnetise, demagnetise!

If you would crash the Dragon's head,
With Fairies wise, with Fairies wise,
Your open hands to Heaven outspread
Demagnetise, demagnetise!

Harris's books appear at first blush to be the ravings of a lunatic, but they are actually exact and extensive descriptions of the worlds of elemental beings long described by magical adepts; and Harris is always cognizant that the "fays" are the effective agents in most magical operations, both black and white. There is the most pronounced "black" tone running through these reports; Harris sees almost exclusively the demonic elementals that have been engendered by human passions. Characteristically, however, he has absolutely no clairvoyance for the "Pandemonium"—his term for possession by entire hosts of demonic fays—that surrounds his own being. Simply put, from 1857 and the publication of his *Song of Satan: A Series of Poems Originating with A Society of Infernal Spirits, and Received, during Temptation-Combats*, Harris was fully possessed by demons, even as he so enthusiastically reported on the activities of demons in those around him.

Site #13: Paschal Beverley Randolph's Recantation of Spiritualism at Clinton Hall, Southwest Corner of Beekman and Nassau, November 1858

Up until an 1855 trip to France, where he encountered mesmerist circles employing magic mirrors, crystals, and hashish, Paschal Beverley Randolph had been a fairly conventional trance speaker, taking as gospel the Spiritualist faith in communication with "spirits of the

Paschal Beverley Randolph

dead." He returned to New York convinced that there were as many worlds *below* the human being as there were above, that modern Spiritualism was a danger because it promoted unconscious trance mediumship, and that adepts and beings in the celestial hierarchies could be contacted by *conscious* clairvoyant means, augmented by a heightened will.

For a decade, Clinton Hall had hosted all the leading local and national Spiritualists; never had its audience heard the blasphemy spoken by Randolph:

> Spiritualism . . . is a masked monster . . . [giving] us a philosophy, unsound, and at best merely speculative, cold, cheerless, selfish and far-fetched, which gradually fastens itself about the soul, devours

the affections, and makes man a locomotive encyclopedia without a heart. . . . It is a bewitching thing—so is a rattlesnake! At first the neophyte rejoices in his new-found freedom, as he falsely supposes it to be. He becomes intoxicated with joy for awhile, revels in rainbow-tinted dreams of bliss; is led on step by step, deeper and deeper into a mazy labyrinth of unintelligible and profitless mysteries; emerges only to embark his soul's fortunes in an exploring expedition to the Land of Shadow; is wrecked on the rocks of doubt, clings to a single plank, dreams on, and not until the cold and chilling fogs of mysticism have frozen his very spirit, does he rouse from his slumber, to find himself on a rough, chaotic sea, which to him, is shoreless, vast and dreary as the icy hand of death.

Randolph broke ranks with his Spiritualist brethren to say that almost all Spiritualist phenomena were the product of an "evil class of spirits"—demons, "Principalities, powers, chiefs of the aerial kingdom," who brought havoc on their hosts.

In fact, ever since the Fox sisters signaled Morse code with the Hydesville poltergeist, there had been in America authors of sound sensibility who neither succumbed to the "spirits'" seductions nor roundly denounced them as humbug sleight-of-hand productions. These authors were mostly Christian ministers whose biblical knowledge combined with long experience wrestling with their parishioners' encounters with demonic beings to allow them to see immediately the chimera that was "Spiritualism." The name itself was a feint, for the beings who produced all the rappings, apparitions, prophecies, and false gospels were not "spirits," in that they lacked spirit as a part of their constitution. They were—as Thomas Lake Harris recognized—fays, elemental beings of a very low order, who had traditionally been the servants of shamans, magicians, and priests around the world but who now, thanks to the blinders of the materialist worldview, were the masters, putting unsuspecting human beings through the most ludicrous steeplechase of soul and spirit.

By the time of Randolph's Clinton Hall recantation, at least two dozen exhaustive "demonological" critiques of Spiritualism had been published; they would continue to come forth at each resurgence of trafficking with "spirits," right into the 1920s. A review of just a single title gives some sense of their tenor: *Mesmeric and Spirit Rapping Manifestations, Scripturally Exposed, as Neither from Electricity nor Spirits of the Dead, but Rather from Infernal Evil Spirits Manifesting Foretold Magic, Soothsaying, Demonology, etc., by an Impartial Examiner* (1852). If one digs a little further, one also finds that similar demonological critiques were readily available for those who were seeking some fuller (than the rationalist antimesmeric polemic) explanation of the phenomena of animal magnetism; a single work, which came just at the cusp of the passage from magnetic to Spiritualist productions, shows the continuity: William H. Beecher's *Animal Magnetism Repudiated as Sorcery, Not a Science; With an Appendix of Magnetic Phenomena* (1846). This was titled in another edition *Mesmerism Examined and Repudiated as the "Sin of Witchcraft," etc., Especially in Its Mysteries, of Clairvoyance.* Clearly, there was in the nineteenth century a widespread comprehension of both mesmerism and Spiritism (the European term, which I prefer) as species of thaumaturgy, that is, demonic/daimonic magic. "Witchcraft" was perhaps the most common appellation at the time, but it smacks too anachronistically of the Salem episode to be useful now as a descriptive term.

It is no coincidence that Paschal Beverley Randolph went on to a fascinating career as a practical occultist, that is, someone who studied, practiced, and taught a broad spectrum of magical techniques, including scrying (divination through mirrors and other reflective surfaces), hallucinogenic drugs, and sex magic. He was the author of more than fifty works on magic and medicine, and his life and writings open up into an entire universe of occult practices, prior to the appearance of Helena Blavatsky. There was a pronounced antinomian tenor running through Randolph's magic; the phrenologist Orson Fowler called Randolph "an out-and-out Radical in everything." It is probably no exaggeration to say that the spectrum of fictional magical operations that J. K. Rowling dreamed up for the Harry Potter series falls far short of the *real* magic practiced and taught by Paschal Beverley Randolph. Certainly Harry's imagined orphanhood cannot compare to the challenges met and overcome by Randolph, an "octoroon" born at 70 Canal Street, a stone's throw from the rough-and-tumble neighborhood of Five Points. Having never met his father, his mother dying when he was just twelve, he shipped aboard the brig *Phoebe* out of New Bedford and spent the next eight years at sea.

Randolph's recantation was significant both for the shock his apostasy brought to fellow Spiritualists and for the exactitude of his magical knowledge, which permitted him to see these variegated spiritual phenomena from the inside. Rather than be buffeted about by the manipulative machinations of the elemental beings, Randolph aimed at *mastery* of them and thereby gained a more comprehensive view. Indeed, any thorough review of either nineteenth- or twentieth-century Spiritualism will show that the only individuals who actually understood its nature were magicians.

Site #14: A Soldier-Mystic Sells His Hermetic Library: Bangs, Merwin and Co., 594/6 Broadway, November 24, 1862

Ethan Allen Hitchcock had begun his military career early, at age sixteen, when he entered West Point in 1814. It was hardly surprising that the boy wished to become a soldier. His mother's father was Ethan Allen, the leader of the Green Mountain Boys, the story of whose capture of Fort Ticonderoga he had heard innumerable times as he grew up. Hitchcock's father, Samuel Hitchcock, had been appointed district judge by President Washington, and upon Washington's death, it was Judge Hitchcock who delivered the public eulogy. Hitchcock's older sister's husband, Major George Peters, was a West Point graduate and secured his nephew's appointment to the academy. An Army officer for almost forty years, Hitchcock taught tactics at West Point, received distinction as commander and

AT PRIVATE SALE.

Catalogue of Books

ON

HERMETIC PHILOSOPHY

Being the Entire Collection of

GENERAL E. A. HITCHCOCK,

Gathered by him during many years, and at much cost, and it
is believed to be the most extensive and valuable
collection of its peculiar class in this country,
and comprises many *unique volumes.* Such
a collection, undoubtedly, could not
now be made.

As General Hitchcock does not design to have the Books
scattered through his immediate agency, the whole
is now offered, in one lot,

AT PRIVATE SALE ONLY.

For further particulars, terms, &c.,

ADDRESS,

MESSRS. BANGS, MERWIN & CO.,

AT THE IRVING BUILDINGS,

594 AND 596 BROADWAY,

NEW YORK.

C. C. SHELLEY, Steam Printer, 68 Barclay Street, N. Y.

Catalogue of Ethan Allen Hitchcock's library of
Hermetic philosophy

peace negotiator in multiple Indian wars, and intermittently lived
in New York City while serving as a recruiter. When the Civil War
began, Hitchcock was the choice of many leaders to lead the Union
army, and though the retired general declined, in 1862 he reenlisted
at the personal request of Abraham Lincoln and Secretary of War
Edwin Stanton. Eight months later, the Broadway bookseller from
whom he had bought his first alchemical work advertised the private
sale of over three hundred Hermetic volumes that Hitchcock had

collected. In America, there was no more complete library of magic than this one.

In the 1820s, in between drilling and recruiting, Hitchcock read Sir Thomas Browne's *Religio Medici*, Hobbes, and Lucretius and filled many volumes with his notes on philosophy and metaphysics. He had, he believed, arrived at a definition of God: "The great whole is one, and all the parts agree with all the parts." His metaphysical speculations early found expression in his conduct. "I am," he said, "determined to regard myself impersonally—that is, as an impartial observer. At times I was under great excitement, though externally as quiet as a child. I was constantly inquiring of myself about myself." Hitchcock's long effort to see justice done to the Seminole had developed step-by-step alongside an intense metaphysical journey. On his voyage to Tampa Bay in 1840, he filled fifty pages of his notebooks with closely written commentary on Kant's *Critique of Pure Reason*. Becalmed with his regiment in the Gulf of Mexico that same year, he declared, "It is plain that Goethe was a pantheist, and I see that a pantheist may be a Mohammedan, and a heathen at the same time. Pantheism ought to be regarded as the very reverse of atheism, being the admission of everything and the denial of nothing. He has the most accurate knowledge of God who has the most comprehensive knowledge of Nature, . . . for these two are one."

By the 1850s, Hitchcock's search for eternal truths had led him from Plato, Spinoza, Jacob Boehme, Swedenborg, Paracelsus, Dante, the *Vishnu Prana*, and the *Bhagavad Gita* deep into the literature of medieval and early modern alchemy. There he had found, in the words of his biographer I. Bernard Cohen, "that mercury is conscience, a quality unevenly distributed in men. The starting point in a person's education is to develop a sense of what is absolutely right. After this, the 'great work' is child's play. A man without conscience is vitriol, arsenic, vipers." He discovered "that all true alchymists pursued not gold but wisdom." While serving in New York as recruiting officer for his Second Regiment, Hitchcock frequented the Nassau Street bookstores, whose proprietors all knew him to be a keen buyer for any metaphysical or alchemical works. After over a decade of reading, in 1857 he published *Remarks upon Alchemy and the Alchemists, Indicating a Method of Discovering the True Nature of Hermetic Philosophy; And Showing That the Search after the Philosopher's Stone Had Not for Its Object the Discovery of an Agent for the Transmutation of Metals: Being Also an Attempt to Rescue from Undeserved Opprobrium the Reputation of a Class of Extraordinary Thinkers in Past Ages.* It was the first modern work to recognize alchemy as a moral path of spiritual—and magical—development. That the alchemists had universally been seen as poor chemists rather than brilliant and brave metaphysicians suggests how deeply disenchanted was nineteenth-century thought.

In the alchemists, Hitchcock had found a stream of wisdom that closely matched his own personal philosophy and practice, developed from a solitary path of reading, reflection, and engagement with the world as a soldier. In 1866, though he was in Washington performing his duties as the nation struggled to heal the wounds of civil war, he had become wholly a mystic.

> I wish to say that I saw, a moment since, what the Philosopher's Stone signifies. I do not omit a statement of it from any desire to make it a mystery. My relation to it is still to be determined. A great number of passages in books of alchemy seem perfectly clear now. I have nowhere told what it is or even what I think it is. It is a kind of revelation, but, when seen, has an effect something like looking at the sun. Personally I have much to fear from it, before I can look forward to its benefits. I have nothing to unsay in my books, and have but this to add: that they are studies to reach the One Thing.

Along with his treatise on alchemy, General Hitchcock elucidated "the One Thing" in seven other works—on Swedenborg, Christ, Spenser's *Faerie Queen*, the medieval allegorical tale *The Red Book of Appin*, the *Arabian Nights*, Shakespeare's sonnets, and the Hindu drama *Sakoontala*.

Hitchcock's very first publication was *De Obfuscastionibus; or, A Glimmering Light on Mesmerism* (1845), a lighthearted but deadly serious assessment of witchcraft as employing magnetism to effect its works. Like Randolph and so many other authors who had not fallen prey to either Spiritualism's error of interpreting elementals as souls of the dead or materialism's error of seeing all the magical evocations as "nothing but" fraud, deception, and hallucination, Hitchcock by way of close personal observation and careful reflection penetrated these phenomena. Reviewing a series of historical cases in which innocent women had been executed as witches, he painstakingly demonstrated from close textual analysis how in each instance, episodes of magnetic or somnambulic behavior had been mistaken—with deadly consequences—as willful sorcery.

Hitchcock concluded his work with a warning: "The salvation this age has reached . . . has not been through any clear account of the natural causes of enthusiasm and fascination: it has been through an undiscerning doubt of all reality in the one, and an absolute denial of all reality even as a basis of the other, the very notion of the power of fascination being held to be ridiculous and absurd in the highest degree; but whether this promises any protection for the future may be reasonably doubted." Hitchcock seemed to intuit that science's ignorance of the reality of the magical power at the foundation of all magnetic phenomena would never make such phenomena go away, and he understood that a society that denied "the One Thing" risked immense dangers.

Hitchcock had met Paschal Beverley Randolph in 1850 in Paris. Both men were "Hermeticists" in pursuing quite solitary, arduous paths toward knowledge and in their apostasy from what Randolph called "false civilization." But while Randolph had forged a path of arbitrary, personal magic, emphasizing always the working of the individual will (his personal motto was the highly Thelemic "Try"), Hitchcock had balanced his magical knowledge with gnosis and mysticism, transforming himself into a vehicle for divine will. His magic was true theurgy, sacred, rather than profane, and his biography demonstrates the supreme distinction between a philosophy of "my will be done" and "Thy will be done."

Site #15: John Tyndall Ponders the Imponderables: Great Hall of Cooper Union, January 1872

At the invitation and arrangement of Joseph Henry, secretary of the Smithsonian Institution, the English physicist John Tyndall made a lecture tour of the Northeast in late 1872 and early 1873, beginning and ending the tour in New York City. His initial scientific fame coming from his study of diamagnetism in the 1850s, by 1872 Tyndall had penetrated other imponderables. He was the first—in 1859—to measure the relative infrared absorptive powers of gases and a year later showed that visually transparent gases emit infrared radiation; in 1864, he was the first to demonstrate that emission of heat in chemical reactions originates in the newly synthesized molecules; he was the first to describe and report thermophoresis in aerosols (1870).

As a proponent of Darwin's theory of evolution by natural selection, Tyndall was a vocal proponent of the strict segregation of science from religion, and yet, as a man of faith himself, he was naturally drawn to the spiritual questions raised by the discovery of "imponderables" all about him, whether in the séance room or in the laboratory. Tyndall was a superb scientific educator, and, reading the *Lectures on Light* that he gave at the Great Hall of Cooper Union that winter of 1872–1873, one can feel how thrilling it would have been to hear the physicist expound on the mysteries of light, from his survey of historical theories to demonstrations of dramatic phenomena produced by crystals on polarized light to the power of spectrum analysis to penetrate deep into the atom. At the farewell banquet at Delmonico's, Tyndall celebrated the spirit of scientific cooperation and gave special thanks to Edward Youmans, the editor of *Scientific American*, for his indefatigable labors representing science to the public.

John Tyndall and Planchette, 1868

In July 1868, from the magazine's editorial offices at 37 Park Row, the *Scientific American* carried on its lead page Tyndall's article on the "planchette"—known to us as a Ouija board. This device is such a commonplace to us now that it is worth feeling the spirit of amazed novelty with which it was met circa 1868: "A peculiar class of phenomena have manifested themselves within the last quarter of a century, which seem to indicate that the human body may become the medium for the transmission of force to inert and dead matter, either in obedience to the will of others, or by the action of the nervous power upon the muscular system, in such a way that those through whom or from whom it emanates, are totally unconscious of any exercise of volition, or of any muscular movement, as acts of their own wills."

Tyndall kindly acknowledged the skepticism shown toward the mysterious machine by Michael Faraday and others, but he faithfully reported the results of his experiments with the English medium Daniel Douglas Home:

> You may hold a conversation with Planchette, provided your own part in it consists of interrogations. Its replies, so far as we have seen, are sometimes true and sometimes false. So are the replies often given by human respondents. It sometimes refuses to write at all, and plays the most fantastic tricks, in apparently willful disregard of the feelings of those who are anxious that it should do its best. When, however, it chooses to be good, it moves gently and steadily over the paper upon which it is placed, the pencil point tracing letter after letter, until the reply is written, when with a rapid sweep it announces its conclusion by rushing swiftly back to the left, and stopping suddenly at the edge of the paper. These motions seem to those whose fingers rest upon the board to be entirely independent of their own wills, their only care being to avoid any resistance to its motions. The fact that it is impossible to suppose that the wills of two persons could be by their own desire mutually coincident, without previously concerted action, forms one of the most puzzling features of the subject, as the nature of the questions asked and answered precludes the possibility of collusion.

Such a fair and judicious—and "innocent"—consideration of the Ouija board would never be found inside the pages of *Scientific American* today. In fact, Tyndall's article was the last in any scientific publication; the debate about the planchette would be conducted instead in popular periodicals like the *Ladies Repository* and *Frank Leslie's Illustrated*.

THE PLANCHETTE MYSTERY

Magic—human employment of supernatural agency—and technology had no more comical but simultaneously tragic collaboration in Manhattan's Magnetic era than in the planchette, or "talking board." By 1868, ads were regularly appearing in *Harper's* and other New York periodicals for "THE GREAT MYSTERY: KIRBY'S PLANCHETTE: Send for a circular at Kirby & Co., 633 Broadway." "HOLMES ALPHABETIC PLANCHETTE: MADE OF MAGNETIC SUBSTANCES" was manufactured at 146 Fulton; its ads claimed, "By this instrument your innermost thoughts will be answered by the invisible power." In December 1868, Mr. Kirby told a reporter from the *Round Table* newspaper that he had already sold over two hundred thousand of his model—no wonder there were dozens of designs competing for attention. A satirical 1869 *Harper's* story, "The Confessions of a Reformed Planchettist," set in lower Manhattan, tells of the author's visit to a pair of scientific-instrument makers to commission the fabrication of an astronomical instrument; the craftsman informs him that he is too busy making "pentagraph wheels," which turn out to be for the smooth operation of the planchette. Samuel Wells (in 1869 operating out of his publishing office at 389 Broadway) devoted three articles detailing his research into the planchette in his *American Phrenological Journal.* "This little gyrating tripod is proving itself to be something more than a nine days wonder," Wells proclaimed. Even the *New York Times* ran half a dozen pieces—all cynically satirical—on the planchette in 1869. Henry Atkins wrote a "Planchette Waltz"; the popular composer August LaMotte penned a "Planchette Polka," dedicating it to Kirby & Company!

Even though Wells reprinted his investigations in an 1872 book reflecting on Charles R. Upham's *History of Salem Witchcraft,* he completely failed to see the relationship between what was visited upon the Salem girls and what was being stirred up in New York,

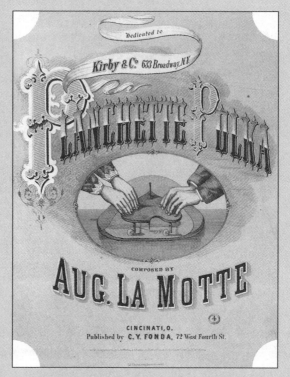

August LaMotte's "Planchette Polka"

America, and throughout the world, by way of the little mahogany tripod. He passed quickly through the half dozen or so theories afloat as to the operation of the mysterious divination device, to hit on a much more effective avenue of inquiry: asking "Planchette" herself. (It was quite common in reports of the day to gender the object.) In the 1872 book, Wells devotes sixteen pages to a transcript of their conversations about the mysteries of the divination device, opening with this simple but reasonable deduction: "Planchette is intelligent; she can answer questions, and often answer them correctly, too. On what class of subjects, then, might she be expected to give answers more generally correct than those which relate to herself, especially if the questions be asked in a proper spirit, and under such conditions as are claimed to be requisite for correct responses?"

The decorum with which the "Inquirer" (Samuel Wells) conducts the interview with the invisible entity is delightful. "Planchette, excuse me if I now treat you as one on whom a little responsibility is supposed to rest. An exciter of curiosity, if as intelligent as you appear to be, should be able to satisfy curiosity; and a creator of doubts may be presumed to have some ability to solve doubts. May I not, then, expect from you a solution of the mysteries which have thus far enveloped you?" Planchette replies with like decorum, explaining to Wells that it would entirely depend on his manner of interrogation. But right at the outset, "she" gives him a key that must have been given up by untold thousands of "spirits" conjured up by the mesmerists, Spiritualists, and planchettists—that the answers would be fitted to his own mind. Referring vaguely and tantalizingly to "conditions and laws which may yet be explained to you," Planchette advises Wells to keep his mind unperturbed and focused.

Wells goes right for the jugular, asking, "What is the nature of this power, intelligence, and will that communicates with us in this mysterious manner?"—to which Planchette replies, "It is the reduplication of your own mental state; it is a spirit; it is the whole spiritual world; it is God—one or all, according to your condition and the form and aspect in which you are able to receive the communication." This is too much for the interrogator, and Wells scales down to asking if she is an intelligence that once occupied a physical body. As 99 percent of the entities did in Wells's day, she claims this to be true: "as has been told a thousand times before," she adds.

The difficulty with Planchette's answer, and the answer told those other thousand times by elemental beings with no moral sense, no ego, and thus no obligation at all to tell the truth, is that they are no such thing. They are the very same beings that an earlier, wiser age than our own pronounced "humbugs."

Site #16: Charles Foster, the "Salem Seer": Oregon Wilson's Studio, 945 Broadway, Summer 1872

No Manhattan wizard, witch, or warlock loved Broadway as much as Charles Foster, the "Salem Seer," whose magical feats and bon vivant ways made him the bosom friend of New York's most celebrated figures. William H. Vanderbilt regularly consulted him for business counsel; he counted among his intimate circle the journalist and diplomat John Russell Young, the painter Frank B. Carpenter, the playwright, actor, theater manager, and inventor Steele MacKaye, the attorney and orator Charles W. Brooke, and the playwright A. E. Lancaster. Even when he was not performing in one or another of a dozen or so hotels or private salons in Manhattan, Foster was a kind of walking theatrical spectacle. Wonders, marvels, and phantasmagoria went on around him all the time. One summer evening around midnight, while Foster was out drinking with his friend and biographer George C. Bartlett and the artist Oregon Wilson, Wilson invited them to his studio to look at some new curiosities. Foster knew this was only a pretext and that Wilson's real object was to induce Foster to give some physical manifestations at a dark séance. Wilson had tried this half a dozen times before, but Foster always refused. On this evening, perhaps due to the drink, Foster's guard was down, and so the three strolled up Broadway to Wilson's studio at 945 Broadway.

Entering the studio, Wilson turned off the gaslights without giving any warning, plunging them into utter darkness. Instantly it seemed as though the world had come to an end, that the building had been blown up by dynamite, or that an earthquake had struck. Assuming that they would find everything in the room a shambles, the two men cried together, "Wilson, light the gas!" When the lights came up, they found only a few things disarranged; Foster, however, was faint, could hardly stand up, and was pale and perspiring. The two men laughed heartily, seeming to think it a good joke, but Foster was shaken. Writing about the evening twenty years later, Bartlett confessed it a total mystery "how to account for the *hurlubrelu.*"

Pandemonium had accompanied Charles Foster—born in 1838 in Salem, Massachusetts—since he was fourteen years old; at school one day, a cacophony of raps were heard coming from his school desk. That night, the raps turned violent, and furniture was tossed about his bedroom. Soon the poltergeists were active even in the daylight, but young Foster learned how to quiet them. As a "test medium"—a kind of Olympian performance for skeptical audiences—he specialized in "pellet reading." People would write names and other information on slips of paper and roll them up into a tight ball, whereupon Foster would pick them up and pronounce their contents. No trickery was necessary; able to telepathically see what was in the sitters' minds, he merely observed their mental images—carried into his mind by his "familiar spirits"—as they wrote. Though he made a small fortune performing with his familiar spirits at an entry fee of a five dollars per person, he was known throughout town as the most carefree spender and as often as not was flat broke.

Before long, a new capacity appeared spontaneously: skin writing. Blood-red letters would appear on Foster's forearm, spelling out answers to questions or even playing practical jokes. When a pair of skeptical men held Foster's arms and demanded he produce some phenomenon, large red characters appeared on his arm, spelling out "Two Fools."

It was not two fools but thousands, for, except for the occasional fellow medium or close friend to whom he confided, Foster left unexplained the nature of his mentalist magic. The scene at Oregon Wilson's studio filled him with dread, for he knew that however firmly he appeared to control his elementals' antics, they might grow restive and vengeful at any time. Living with poltergeists all his life, Foster knew better than to encourage their activity with twilit rooms.

By age forty-eight, Foster's profligate drinking had given the imps the upper hand, and as they possessed him further and further, he lost his sanity. In 1888, he died in Danvers Lunatic Asylum in Massachusetts, two years after being committed there.

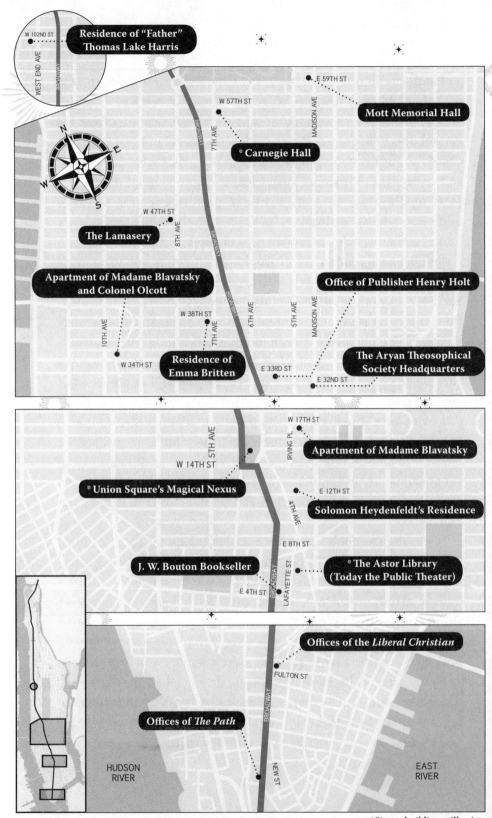

4

Occult Manhattan

1875–1914

Map of the Borough of Manhattan, New York City, 1900
(Library of Congress)

O ccultists—almost exclusively a male club—the world over were taken by surprise at the appearance of Madame Helena Blavatsky, a woman with a mysterious past and prodigious innate magical gifts. Though an outpouring of recent scholarship has provided a rich portrait of "HPB" and her activities, none of these works have adequately understood her seminal position within a titanic magical battle that was coming to a head in the late nineteenth century, waged by secret brotherhoods. Blavatsky wrote her first major work—*Isis Unveiled* (1877)—while living in New York, the birthplace of the Theosophical Society, arguably the most influential magical organization in the world for the past century and a half. Gilded Age Gotham actually sported a whole golden web of occult practitioners, whose identity and history have yet to be fully elaborated.

The world of magic is surrounded and shot through with secrets, arcana that include Manhattan's magical history. There were hidden hands behind both Blavatsky and the productions of Spiritualism; bringing them into the light is essential before the United States can see its own proper magical self.

While making this long journey through physical space—from 214 Broadway, across the street from Trinity, the city's first church, to 308 West 102nd Street—we will amble only four decades in time, ending just before the outbreak of World War I, a catastrophe with deep magical occult roots, some of which grow under Manhattan's good but always magically ambivalent ground. The leitmotif for all this ambling is literary; New York City's publishing industry made *exoteric* immense landscapes of magical knowledge and practice that had once been occult, secret, that is, *esoteric*. Whether from your reading chair or at the sites themselves, think of this chapter as a magic carpet ride into Manhattan's "Occult Revival," as you pass over lower Broadway's *Liberal Christian* offices to Madame Blavatsky's successive quarters on Irving Place, in Hell's Kitchen, and the Lamasery on West Forty-Seventh and to public arenas like Mott Memorial

Hall, fronting on the Grand Army Plaza at Fifth Avenue, the Theosophical Society headquarters on Madison Avenue and the Astor Library, and Carnegie Hall, where a small band of singers explored artistic avenues into the New Age.

Site #1: A Unitarian Minister Reports on the Magical Milieu: Offices of the *Liberal Christian*, 214 Broadway, September 4, 1875

If you were a faithful reader of the *New York Times* in September 1875, you had absolutely no reason to fear—or hope—that magic was about to bust lustily into the metropolis. Yes, there were reports of the popish convention in New Jersey and Rome's attempt to influence the voters, and *Madame L'Archiduc*, the new play at the Lyceum, pivoted on royal European conspiracies; but the Astor House was reopening after a major renovation, the markets were all humming along, and Henry Ward Beecher's adultery trial, however scandalous the paper might try to make it out to be, was pretty bourgeois stuff. The *Times* boasted its own conventionality right under its masthead: "The *New York Times* is the best family paper published. . . . It contains the latest news and correspondence. It is free from all objectionable advertisements and reports, and may be safely admitted to every domestic circle. The disgraceful announcements of quacks and medical pretenders, which pollute so many newspapers of the day, are not admitted into the columns of *The Times* on any terms."

Then again, from the Broadway offices of the *Liberal Christian*— only a block from the *Times* building on Park Row—there issued on September 4, 1875, this provocative report, from the pen of one Rev. James Henry Wiggin, Unitarian minister and progressive editor, about "Rosicrucianism in New York":

> That a brotherhood of occultists has existed and still exists, reaching perfection in the far East; hating black magic and encouraging white; that Jesus belonged to it and initiated into it John, who wrote the *Apocalypse*; that Jesus died at forty-seven instead of thirty-three; that

he was an Essene and studied pure magic in India; that in the fraternity's archives are preserved grand records of truths about men and nature, which shall be revealed to the world when it righteously hungers therefor; that Rosicrucians can work what are falsely called miracles, by their knowledge of the true essence of things; that in Siamese temple-worship the dead are brought to life, the young grow suddenly old and the old young, women dance in the air; that some of the Rosicrucian disciples never die, having the elixir of life; that they possess the philosopher's stone; that gold rings can be brought today, and are, from rose-buds; that human bodies can disappear and reappear at will; that they can float in the air; that flying is as easy as to dream it; that the fraternity, seen and unseen, control the fate of nations; that its members directed Washington through his few degrees of freemasonry; that they paid the six milliard Prussian war debt of France; that they control the Carbonari (secret society), of Italy; that all nature is subject to their decrees through their knowledge of divine laws.

Such was the talk of the day about Rosicrucianism, at least in some circles.

Others might merely know of the mysterious order from Edward Bulwer-Lytton's *Zanoni* or certain Freemasonic utterances about Count Cagliostro's role in the founding of modern Masonry, but Reverend Wiggin's remarks were inspired from a recent visit that he had made, at the invitation of his friend Charles Sotheran, of the *American Bibliopolist,* to the home of Madame Helena Petrovna Blavatsky, at 46 Irving Place. Joined there by the lawyer, "war detective," and journalist Colonel Henry Steel Olcott; Signor Bruzzesi, former secretary to Giuseppe Mazzini; "Judge M" from New Jersey and "Mr. M" of Boston, Madame Blavatsky had presided past midnight over a rollicking conversation touching on not just the magical claims of Rosicrucianism but also "the Phallic element in religions; the souls of flowers; recent wonders among the mediums; history; Italian character; the strangenesses of travel; chemistry; poetry; Nature's duality; Romanism; Gravitation; the Carbonari; jugglery; Crooke's new

Madame Blavatsky, 1876

discoveries about the force of light; the literature of magic." Reverend Wiggin expressed his fervent hope that Madame Blavatsky could, as she had promised, bring order out of the chaos of modern Spiritism. The very sane and sober Colonel Olcott declared to Wiggin that until he met her, he could find no philosophy that could adequately explain the contradictory phenomena he had witnessed. With her help, he now saw a possible path to order and clarity.

The Rosicrucian philosophy, as given by Madame Blavatsky to her guests, held that "God dwells alone and is unapproachable. Souls pre-exist. They enter bodies at birth for developing discipline. It is the operation of the undeveloped spirits who have not yet been born into this world and have no consciences that make the vagaries of Spiritualism and their demonized revelations. Only by conformity to God's law can truth be reached. Only the pure are entitled to it. Prestidigitateurs like Houdin and Hermann have not the true power, but Magicians have it in the farther east." Though Wiggin found it a little startling to find oneself associating with those who possessed, or claimed to possess, such magical powers as were linked with the Count of St. Germain, Cagliostro, Eugenius Philalethes (Thomas Vaughan), Robert Fludd, Roger Bacon, and a hundred other ancient astrologers and worthies, and to hear talk of superiors and inferiors in the Brotherhood, he admitted that these were the statements put forward by those who constitute what might be called "the aristocracy of Spiritualism."

The anonymous Mr. M. was just such an aristocrat; Wiggin reported that this Boston gentleman had been "in many lands, travelled miles by the hundred thousand, is a practical scientist, served his country in the suppression of the African Coast slave trade before the war, journeyed with Livingstone, loves his many flowers, which love him back again, and brings a store of things new from his treasury." In his honor, Madame Blavatsky had magically transported from Scotland a bundle of blossoming heather.

This compelling Russian thaumaturgical wonder was the talk of New York. Newspapers had complained about the audacity of her fondness for cigarettes, her eccentric dress, and her thick Russian accent, but Wiggin found her English remarkably fluent and accurate and was charmed by the large jewels—one, it was rumored, brought from her father's Russian tomb to her through a spirit who talked Russian, in the presence of a host of witnesses; the other a fantastic Rosicrucian diadem—which she wore about her neck.

She is perhaps forty years old, strong-built, brusque and generous appearing. Interesting were the stories she had to relate about her residence in Asia and Africa—like Lady Mary Wortley Montague, living long away from the sight of European women. Marvellous were her narratives of her attempts at commerce, selling a cargo for cocoanuts which the unseaworthy ship could not bring away. Strange sights had she seen among the tribes of sorcerers in Africa; a negro, who, by black art, could submit to seventeen shots while the muzzle touched his body, causing each bullet to describe a triangle, spin into the air and finally bury itself in the earth; and a child whirled about in the air by invisible hands.

Though of a lesser order, her own magical feats were still spectacular, and she was admirably circumspect about her own abilities.

In that decade when New Yorkers had mostly moved on from merely crying "humbug!" at reputed miracles to a state of smug satisfaction that the Age of Miracles was soundly defeated, Reverend Wiggin was a fair and honest observer of both Blavatsky and her extravagant science. Reflecting on the implications of a suite of marvels produced not by machines but by the innate powers of humanity, he struggled mightily to reconcile the challenge posed:

If Siam and Hindostan have possessed this sacred truth, why are they so behind the age in their progress? Without it, behold what the Anglo Saxon has done for the earth and himself. Nor does it require a profound observance of the moral and humane condition of the Occident as compared with the Orient, to conclude that whatever we may lack in metaphysics, we are in no wise behind in the practices of the domestic virtues and philanthropy. Yet far be it from any mind to doubt that there may yet be something more to learn; "more things in heaven and earth than are dreamt of in our philosophy."

Little did the good Reverend Wiggin know just how true this truism was, when applied to the mysterious Madame Blavatsky.

Site #2: The Birth of Theosophy: Apartment of
Madame Blavatsky, 46 Irving Place, September 7, 1875

For the small group of people who assembled at Madame Blavatsky's modest Irving Place apartment on September 7, 1875, the advertised lecture of the evening—"The Lost Canon of Proportion of the Egyptians"—seemed to promise lesser entertainment than at any of the half dozen theaters a block away on Union Square. *Hamlet* was playing at both Booth's Theater and the Grand Opera House.

Standing before a set of colored drawings he had prepared for the occasion, the former Union army officer, inventor of telegraph devices and rockets, and avid Egyptologist George Henry Felt—a "remarkably clever draughtsman," according to Colonel Olcott—pointed to the chief illustration, of an Egyptian temple hieroglyphic he called "The Star of Perfection." Consisting of a circle bounded by a square and enclosing another square, a common triangle, two Egyptian triangles, and a pentagon, Felt shared his discovery that the figure could be applied to a whole range of Egyptian temple architecture—doors, pyramids, tombs, as well as elements within, such as statues, paintings, and hieroglyphs—to show that these were all ruled by the figure's proportions. Felt even asserted that the Egyptians had used the figure as the basis of all their astronomical calculations and religious symbolism.

Felt then added that while he had been researching the mathematical revelations in several Egyptian zodiacs, both his terrier and his Maltese cat acted very strangely. The cat would become upset, then the dog, and both ran against a glass window, trying to escape. Let out of the room, they continued to mew and bark, as if calling Felt to come out. Further research led Felt to conclude that he had unwittingly evoked spiritual beings both human and animal in form and that these could, by "chemical means," be rendered visible to his own eyes as well as his pets.

Dr. Seth Pancoast of Philadelphia challenged Felt on his ability to evoke these elemental beings, which everyone present under-

Madame Blavatsky and Colonel Olcott, 1888

stood to be the active agents of all magical operations, both ancient and modern. Felt offered to produce them before the group, if they would bear the cost of his work, and even promised to teach "persons of the right sort" how to produce and control the elementals—which, he warned, could become maliciously dangerous if not properly controlled.

At that moment, the thought came to Colonel Olcott that it might be worthwhile to organize a society to undertake exactly this sort of occult research, and he wrote this out as a question on a slip of paper and passed it to HPB (Olcott's favorite nickname for his friend), who read it and nodded. Years later, Olcott wrestled with the possibility that this had not been his own idea but the idea of some invisible "adept," who planted the thought in his mind.

The seventeen men and women who heard Felt's lecture were unanimous in their belief that magic was real, that it was capable of cultivation in the present era, and that it offered a path of investigation into nature's mysteries. When Olcott stood up to propose the formation of a society for the study of occult science and esoteric philosophy, in theory and practice, there was also unanimity. Thus was born the Theosophical Society—in 1875, the year that the Count of St. Germain said that he would reappear.

Two blocks from Madame Blavatsky's apartment, at the corner of Fourteenth Street and Irving Place, stood the Academy of Music, where, along with opera and orchestral concerts, respectable New York audiences gathered to witness the prestidigitation feats of the world-famous stage magicians Alexander Hermann and Robert Houdin. As they had since the late eighteenth century, stage magicians comforted the materialist masses that all the inexplicable phenomena of mesmerism and Spiritualism—and soon, Theosophy—were but sleight-of-hand.

Olcott, who had first met HPB in November 1874 at the Eddy household in Chittenden, Vermont, had come a long way in the past year. Sent there by the *New York Sun* to report on the Eddy brothers' mediumistic productions, Olcott watched the steady stream of discarnate spirits' antics through the same lens as all Spiritualists— that these were indeed spirits of the dead. Despite the protestations of many Christian circles, who recognized the activity of "infernal" agents in the séance room, the vast majority of people who did not condemn all Spiritualist phenomena as fraud believed the mediums were communicating with the dead. Having witnessed a most extraordinary series of events around Madame Blavatsky, Olcott now knew just how erroneous the Spiritualist worldview was.

HPB regularly astonished all but her fellow adepts. A week after Felt's lecture and the founding of the Theosophical Society, an Italian artist, "Signor B.," formerly one of Mazzini's Carbonari, arrived at the Irving Place apartment while Olcott was sitting in the drawing room with HPB. In the midst of an animated discussion about Italian affairs, the stranger mentioned the name of one of the greatest adepts; reacting as if touched by an electric shock, Blavatsky then began to speak solely of magic, magicians, and adepts. Though it was a bitter December evening, Signor B. stepped to one of the apartment's French windows, threw it open, and made a series of beckoning passes toward the outer air. Instantly, a pure white butterfly flew into the room and fluttered up toward the ceiling.

"That's pretty, but I can also do it!" laughed HPB, who then opened the window again and made similar gestures, until a second, identical white butterfly entered. Climbing toward the ceiling, it chased the other around the room, playing tag with it, until they both flew into a corner and—PRESTO!—disappeared while Olcott's eyes were fixed upon them.

"What does this mean?" he asked.

"Only this," his friend replied, "that Signor B. can make an elemental turn itself into a butterfly, and so can I."

Site #3: The Quixotic Quicksands of Occultism: Apartment of Madame Blavatsky and Colonel Olcott, 433 West Thirty-Fourth Street, October 16, 1875

There are many other players—human, nonhuman, human posing as nonhuman, and nonhuman posing as human—in the drama that saw both the original inspiration for the Theosophical Society and its subsequent fate. Before the departure of HPB and Colonel Olcott for London and then India, they jumped about Manhattan as promiscuously as did the "spirits"; in late 1875, they departed the swanky Irving Place / Gramercy Park neighborhood for a modest apartment in Hell's Kitchen. New York City continued to be a locus of magical activity by individual "spirits" with a bewildering roster of names and pseudonyms, occult brotherhoods like the Hermetic Brotherhood of Luxor, and single individuals—such as the artist and early lover/ companion of HPB Albert Rawson; the English antiquarian, bookseller, and journalist Charles Sotheran; the child seeress, Spiritualist medium, and first historian of Spiritualism Emma Hardinge-Britten; the physician and former Universalist minister turned Episcopalian turned Spiritualist turned Theosophist James Martin Peebles—with multiple and confusing affiliations and allegiances.

Portrait of John King
(Boris de Zirkoff Papers, Theosophical Society in America Archives)

Scholars are still sorting out—with great difficulty—the details of this history. Let us step lightly around the occult quicksand and consider just one itinerant spectral figure from HPB's biography, who put in the occasional appearance during her signal three years in New York. During those years, HPB often referred to a "JK"—for "John King"—whom she called "my only friend," who faithfully watched over and instructed her. A name that had appeared in countless séances for over twenty years, it seems clearly a pseudonym—whether chosen by JK himself or HPB. Just before her return to New York at the end of the summer of 1875, Blavatsky had badly injured her leg; doctors recommended amputation, but JK attended and healed her. At the same time, her occult powers grew considerably, under his guidance. These she attributed wholly to JK (also called by her "host," "Sahib," and "No"), whom she said had saved her life on three other occasions. At these and other times, she felt JK merge with her body and mind. He also aided her in astral travel.

Or did he? Olcott reported that JK had told him that for each time that he genuinely appeared, twenty elemental beings had impersonated him. Such is the nature of Faerie; *all* of the beings from this realm are capable of instantaneous and manifold shapeshifting. As with the thousands of mediums who had none of Blavatsky's innate occult gifts, once entrance was permitted for one elemental, unless one practiced the most rigorous spiritual hygiene, a whole circus train of elementals might gain admittance to the host's consciousness. For all but those with the strongest constitutions, this circus inevitably always proved debilitating and often fatal. Somehow, the blind spots of the Spiritualist enthusiasts of the nineteenth century have continued to afflict contemporary historians, who have failed to take note of the tragic roll call of insane, suicided, and fatally diseased Spiritualist mediums.

JK—the authentic, original JK—was clearly the author of the message that HPB was bringing to the world: that the strange phenomena of Spiritualism were entirely real but had nothing to do with spirits of dead people. The elementals who were responsible for the vast majority of mediumistic phenomena were an unprecedented window into the invisible aspect of nature and the Cosmos. "It is not I who talk and write; it is something within me," said HPB and any other honest medium.

When, on July 7, 1873, HPB had first arrived in New York City on what she said was her master's order, did she mean John King? Was John King a Hindu political occultist or a Rosicrucian? Was he, as the leading scholars of this episode believe, the same individual as the Coptic Greek Paulos Metamon, aka "Hilarion"? A later Christian initiate stated that John King was the inspirer working to introduce neo-Hinduism into the world, which he also did through the Englishman A. P. Sinnett's works. "A mahatma behind a mask" is what this initiate termed John King, who placed himself in contact with

Blavatsky over her original Rosicrucian inspirer and guide—the one who had looked after her since childhood. It is *this* John King whose identity remains a mystery, but it is again most suggestive that he took hold of Blavatsky's destiny in exactly the year prophesied by St. Germain and that Blavatsky herself held him in such high esteem.

From this brief episode, one begins to see how high the stakes were for human destiny; immense occult magical powers had been revealed, stimulated, and circulated, and now anyone was at liberty to take hold of them and by doing so take hold of both individual and collective human consciousness for selfish ends. Magic's entry onto the modern historical stage in the form of Spiritualism wreaked havoc both because of disenchanted science's and enchanted Spiritualists' inability to discern its true nature.

Site #4: H. S. Olcott's Theosophical Society Inaugural Address: Mott Memorial Hall, 634 Madison Avenue, November 17, 1875

In the 1870s, Mott Memorial Hall was tony Madison Avenue's lyceum for all things au courant for bourgeois society—everything from natural science (the New York Academy of Science was housed there) to Vedantism (various swamis gave lectures there for decades) to occultism, referred to by many of its practitioners as "occult science." The sort of promiscuous mingling of science and the supernatural that was a commonplace at Mott Memorial Hall was true of other cultural centers throughout the city in that era. The towering apartment buildings now lining Madison Avenue on these blocks obscure an era when every neighborhood in the city had public venues for the earnest seeker of spirit to hear and discuss the frontiers of knowledge, both magical and mundane.

The eminently empirical, practical, go-along-to-get-along Colonel Olcott was the perfect collaborator for HPB in founding the modern world's first cosmopolitan, wholly *exoteric* mystery school. He was just down-to-earth enough to play Watson to HPB's Sherlock Holmes, and he was honest enough to admit that when he thought

Henry Steel Olcott

back to that evening at Irving Place—when, out of the blue, he proposed that the circle of seventeen form a permanent circle to investigate magical phenomena (the very thing that *had not* happened in
response to the Hydesville poltergeists)—he was not sure that the
idea did not come from someone or somewhere else.

Olcott was nothing if not *active*, and so he charged in, with a New
Yorker's bluster. As president of the newly formed Theosophical
Society, he addressed those who were assembled for the ceremo-
nial inauguration at Mott Memorial Hall on November 17, 1875. His

reflection was humble, appealing to future historians to make some sense of an event that irked both the magic-denying Philistine scientists ("exhibitions of medieval sorcery") and the Church ("the worst forms of fetishism"). The ones who really got their knickers in a knot were the Spiritualists, whose imagined happy democratic relations were threatened by the "aristocratic elitism" of the Theosophists.

Olcott was a Jersey-born Columbia dropout, but his address had the ring of Broadway and Barnum about it:

> What is it then, which makes me say what in deepest seriousness and a full knowledge of its truth I have said? . . . It is the fact that in my soul I feel that behind us, behind our little band, behind our feeble, new-born organization, there gathers a MIGHTY POWER that nothing can withstand—the power of TRUTH! . . . Because I feel, as a sincere Theosophist, that we shall be able to give to science such evidences of the truth of the ancient philosophy and the comprehensiveness of ancient science, that her drift towards atheism will be arrested, and our chemists will, as Madame Blavatsky expresses it, "set to work to learn a new alphabet of Science on the lap of Mother Nature."

Those who turned to Spiritualism "encounter such a barrier of imposture, tricky mediums, lying spirits, and revolting social theories, that they recoil with loathing; secretly lamenting the necessity which compels them to do it." Both Protestantism and Catholicism were bankrupt, especially the latter, due to its "secret machinations."

Asking what might be the Theosophical Society's historical archetype, Olcott reviewed centuries of theurgic impulses—Cabalism, Neoplatonism, Stoicism, Hermeticism, mesmerism, Spiritualism—and found them all wanting. The times demanded a wholly *exoteric* order of associated adepts, who could carry out the task that had been so badly bungled by the Spiritualists—to demonstrate that nature was woven out of invisible elemental beings. Olcott challenged his audience to contemplate the implications for both science and superstitious Spiritualists of a wholly "daylight" magical practice:

Without claiming to be a theurgist, a mesmerist, or a Spiritualist, our Vice President [George Felt] promises, by simple chemical appliances, to exhibit to us, as he has to others before, the races of beings which, invisible to our eyes, people the elements. Think for a moment of this astounding claim! Fancy the consequences of the practical demonstration of its truth, for which Mr. Felt is now preparing the requisite apparatus! What will the Church say of a whole world of beings within her territory but without her jurisdiction? What will the academy say of this crushing proof of an unseen Universe given by the most unimaginative of its sciences? What will the Positivists say, who have been prating of the impossibility of there being any entity which cannot be weighed in scales, filtered through funnels, tested with litmus, or carved with a scalpel? What will the Spiritualists say, when through the column of saturated vapour flit the dreadful shapes of beings whom, in their blindness, they have in a thousand cases revered and babbled to as the returning shades of their relatives and friends? Alas! poor Spiritualist "editors and correspondents" who have made themselves jocund over my impudence and apostasy. Alas, sleek scientists, overswollen with the wind of popular applause! The day of reckoning is close at hand, and the name of the Theosophical Society will, if Mr. Felt's experiments result favourably, hold its place in history as that of the body which first exhibited the "Elementary Spirits" in this nineteenth century of conceit and infidelity, even if it be never mentioned for any other reason.

More than the Church, the Academy, the Positivist and Spiritualist naysayers, some other institution stood firmly in the way of Olcott's inspiring vision. Not he or HPB or Felt or any of those assembled saw this threatening specter, for it was altogether invisible. This was a *magical* battle, and the innocent Colonel Olcott had no idea that he was with his address summoning dreadful powers upon himself and his partner, Blavatsky.

Site #5: *Art Magic*: Residence of Emma Britten, 206 West Thirty-Eighth Street, January 1876

Back on October 2, 1875, in between the Irving Place imagining of the Theosophical Society and the November formal founding of it as an institution, a small advertisement appeared in the *New York Herald Tribune*: "[*Art Magic; or, Mundane, Sub-Mundane, and Super-Mundane Spiritism*] . . . will be the first and it is believed only publication in existence, which will give an authentic and practical description of art magic, natural magic, modern spiritism, the different orders of spirits in the universe related to or in communication with man, together with directions for invoking, controlling, and discharging spirits, and the uses and abuses dangers and possibilities of a magical art." The notice was signed, "Mrs. Britten. 206 W. 38th St." Before marrying William Britten in October 1870, she had been Elizabeth Hardinge, English actress and Spiritualist trance medium. In both of these careers, she had lived and worked for a considerable period in New York and was both a central figure in American Spiritualism (which she as often termed "Spiritism") and the early Theosophical Society. Her residence in New York gave her the vantage point to pen, in 1869, *Modern American Spiritualism* (favorably reviewed by the *New York Times*), an impressively complete history of antebellum America's most spectacular explosion of magical activity, mistaken until this very day as a "social movement."

Some picture of the exclusiveness of the city's magical community may be gathered from the publication prospects for *Art Magic*; Mrs. Britten said that just five hundred copies would be printed and that given the potential dangers of the book's misuse, she as editor and bookseller reserved the right to refuse unworthy buyers. If we could see the list of subscribers, we would be given today a fairly representative picture of this magic isle's impromptu Hogwarts Academy, circa 1876—the nation's centennial year. But absent that list, we can still be pleasantly and rightfully dumbfounded at the content of *Art Magic*. Just a decade or two after antiquarians and Hermetophiles

ART MAGIC;

OR,

MUNDANE, SUB-MUNDANE AND SUPER-MUNDANE

SPIRITISM.

A TREATISE

IN THREE PARTS AND TWENTY-THREE SECTIONS:

DESCRIPTIVE OF ART MAGIC, SPIRITISM, THE DIFFERENT ORDERS OF SPIRITS IN
THE UNIVERSE KNOWN TO BE RELATED TO, OR IN COMMUNICATION WITH
MAN; TOGETHER WITH DIRECTIONS FOR INVOKING, CONTROLLING,
AND DISCHARGING SPIRITS, AND THE USES AND ABUSES, DAN-
GERS AND POSSIBILITIES OF MAGICAL ART.

PUBLISHED BY THE AUTHOR,
AT NEW YORK, AMERICA.
1876.

Title page of *Art Magic*, 1876

might have scoured the bookshops of Broadway for rare *grimoires* from East and West, a thoroughly modern magical manual appeared in their midst. Erudite and comprehensive, *Art Magic* was a wonder, right down to its novel title. The anonymous author, who said that he had written the book at the invitation of "highly esteemed European friends," identified himself only as the author of another anonymous work, *Ghost Land; or, Researches into the Realm of Spiritual Existence*, which had been serialized in Mrs. Britten's *Western Star* magazine. That work's putative narrator was a "Chevalier Louis," or "Louis de B——."

After some one hundred pages or so of cosmology, anthropology, and history—including a fairly unabashed résumé of sex magic—the author coins the term "Art Magic." "Magic arts" and "the art of magic" had long been common coin, but this was an altogether novel phrase. "Louis" says merely that he adopted the term to distinguish modern magical practices from the ancient. "Every mind of ordinary intelligence and indomitable purpose may by the perusal of these pages become an Adept in Art Magic," he promises. To communicate the essential foundations on which Art Magic is based, Louis draws on Hindu concepts and language, most importantly, *Akasa*—the "pure, all-pervading fluid, invisible, fiery, radiant, wholly divine, free from the taint of matter, purer than ether, stronger than loadstone, mightier than the thunderbolt, swifter than the winged lightning"—which he equated with the Rosicrucian "Astral fluid." Using *Akasa* as instrument, any human soul could reach a level of adeptship that allowed it to escape the bonds of matter; such individuals were known as saints.

When we, denizens of the twenty-first century, walking this same Broadway as did Gilded Age New Yorkers, read from this 1876 book that "a Soul having at command an earthly vehicle in which to approach matter, is yet, by the subjugation of matter and the exaltation of Soul, at once a man, a spirit—a God"—we perhaps hear it today not so much as brazen blasphemy but as bittersweet missed opportunity. Supernatural technologies—electric light, the telephone, the Remington typewriter, the Corliss steam engine, the monorail (as well as Heinz ketchup and Hires root beer)—were all birthed in 1876. Supernatural humans such as Mandrake the Magician and Superman in 1876 might still be half a century away, but there were already prototype magical superheroes—the dashing protagonists of Brady's Mercury Stories, Beadle's Dime Novels, Chaney's Union Novels, DeWitt's Ten Cent Romances—dancing about in American literature at the centennial. At the risk of reductionism, one could say that all the American superheroes from Nick of the Woods (1837) to Hugo Hercules (1902) to Superman (1938) to Black Panther (2018) are *magicians*, possessed of supernatural abilities over nature and/or their fellow human beings. Had *Art Magic* sold more than five hundred copies and *Isis Unveiled* caused a wholesale soul search on the part of American natural science, the Marvel and DC Universes, Industrial Light and Magic, and Harry Potter would never have been necessary as intermediate detours on our destined path toward becoming Art Magicians.

What can *Art Magic*'s magicians do? "He can ride upon [*Akasa*]; sail in it; stand upon it; use it as the chemist uses airs, fluids, solids." Accumulating a vast reservoir of *Akasa*, the Art Magician can "cause . . . the heaviest bodies, even rocks, to move, transport them through the air, dissolve solids into fluids, fluids into airs, and recombine them again; . . . subdue the fiercest beasts by stupefying their senses; fascinate the serpent, charm the Boa, and palsy the Cobra de Capello." Upon the will of a powerful Art Magician, *Akasa* might be "diffused like a gauzy veil all through the atmosphere . . . [to] paint any images he pleases, and thus a whole assembly can see the objects created by that will at one and the same time."

Harry Potter's Cloak of Invisibility? The mysterious Chevalier informs us, "The magician can envelop himself in *Akasa*, and thus become invisible or visible at pleasure." Such feats relied solely on the fiercest, most ascetic discipline—something that was about as foreign as Hindu fakirs to Gilded Age New Yorkers.

Elder Wand? The author of *Art Magic* was experienced enough to know that no magical tool is inherently imbued with magical power but acquires that potency from those who employ it. "In the use of spells, charms, amulets, consecrated names and words, can we assign virtue to such objects? Some magnetic virtues, some narcotic essences, and some sublunary as well as Astral influences, inhere in every plant that grows, on every stone beneath our feet; yet we tread on Cabalistic stones, pluck Cabalistic plants, aye, and make use of Cabalistic words every day, and—nothing comes of it!"

Madame Blavatsky's spirit drawing of "Louis"

Resurrection Stone? A Hindu lama (*Bokt*), Louis says, quoting some unnamed source, "can rip up his abdomen, withdraw the intestines, and inspect them as calmly as the Priest examines the entrails of the sacrifice to discover oracular meanings. . . . This slain Bokt truly dies, but he feels nothing. . . . The body is whole again; it cannot be hurt, since *Akasa* makes, unmakes, and remakes again."

Just *who*, pray tell, is this "Louis" who seems so omniscient about the Mundane, the Super-Mundane, and the Sub-Mundane, as realms in which to effect magical action? See his portrait reproduced here, as created by HPB one cold evening in December 1875 at the home of the Theosophical Society treasurer H. J. Newton, at 128 West Forty-Third Street. Asked by a Spiritualist named Miss Pauline Liebert to produce a spirit photograph of the mysterious author of *Art Magic*, HPB obliged by snatching up a piece of cardboard, laying it on a table before her, rubbing the palm of her hand over it three times, and then turning it over to reveal this image. Not only had the author himself signed the portrait, but it also captured the image of one of the elves (to "Louis's" right in the image shown here) who effected it!

Despite the evidence of this unimpeachable spirit photograph, and a great deal of scholarly sleuthing, there remains a question as to who authored *Art Magic*. Mark Demarest, the indefatigable curator of the Emma Hardinge Britten Archive, believes that Emma is the author, just as she authored *Ghost Land*. There is something significant in the identity of *Art Magic*'s author having remained a mystery. It is as if, now that the era of protective secrecy that had for millennia enveloped magical practices had passed, the final step on the threshold of the exotericization of the ancient mysteries still saw a Victorian demurring, to protect the good lady's name and reputation. But Isis was about to be unveiled with the candor and bravado of a Broadway showgirl.

Site #6: Magical Hijinks at the Lamasery, 302 West Forty-Seventh Street, Summer 1876

Madame Blavatsky was by nature exotic, but she was also wholly aware of how effective a little exotic stage setting was to put an audience in her power—and given who she was and what New York was in the Gilded Age, there were audiences aplenty. Journalists came to see her almost daily, as did a steady stream of wonder-gawkers both highbrow and lowbrow and middlebrow too. She did not disappoint them. The "Lamasery"—her name for her Forty-Seventh Street apartment and the headquarters of the Theosophical Society, sported a mechanical bird and golden Buddha on the mantelpiece;

The Lamasery

huge potted palms on the floor; and stuffed owls, snakes, and lizards in the bookcases. A bespectacled stuffed baboon holding a journal article about Darwin's *Origin of Species* gawked from the corner. Celebrities like Thomas Edison came to séances there and found the outlandishly attired HPB chain-smoking cigarettes while she casually performed her "phenomena"—raps, wind chimes and other sound effects, and pictures appearing on blank slates. All the standard gimmicks of stage and parlor mediums she could effect easily, while fully conscious. Late one snowy night, having eaten some salty food for dinner, Olcott suggested to HPB that it would be nice to have some hothouse grapes to clear their palates. She asked Olcott to turn down the lights, but he accidentally extinguished the gas. "Light it again, quickly!" she commanded, and there hanging from the end of a bookshelf were two large bunches of Hamburg grapes. Asked how she did it, she replied that the grapes were the gift of elementals under her control.

For a tour through the magical kingdom that was Madame Blavatsky, one can do no better than Olcott's *People from the Other World* (1875) or *Old Diary Leaves, 1874–1878* (1895). Neither these eyewitness accounts nor the sensational newspaper articles adequately convey her penetrating understanding of the magic that she could perform or the degree to which her magical performances were a duty and sacrifice. She was as gifted a writer as a wizard, and a review of just the pieces she wrote during her New York years (1875–1878) gives some glimpse of her wit, her courage, and her wide-ranging comprehension of the invisible world lying just over the threshold of the physical.

Blavatsky published dozens of articles in these years in Spiritualist-oriented journals like the *Spiritual Scientist* and the *Religio-Philosophical Journal*, but she also regularly penned pieces for two of Colonel Olcott's old publication outlets: the *New York Sun* and the *New York World*. Wittier than a dozen Barnums, wiser than a roomful of Columbia dons, here is a sampling of her spirit:

On the limitations of science:

Among the numerous sciences pursued by the well-disciplined army of earnest students of the present century, none has had less honours or more scoffing than the oldest of them—the science of sciences, the venerable mother-parent of all our modern pigmies. Anxious in their petty vanity to throw the veil of oblivion over their undoubted origin, the self-styled positive scientists, ever on the alert, present to the courageous scholar who tries to deviate from the beaten highway traced out for him by his dogmatic predecessors, a formidable range of serious obstacles.

On the dangers of magic:

As a rule, Occultism is a dangerous, double-edged weapon for one to handle who is unprepared to devote his whole life to it. The theory of it, unaided by serious practice, will ever remain in the eyes of those prejudiced against such an unpopular cause an idle, crazy speculation, fit only to charm the ears of ignorant old women.

On love as a magical power:

There is a Power in this world which can command spirits—at least the bad and unprogressed ones, the elementary and Diakka. The *pure ones*, disembodied, will never descend to our sphere unless attracted by a current of powerful sympathy and love, or on some useful mission.

On the two streams of evolution—spiritual and physical:

There can be no real enfranchisement of human thought nor expansion of scientific discovery until the existence of spirit is recognized, and the *double* evolution accepted as a fact. Until then, false theories will always find favour with those who, having forsaken "the God of their fathers," vainly strive to find substitutes in nucleated masses of matter. And of all the sad things to be seen in this era of "shams," none is more deplorable—though its futility is often ludicrous—than the conspiracy of certain scientists to stamp out spirit by their one-sided theory of evolution, and destroy Spiritualism by arraigning its mediums upon the charge of "false pretences."

HPB's personal magical code:

I never claimed that Magic was anything but Psychology practically applied. That one of your mesmerizers can make a cabbage appear a rose is only a lower form of the power you all endow me with. You give an old woman—whether forty, fifty, sixty or ninety years old (some swear I am the latter, some the former), it matters not; an old woman whose "Kalmuco-Buddhistico-Tartaric" features, even in youth, never made her appear pretty; a woman whose ungainly garb, uncouth manners and masculine habits are enough to frighten any

bustled and corseted fine lady of fashionable society out of her wits—
you give her such powers of fascination as to draw fine ladies and
gentlemen, scholars and artists, doctors and clergymen, to her house
by scores, to not only talk Philosophy with her, not merely to stare at
her as though she were a monkey in red flannel breeches, as some of
them do, but to honour her in many cases with their fast and sincere
friendship and grateful kindness!

Far away and exotic as Blavatsky's perspectives might sound to
our contemporary ears, there is also something uncannily familiar to them. We live in an age when science still strains our souls
with its Promethean tendencies and when the proliferation of
"psychologizers"—and supposed communicants with the dead—
continues apace. A hearty swig of her witty observations on magic's
pitfalls and possibilities is still a powerful tonic for the modern soul.

Site #7: *Isis Unveiled*: J. W. Bouton Bookseller, 706 Broadway, September 1877

Beginning at the Irving Place rooms (visited in Site #2 in this chapter) and then at a series of apartments and finally at the Lamasery,
Madame Blavatsky labored steadily at writing a book. Sitting at a
large library table by a window with rose-pink curtains, hundreds
of sheets of paper strewn about her on the floor, her hand guided
by an unseen amanuensis, she told a reporter in January 1877, "Yes.
I am writing a book. It is to be called 'The Veil of Isis' and is in two
parts. In the first part, I attack science, and in the second part,
dogmatic theology."

*Isis Unveiled: A Master-Key to the Mysteries of Ancient and Mod-
ern Science and Theology* was just that. America appeared to be
waiting for it; it sold one thousand copies in ten days after its publication by James W. Bouton, a seller of rare (and some "licentious")
books on Broadway. The unwieldy mammoth manuscript that
Olcott first brought to Bouton was rendered much more intelligible

New York Tribune ad for *Isis Unveiled*, 1877

by Dr. Alexander Wilder, professor at the Eclectic Medical College of the City of New York. A scholarly student of Platonism and alchemy, Wilder had long been steeped in the language and concepts necessary to interpolate Blavatsky's revolutionary tome.

Isis Unveiled is many things, indeed, as manifold as magic itself, and so it takes a stout-hearted soul to penetrate it. Focused rigor and a light heart are both required as one turns its pages—which are many and dense. Even though volume 1 bears the title *Science*, it is a book about magic, and even today it has the potential—as do all *grimoires*—to also *be a magical book*. When you take it up, begin with just the table of contents: Old Things with New Names; Phenomena and Forces; Blind Leaders of the Blind; Theories Respecting Psychic Phenomena; The Ether, or "Astral Light"; Psycho-Physical Phenomena; The Elements, Elementals, and Elementaries; Some Mysteries of Nature; Cyclic Phenomena; The Inner and Outer Man; Psychological and Physical Marvels; The "Impassable Chasm"; Realities and Illusion; Egyptian Wisdom; India the Cradle of the Race. *Isis*

Unveiled was the first book in history that divulged the essence of magic, while also critiquing modern science as a materialist idol that might also function as a species of magic. Blavatsky reserved her most pointed criticism for hypnotists, calling them "unconscious sorcerers" who were oblivious that they were interfering with the most dangerous forces of nature.

Blavatsky's own magical touch lay lightly on the cover page, in the form of an epigram from Montaigne: "Cecy est un livre de bonne foy"—Here is a book of good faith. It is no idle choice for a motto, but still it is easily passed over. Montaigne's words could be taken to play with the double entendre of "faith," introducing at the outset of a book whose subject was said to be science its assumed antagonist: faith. One might hear that epigram as a direct and heartfelt plea by HPB that the reader accept each of its more than five hundred pages as genuine, as she herself was genuine. It takes a very noble soul to publicly play at magic in an age that disbelieves it, all the while flogging so-called science with as much passion as she musters.

Brilliant as she was, witty as she was, canny as she was, one need only enter a few pages into *Isis Unveiled* before one hears and feels a voice even larger than Blavatsky's—a prophetic, Abrahamic roar. Magical books are produced by magical means, and there is surely a stream of sacred magic flowing freely through the pages of *Isis Unveiled*. Taking nothing away from her vast accomplishment in its authorship, one can safely assume that this gospel came from above, from some impeccable Rosicrucian source. The text of *Isis Unveiled* suggests that Blavatsky's inspirer, the *original* John King, was Christian Rosenkreutz himself.

THE HIDDEN HAND: SPIRITUALISM AS MAGICAL EXPERIMENT GONE AWRY

Given Madame Blavatsky's opening of the floodgates of esoteric wisdom, it fell to the British Christian esotericist C. G. Harrison to comment on HPB's work and life—including the East/West occult struggle over her destiny—in a series of six lectures in 1893 to the Berean Society in London. The issue of HPB was closely tied to an earlier episode in the dance between the material world and the magical world: the appearance of "Spiritualism." Harrison's lecture series represented the "coming out," the exotericization, of what was widely known for decades among the Illuminati (not Weishaupt's Illuminati but the worldwide diaspora of members of truly occult brotherhoods). That to this day Spiritualism's true origin remains quite unknown—despite an enormous volume of scholarship—is a testament both to the effectiveness of circumspection among the brotherhoods and to the difficulty of relying on wholly exoteric scholarship to comprehend the full history of magically potent historical events.

In fact, it was the very issue of circumspection that decided the experiment in the first place. Occult orders in the West that saw themselves as the guardians of human spiritual evolution shared the view that the year 1841 marked "the abyss of materialism," the low point of humanity's spiritual life, when opponents of spiritual life were afforded the strongest point of attack on the evolution of humankind. Along with the telegraph (1837) and railroad (steam locomotive, 1840) as significant markers of the zeitgeist, other inventions included inexpensive photographic equipment (1840s) and the transoceanic cablegram (1844). An unprecedented outpouring of discoveries in the natural sciences paralleled these technological innovations. If one theme emerges from all of these developments in nineteenth-century natural science, it is the *extension of vision*. Optical instrumentation, spectroscopy, and new imaging techniques

THE

TRANSCENDENTAL UNIVERSE

𝕾𝖎𝖝 𝕷𝖊𝖈𝖙𝖚𝖗𝖊𝖘

ON OCCULT SCIENCE, THEOSOPHY, AND
THE CATHOLIC FAITH

BY

C. G. HARRISON

SECOND EDITION

LONDON
GEORGE REDWAY
1896

Title page of C. G. Harrison's
The Transcendental Universe, 1896

all vastly extended the range of the human eye into nature at every scale of perception. Concomitant with this visual enhancement came an acute sharpening of analytical capacity. Nature was inevitably reduced into smaller and smaller parts: cells became mere epiphenomena of their nuclei; nuclei dissolved into "genes"; animal and plant species shattered into populations; molecules were rendered into stochastic probabilities; stars dissolved into constituent

gases, which became mere spectral lines. All formerly fleshy phenomena hovered precariously, threatened by the prospect of being
reconstituted as mere statistics. In but three short decades of the
mid-nineteenth century, the groundwork had been completely laid
for what René Guénon termed "The Reign of Quantity."

Determined to do something to respond to this low point in
human spiritual history, a number of esoteric brotherhoods made
plans to use ceremonial magic to introduce certain phenomena into
the public realm, in hopes that they would stimulate scientific interest. To be candid, these orders—"Brothers of the Left," so called by
their more conservative and circumspect brethren (and so "Brothers of the Right")—wished to perform magical actions that would
use elemental beings (gnomes, undines, sylphs, and salamanders) to
excite the attention and investigation of the unseen "forces" (really,
beings) of nature. The "exotericist" Brothers of the Left argued for
full public disclosure; the "esotericist," conservative Brothers of the
Right wished to keep the public in the dark about magic. A compromise solution was proposed from the Left: let us bring about
mediumship as a way to show humanity the reality of the spiritual
world. The Right agreed to enter into this experiment.

It is as yet unclear if the Hydesville rappings were one of these
magical experiments, but it is the one that "stuck." After the Fox
sisters appeared on Broadway at Barnum's Hotel, the Spiritualist
craze infected the entire nation and world. Having taken a calculated risk that critical—but open—minds would honestly ask what
in the world might cause tables to tilt, raps to sound, and objects to
appear and disappear as routinely as a stage magician might cause
them to do, the Brothers of the Left (and Right!) were dismayed to
see that the elementals were mistaken as "spirits of the dead."

By the time of Madame Blavatsky's appearance in New York in
1875, there had been dozens of prominent commentators on Spiritualism who had correctly identified elemental beings as the cause

of all the mayhem and phenomena. But HPB was a phenomenon unto herself. She was capable of reproducing at will the antics of the performing mediums, as well as phenomena they were quite unable to produce—like that magical butterfly or the Scottish heather. She was also able to contextualize her magical feats, colorfully comparing and contrasting them with fakirs and wizards both celebrated and anonymous. HPB added to this her vast erudition and her playful good humor; she could ecumenically cite alchemical, scientific, and mystical literature chapter and verse, while at the same time rip to shreds the latest so-called scientific literature, from Darwin and Huxley to Tyndall and Laplace.

Long before Blavatsky and Olcott met up at the Eddy farm in Chittenden, Vermont, the Brothers of the Left had quit their magical experiment. Not only had they completely failed to inspire the natural scientists to formulate a new alchemy; they had thrown wide open a barn door that could not be shut, and the amoral, attention-seeking, pandemonium-causing tommyknockers continued to pour through the portal into the material world. In some way, Blavatsky was their last hope, a wizard so wily and whimsical that even the most mischievous elementals would be charmed into helping her cause of bringing "Truth, Higher than Religion." But there were human, not elemental, beings who would—and did—thwart her high mission to usher in a Rosicrucian order on this magic isle.

Site #8: Union Square's Magical Nexus, 1879

As 1878 was passing into 1879, Mozart's *The Magic Flute* had just finished a successful run at the Academy of Music—at that time located at the corner of Fourteenth Street and Irving Place, just a block off Broadway. Indeed, in 1879, Manhattan's mammoth theatrical industry was centered on Union Square. In 1879, "Broadway" essentially meant the blocks between Niblo's Garden and Tony

Pastore's Theater at Houston, north to the Academy of Music, Tammany Hall, and Irving Hall on Fourteenth Street. The favorite watering hole of New York's actors, directors, and playwrights was the Lotos Club, adjacent to the Academy of Music on Irving Place. Steinway's showrooms took up a quarter of the block across from the Academy, fronting on Union Square. The Martinka Brothers stagemagic emporium—opened in 1873—was just two blocks west. Tiffany's had just opened its new store on the other side of the square; the most popular luxury items this season were brought back by Tiffany from last year's Paris Universal Exposition—paperweights of hollow glass balls filled with water and a flocculent white powder of imitation snow. This novelty item would soon come to be called a "magic globe."

From the foot of Broadway at Castle Garden to Madison Square Garden, a block off Broadway at Thirty-Fourth Street, the greatest avenue in the world was lined with theaters sporting enchantment in all its many iterations. One could stroll out any evening and witness, from conjurors, thaumaturges, and "professors," cremation, decapitation, second sight, sword play, botanical miracles, vanishing ladies, hypnotism, mind reading, instantaneous memorization, and a cacophony of anti-Spiritualists who deftly displayed by mere sleight-of-hand the threshold-crossing feats of the séance parlor. On a walk up Broadway in 1879, one could have come face-to-face with the Swedish Wonder; William Robinson, the Man of Mystery; Zanzic; Roltair; Morphet; Clever Carroll; Marvelle; Verona, the King of Fire; and thirteen different "Signor Blitzes"—including "Jr.," "The Original," "Son," "Nephew," "The Great," "The Wonderful," "The Unrivalled," "The Mysterious," "By Purchase," and "The Great Original"—as well as the *real* original Signor Blitz, who frequently received hotel bills left unpaid by these impostors.

Theater historians dub 1879 the year of the "Grand Transformation" in New York's theater world. The theater impresario E. G. Gilmore had a hit at Niblo's with a spectacle called *Enchantment* this season, but the production's title might justly be employed to

Thomas Nast illustration for *Harper's Weekly*

characterize Manhattan's entire atmosphere and attitude that year. Wizards like Steele MacKaye—whose home was on Irving Place—were revolutionizing the theater with technical improvements in lighting and stage machinery that added to the level of marvel experienced by audiences. But Manhattanites, Americans, and the wide world in 1879 were much more deeply mesmerized by developments offstage. The telephone and Edison's incandescent electric light were both extending their mechanical magic by leaps and bounds this year, and Manhattan was the epicenter of innovation for both technologies. The city's landscape was metamorphosing apace: spires of the newly opened St. Patrick's Cathedral soared above Fifth Avenue; the Third Avenue El reached 129th Street only a year after it had come as far north as Sixty-Seventh Street; construction began on the Metropolitan Museum's new home on the east side of Central Park. Manhattan was in 1879 truly a prodigy, a wonder, altogether a place of *magic*.

The occult brotherhoods of New York and the whole world approached 1879 with an entirely different understanding of its significance, holding that in the spiritual world—the source of all magical power—an event occurred in 1879 that potentially marked the end of the "Abyss." The Rosicrucian understanding was that a battle had taken place between Archangel Michael and Satan—the "Dragon"— from 1841 to 1879. In the autumn of 1879, the Archangel Michael assumed the regency that had previously (since 1525) been the province of the Archangel Gabriel. With the assumption of Michael's rightful regency, a host of dark spirits were cast out of heaven, into the earthly realm. If one considers that this "fall of the spirits of darkness" transpired all through those decades, one has an entirely different perspective on the macabre productions of modern Spiritualism in those very years.

Michael had been from the beginning of human evolution the companion of humanity as it strove toward independent thinking, and now Michael's mission was to serve all those who would call on him freely and faithfully, to aid in cultivating a new, independent, daylight clairvoyance to dispel the spectral visions brought so recently down to Earth. The brotherhoods believed with weighty heart that if humanity did not proceed aright on the destined magical path, the Dragon and his demons would invade human thinking, to take up residence within us.

Site #9: Offices of *The Path*, 35 Broadway, August 1890

The attorney and editor/publisher William Q. Judge launched his small but insightful little review *The Path: A Magazine Devoted to the Brotherhood of Humanity, Theosophy in America, and the Study of Occult Science, Philosophy, and Aryan Literature* from a Park Row office in 1886; by 1890, he had moved it to his new quarters at 35 Broadway. Folding its tent in 1894, the short-lived periodical provides a superb window into the mélange of magical activity in New York City in the wake of Madame Blavatsky's departure. HPB had truly unveiled Isis, occasionally for the better but more often for worse.

In August 1890, there appeared in the pages of *The Path* a notice regarding a circular that had been sent to members of the "H.B. of L."—the Hermetic Brotherhood of Luxor—offering what was essentially a correspondence course in ceremonial magic, twelve months of lessons for sixty dollars. The instructor, T. H. Burgoyne, was a shady occult con artist whose dishonesty put him in trouble with the law but who meanwhile unleashed a stream of black magic masquerading as "Egyptian and Chaldean Magic." Burgoyne promised his prospective students that "all argument or superfluous matter will be strictly omitted" and the laws and teachings "concisely stated." A decade after Blavatsky parted the veil of Isis, Burgoyne had pared down to basics the vast oeuvre of Hermetic philosophy and practice. To do so, he had tossed together scraps from Swedenborg, Anna Bonus Kingford's *The Perfect Way* (1882), Thomas Lake Harris's dangerous "soul-blending," and a great deal of Paschal Beverly Randolph's sex magic and scrying. The result was a sorry mess of absurdities and obscenities. As recapitulated in *The Light of Egypt; or, The Science of the Soul and Stars* (1889), Burgoyne's stripped-down thaumaturgy took aim at both Blavatskian Theosophy and Western Christianity. Lifting plenty of material from HPB's *Isis Unveiled* and *The Secret Doctrine* (1883), Burgoyne's special hatred was saved for Christianity. "The names of Christ and Christianity ought to be

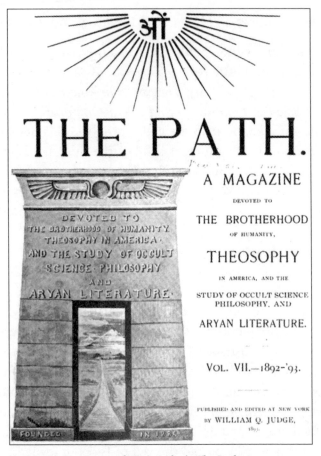

Cover of W. Q. Judge's *The Path*

banished forever from the minds of all students of Occult Science. Let us have the simple teachings attributed to the man Jesus, if you will, but never call anything divine by the name of Christ or Christian, although Christ or Christos anciently referred to the inner light of man.... The Gospel Jesus, as taught by Christianity, never existed."

"Zanoni"—Burgoyne's pen name for these lessons (tellingly, in Edward Bulwer-Lytton's novel of the same name, the main character is an adept whose occult powers divorce him from human emotion)—always signed his name with a swastika, and when one reads his mad magical pronouncements, one wonders if the being who later inspired the corruption of that ancient symbol of life had not taken hold of Burgoyne. It certainly was an "Imperial" vision that he soon expected to reign:

> Empires will shine full of glory, the human intellect will have full play and all Churches, Religious Creeds and Ecclesiastical Dogmas will fall to the ground and become things of the past. . . . This era shall proclaim the rights of man. It is essentially the age of reason dreamed of by Bruno and Thomas Paine. During the reign of this Angelic Intelligence, the Masculine Element will receive the Solar influx and obtain its highest development. Intellect and reason will remove most of our social disorders. . . . Mankind under this rule will become physically and intellectually immensely superior to what they are now. Startling discoveries in Chemistry, Electricity and all the physical sciences will be brought to light. . . . In fact, a new era of progress will dawn upon the world, as time and space will be annihilated by the new transportation and communication; and last, but not least, Science and Religion will become blended, spiritual intercourse an acknowledged fact, and Psychology the special study of the great scientists of the day.

This sort of materialist Utopianism was bad enough; the highest mysteries—karma, reincarnation, death, birth—all were profaned at fifteen dollars per quarterly payment, making a "hell" of "heaven." This would soon become the hallmark of a whole array of false gospels issuing from surface-skimming mystagogues, repeating with even more dangerous results the "unveiling" that had accompanied the brotherhoods' introduction of mediumism decades earlier.

THE COLUMBIAN: SECRET SOCIETIES AT COLUMBIA UNIVERSITY, 1891

In 1891, secret societies were at the height of their popularity. A glimpse at the pages of *The Columbian* shows how magically charged are the insignia of the fraternities: Delta Kappa Epsilon's winged Egyptian crystal ball; the Athenian owl atop Psi Upsilon; Zeta Psi's alpha and omega. Many of the fraternities' symbols bore a pair of hands in magical grips. The insignia for Cyclopes, along with bearing a full-blown third eye in the center of the skull, had a cobra coiled around it, its triangular face looking out from above the Cyclopean eye.

There was perhaps no place better than college fraternities to see the apotheosis of *disenchantment* that began in the old Freemasonic orders; any magical arcana were now merely the source of cheap masculine thrills and empty bravado. Divorced from a course of moral and ethical development, as well as from the magical sciences, "Greek" life on American university campuses was a caricature of the ancient mysteries, emblazoned on the Ivy League soul at the very moment that those mysteries were yielding up their magical secrets.

Insignia of Columbia University's
Cyclopes fraternity

Site #10: Solomon Heydenfeldt Seeks Senate Action against
Magical Orders: Heydenfeldt's Residence,
107 East Twelfth Street July 29, 1892

On Friday, July 29, 1892, Vice President Adlai Stevenson presented to
the United States Senate the petition of Solomon Heydenfeldt Jr., pro-
posing the passage of legislation to "prohibit the use of electricity on
human beings where it affects others." In 1892, electricity was hardly
a mystery to Americans, and the senators present no doubt imagined
that Heydenfeldt's petition was directed at the exaggerated dangers
of urban electrification plants or telegraph lines. Back in their Senate
offices, opening the petition, they read the heading, "Danger to Your
Wives and Daughters—Theosophy & Demonology—the Mysteries
of Satanism—Unison of the Conscious Force."

In the most sanely scientific language, Heydenfeldt—a prominent San Francisco attorney and son of California's first Jewish
state supreme court justice—stated that millions of Americans in
large cities were unknowingly under the influence of currents of
electromagnetism, which allowed their thoughts to be controlled
from a distance. Unnamed magnetizers passed an electrical current
through thousands of persons; even after the chain of persons was
decoupled from the current, according to Heydenfeldt, the Earth's
natural magnetism would continue to connect them in "sympathetic
relation, unless supernatural power intervenes."

Supernatural power was indeed at the center of Heydenfeldt's con-
cern; the full title of the report he published in 1891 hinted at the scope
of this power: *The Unison of the Conscious Force: To the Medical Profession: Electro-Magnetizing and Hypnotism: Outline of the Secret of
the Buddhists: The Doctrine of Secrets: The Augmentation of Sound:
Electro-Magnetizing—Natural Insulation of Man—The Condition
of Electro-Magnetism—Hyperaesthesia—Etheropathy—Insanity—
Neurasthenia—Epidemics—Transmission of Disease–Dangers
of Electro-Therapeutics—Power of Magnetizers—Hypnotism—
Somnambulism—Suggestion—Transmission—Subjectiveness—*

"Lobster-cracking" device drawn by James Tilly Matthews,
from John Haslam's *Illustrations of Madness*, 1810

*Semi-Suggestiveness—Telepsychological Action—Thought
Transference—Mind Reading—Muscle Reading—Visualizing—
Dreams—Victim System—Opium Leprosy—Distributing
Subjects—Cystic Punishment—Secret Societies—Theosophy—
Spiritualism—Legislation—Treaties—Galvani—Grimes—St.
Sauveur—Gall—The French Academy—Lecky—Hucker.* The preface
to the book Heydenfeldt signed simply, "New York, December, 1890."
In 1869, when he was a student at Columbia University, Heyden-
feldt's address was 107 East Twelfth Street; in 1892, he was living in
San Francisco but had spent nearly a year back east, doing research
in the Astor Library and the Library of Congress.

Heydenfeldt especially accused the Mormon leadership of practicing demonic mind control and went on to suggest that secret

societies used electricity to spread epidemic disease and even to disturb or destroy "national independence." As evidence, Heydenfeldt cited over fifty published works, from the principal demonological treatises of the early modern period—Pierre de Lancre's *Tableau de l'inconstance des mauvais anges et demons* (*Portrait of the Inconstancy of Evil Angels and Demons,* 1612); King James I's *Daemonologie* (1597); Bodin's *De la démonomanie des sorciers* (*Of the Demon-Mania of the Sorcerers,* 1580); and the "Hexenhammer," the *Malleus Maleficarum* (1487)—to recent Theosophical and other works of popular occultism like HPB's *Isis Unveiled* and A. P. Sinnett's *The Occult World.* The only overtly political treatises Heydenfeldt cited were works like Abbé Barreul's *Memoirs Illustrating the History of Jacobinism,* which Heydenfeldt believed proved that all the people of France were magnetized during the French Revolution. Heydenfeldt also included Orestes Brownson's *The Spirit-Rappers: An Autobiography,* which, though a work of fiction, presented Brownson's conviction that the European revolutions of 1848 were also precipitated by magnetic contagion set in motion by secret brotherhoods. Heydenfeldt had recently written to Brownson's son Henry to ask for access to his father's notes on the subject.

Heydenfeldt's petition was full of incendiary charges: the Mormons used magical practices in their efforts to overthrow all other religions and the United States government; "Magnetical Somnambulisms" and other centers of thought transfer and control existed throughout the world; there were adepts who could imitate God, Jesus, the saints, philosophers, angels, and archangels, to guide the vast army of *dédoubles*—unwittingly hypnotized dupes. In a letter enclosed with the petition, Heydenfeldt expanded on his allegations. Using electromagnetic currents, secret societies could create "magnetical unions" and control the actions and opinions of large numbers of citizens without being detected. "Passions" could be transmitted during these magnetic chains, leading to epidemics of crime, neurasthenia, epilepsy, and other afflictions. Even torture could be practiced remotely.

Heydenfeldt promised that he was not currently a member of any secret order, and the former Freemason claimed to have been "electromagnetized" without his consent. He had been diagnosed by experts and, through his inner ear, had been spoken to for three and a half years by "operators" throughout the United States, France, England, Germany, Switzerland, and other countries. The operators used fictitious names and refused to be identified, but he had made a list of names that had been transmitted to his inner ear. Having moved from New York to Washington, DC, so that he might call on both the police and Secret Service for help, he had been informed that there was no law to prevent hypnotism. He had then turned for help to Masonic orders, the Ancient and United Order of Druids, and the Mormons, with no success. Physicians too were ignorant of the diabolical practice, and so he had come to DC and spent nearly a year researching the magic and mesmeric arts at the Library of Congress.

"The people of the United States have been kept in ignorance of the subject of magic," Heydenfeldt declared at the conclusion of his letter. Since magic could be used across state lines, federal judicial action was required, Heydenfeldt reasoned. What the United States needed was a Declaration of Independence of the mind, to protect its citizens from secret enemies; Congress should also seek an international treaty to guard the army, navy, and overseas ambassadors and public ministers from the conspiratorial, treasonous machinations of magnetizers. Despite Heydenfeldt's efforts, which included the publication and dissemination of *Unison of the Conscious Force*, an eighty-six-page expansion of his argument that the United States was under threat from a vast magnetic conspiracy, the Senate Judiciary Committee failed to take up the proposed legislation.

Heydenfeldt was particularly concerned with the political dimension of the magical employment of electricity:

At various periods in past centuries, the knowledge of electro-incysting, called "taking possession of," and the method of affecting one person through another by a current of electricity, generated from some form of battery, was more generally known.

The power which it gave, led the ambitious to conceal and control it, by false arguments of its dangers, if generally known, by ridiculing those asserting it, by charging them with superstition, and by inducing others to become members of secret orders, which prohibited even its discussion. Also by buying up entire editions of publications, which would lead to its exposure.

The only *safety which the present and future generations* have, is to keep the *explanation* of the subject *before the people.*

The diagram at the beginning of the description of this site is from John Haslam's 1810 account, *Illustrations of Madness: Exhibiting a Singular Case of Insanity, and a No Less Remarkable Difference in Medical Opinions: Developing the Nature of an Assailment, and the Manner of Working Events; With a Description of Tortures Experienced by Bomb-Bursting, Lobster-Cracking and Lengthening the Brain. Embellished with a Curious Plate.* In 1797, the London tea broker and hopeful broker of peace between Britain and France James Tilly Matthews was committed to Bethlem (aka "Bedlam") Royal Hospital after he shouted "Treason!" in the House of Commons. Matthews maintained that a gang of spies skilled in "pneumatic chemistry" tormented him and others using a machine he called an "Air Loom," whose rays could be used all over London, to "premagnetize" victims—mainly important ministers—with "volatile magnetic fluid" so that their minds could be read and otherwise influenced. The "curious plate" shown here is Matthews's own drawing of the Air Loom.

Just as has happened regarding Mesmer's healing magic, searing, satirical hay has for two centuries been made of the Air Loom, but Heydenfeldt's little manifesto—when considered against the backdrop of the true magical history of Anglo-America in the nineteenth century—suggests that occult brotherhoods were using their predecessors' techniques all the same. In the twentieth century, these occult methods would be refined further and continue to be diabolically—and successfully—employed, all the while guaranteed secrecy by a sort of Cloak of Invisibility created by the Muggle world.

Site #11: The Aryan Theosophical Society Headquarters, 144 Madison Avenue, 1893

Sometime in 1893, under the direction of the organization's president, William Q. Judge, the Aryan Theosophical Society of New York purchased for $42,500 a brownstone building on Madison and Thirty-Second Street. From the basement were published works from the Aryan Press, and the office for *The Path* and the library were housed on the second floor. There was on the third floor a space for a receptacle to hold the ashes of Helena Petrovna Blavatsky. The year 1893 saw a dozen or more members of the group travel to the World Parliament of Religions at the Chicago World Columbian Exposition; by this moment, New York City's branch—the founding branch—of the Theosophical Society was turning more into a neo-Buddhist religious organization or study group, losing the initial theurgic magic emphasis. In that same year, at the Theosophical Society's annual convention, the members assembled on the steps of the new headquarters building for a group photo.

This surely is no "Miracle Club," as HPB, Olcott, and other founding members jokingly referred to their tribe in 1875, but then again, it is terribly hard to say anything at all about the people in the photo. Of ninety-seven individuals, forty-two are women, and two are children (probably the children of W. Q. Judge, who sits in the front row, to the right of the center railing). Two people seem to be over the age of seventy, a dozen or so seem to be under forty, perhaps ten are in their sixties, and half the group are in their fifties. Their costume and demeanor are conspicuously bourgeois. From this distance, only one or two appear—from the light in their eyes—to possibly be Art Magicians.

1893 Theosophical Society convention attendees

One young man alone reaches forward to place his hand on the shoulder of a fellow in front of him. A man with a robust beard and mustache is playfully putting his top hat up behind the head of the man in the row below him. Facing the formerly magical, now growing increasingly prosaic alchemical invention that used silver to capture and freeze light, the Theosophists almost all look with great intensity directly at the camera. Perhaps this is the closest approach to Hogwarts made by any gathering of hopeful magicians, up until now.

Site #12: Fountaingrove: Residence of "Father" Thomas Lake Harris, 308 West 102nd Street, 1894

No Manhattan magician can rival Thomas Lake Harris for the length of his wizarding career. Having set himself up as a viticulturist in

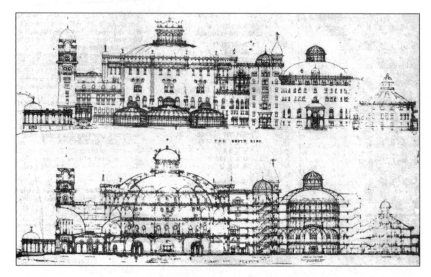

Fountaingrove plans
(Edwin Markham Papers, Wagner College)

Santa Rosa, California, in the 1870s, Harris was back in New York in 1894, living in a modest Upper West Side apartment where he dreamed of re-creating his California Xanadu on the Hudson River. His architectural plans include drawings of elaborate Halls of Music and Feast, a Rotunda of the Dance, a "Commandery" and "Familis-tery," a Calling Choir Loft, Armory, Exposition Hall, Bathing Pool, Boat House, Social and Business vestibules, and "a hundred bowers of love's repose."

By 1894, Thomas Lake Harris was completely possessed by a host of very eccentric, epicurean demonic beings whose ever-enlarging appetite for grandeur was expressed in both this New York palatial scheme and in the books Harris wrote. A quick glance at any of the works after 1880—*The Wisdom of the Adepts: Esoteric Science in Human History* (1884), *The Joy Bringer: Fifty-Three Melodies of the One-in-Twain* (1886), *The New Republic: A Discourse of the Pros-pects, Dangers, Duties and Safeties of the Times* (1891), *God's Breath in Man and in Humane Society* (1891), *Conversation in Heaven: A*

Wisdom Song (1894)—shows that Harris's penetrating clairvoyance for the activity of what he termed "the Infernals" did not prevent him from becoming their plaything, turning him into an "Inversive"— Harris's term for "men of *Ob*, men of an evil destiny." Each of Harris's books is an immense and disturbing chronicle of magical practice within which one finds a close chronicle of the magical methods of the occult brotherhoods of Harris's era. Harris's *Wisdom of the Adepts* is a blood-curdling account of the ceremonial magical machinations of the black brotherhoods, but it is equally a record of his own Faustian destruction.

Harris—whose eyes in photos from the 1890s have the far-off, vacant, shiny stare of the lunatic—had taught two generations of acolytes a magical yogic technique he called "Divine Respiration," which was actually a form of psychic vampirism. Harris repeatedly and regularly black magically stole the life force from his followers, who, after he died on March 23, 1906, at his home on 102nd Street, continued to believe for quite some time that he would be physically restored to life. "The Brotherhood of the New Life" was a very old conceit, the dark conceit of material resurrection, and we would do well to study Harris's life as an object lesson in the chaos and destruction that such a black-magical belief engenders.

Site #13: A Magical Librarian at the Astor Library (Today the Public Theater), 425 Lafayette Street, March 1895

Most of the New Yorkers in that 1893 Theosophical Society photo would have been acquainted with Carl Henrik Andreas Bjerregaard, if not from attending his lecture series at the society's rooms, then from visits to the Astor Library (now the Public Theater), where he had been a librarian since 1879. By the time the New York Public Library opened in 1911, he was the chief of the Main Reading Room. With this vast collection at his fingertips, he became a most accomplished mystic vagabond, writing books on Sufism, Taoism, Jesus, mysticism, and nature worship. He taught himself painting at the age

Carl Henrik Andreas Bjerregaard (1845–1922)

of seventy, producing several hundred works entirely from memory, some of scenes beheld in his dreams. It is quite characteristic of this magic isle's perennial cosmopolitanism that a man who spent nearly forty years classifying, locating, and delivering books to patrons (he was the staff member who originally arranged the "pastel cards" that were cut from the original catalogues of the Astor Library when it was consolidated with the Tilden and Lenox libraries to become the New York Public Library; this became the foundation of the New

York Public Library's classification scheme) should have been a former spy in the Danish army, a Knight of Danebrog, and as sensitive a commentator on mysticism both East and West as was writing in the early twentieth century.

Bjerregaard was deeply acquainted with the principles and practice of magic, and this informed all of his research and writing. In his *The Great Mother: A Gospel of the Eternally-Feminine; Occult and Scientific Studies and Experiences in the Sacred and Secret Life* (1913), he displays an alchemist's appreciation for all the occult qualities of nature and an initiate's love for those who have walked the narrow path, be they Sufi, Hebrew, or Hindu. One feels when he is writing about Jesus Christ that Bjerregaard—who for years led nature walks around the metropolitan area—had walked with the master himself. How refreshing to find in him a kind of modern Paracelsus, who can liberally quote both Thoreau and Emerson and the Gospels and *Bhagavad Gita*: "In the Air there are an immense number of 'airs,' living, dead, healthy or noxious. They produce ferments and disturbances as well as health and happiness. They are occult in their character and only controlled by 'magic.' Air envelops us everywhere and always. Our body or personal temple is built out of Air solidified for the time being and stands in constant rapport to it, changing into it, drawing from it, and at times being a magic agent."

In "The Elementals, the Elementary Spirits, and the Relationship between Them and Human Beings," a two-part essay in 1887 in *The Path*, Bjerregaard displayed as complete a knowledge of the beings "at the bottom of the garden" as even HPB. He draws fine distinctions about the capacities and proclivities of elementals versus elementaries, draws on a wide knowledge of past writers from Leibnitz to Swedenborg, and makes his own contributions, always stressing the moral development that must precede the cultivation of magical faculties:

It is a truth well understood that Spirit does not act immediately upon Matter. There always is a medium between them. It seems rational that it should be so. Spirit and Matter being the two poles of one and the same substance need the intermediate middle as a point of conjunction and exchange of energy.

Applying this general law to the particulars before us, it seems most natural to conclude that the Elementals are the media by means of which all our spiritual efforts are exerted upon Nature, and that nothing can be done without their intervention.

But the question also arises: how do we make the Elementals perform this work for us? By what means do we influence them?

Occult Science teaches that "the pure of heart," those that, having travelled over "the Path," have come to "freedom," can, by a mere mental effort or by stretching out the hand, "do these things."

Reading this, reading all of Carl Bjerregaard's essays and books, one may take heart that whatever distortions the human being may introduce into the realm of the Great Mother, whatever manipulations might be attempted on the fabric of the *Akasa*, these are but the most transient of things and that at every moment in human history, especially now, there are among us great sages and mages who can help us on our path.

MANHATTAN'S FIRST UFOS? SEPTEMBER 1909

By dusk on the inaugural evening of the Hudson-Fulton three hundredth anniversary celebration, a war fleet had made a midstream line up the Hudson for ten miles, from Forty-Second Street to Spuyten Duyvil Creek to the north. The ships were eerily quiet, their presence revealed to the mass of spectators only by their faint silhouettes and an occasional signal flashed from ship to ship. Then, at the sound of eight bells, the entire fleet burst into outlines of light, as if suddenly touched with the propitious augury of St. Elmo's fire—the masts, decks, water lines, and other chief features glowing with thousands of sparkling electric globes. And for hours these

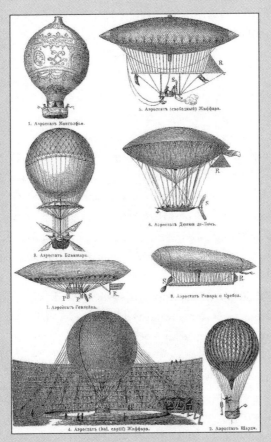

Air balloons and airships
(*Brockhaus and Efron Encyclopedic
Dictionary, 1890–1907*)

ponderous, death-dealing machines, lying peacefully on the bosom
of the Hudson in friendly association, scintillated like the airy fab-
rics of a magician or the unsubstantial dreams of an Oriental fairy
tale. It was a scene of exquisite beauty that will never be forgotten by
the millions of people who thronged to the riverside to see it.

The plan was for this surprise illumination to be augmented
by a massive fireworks display that had been set up on four floats

anchored at intervals of one thousand feet along the New Jersey shore directly across from Riverside Park. Just after the fireworks began, as the crowd watched, the floats were cut loose from their moorings and drifted downriver. That evening, the telegraph operators were reporting problems with their lines, and it was attributed to the fireworks operation, since the floats were very close to the telegraph cable crossing the river.

New York City telegraph operators were not the only ones having trouble with their lines. Since dawn that morning, telegraph service all over the world had been disrupted. Calling it an "aurora"— knowing from experience that brilliant displays of the northern lights typically followed such disturbances—telegraph operators wrestled with the strange force, which peaked at about noon but then continued to "throb" in the afternoon and evening. Wires would go dead for a few moments, pick up slowly, and then die again. Telephone systems were useless as well. New York City, with the nation's densest grid of electrical communications, was most severely affected, but the pulsing wave of electromagnetic energy moved steadily westward, knocking out telegraph service in Cincinnati, Chicago, and beyond, all the way to Seattle and San Francisco. Instruments in telegraph offices measured a current of five hundred volts in the atmosphere—greater voltage than was usually supplied along the lines. In western Australia, from Perth to Kalgoorlie, a distance of 350 miles, the line kept operating for a half hour even though the batteries had been disconnected. Incandescent lamps attached to the wires lit up from the atmospheric electricity, and brilliant sparks flashed across the gaps whenever operators opened their telegraph keys. Reports from around the world the next day showed that the aurora borealis was seen generally as far south as thirty degrees north latitude, but Jakarta and Singapore—at one degree north and six degrees south—had also experienced the aurora.

The presumption by the telegraph company that the fireworks might have been the cause of the problem suggests how new and mysterious electromagnetism was, even a half century after the first telegraph lines were strung across America. Newspaper reports discussed the theory that the magnetic storm was caused by sunspots as just one of a number of competing theories. At the time of the September 25 storm, Guglielmo Marconi was in New York, and when the *New York Times* asked him for his explanation, he said that sunspots might have little to do with it. He did, however, gloat over the fact that his new wireless telegraph was not as adversely affected as standard telegraph systems were by the auroral storm. "I can't help being a little glad the telegraph companies have had this object lesson," Marconi told the *Times*.

The sky was full of all manner of signs and wonders in 1909. Underneath the Marconi interview in the *Times*, a tiny filler item from the newswire noted that in Hawaii on the twenty-fifth, there had been a display of spectacular fireworks—attributed to a meteor shower. But in recent months, there had been stranger sightings: a report of an hourlong storm of hot globular rain in Santa Cruz, California; a meteor that had dropped through the roof of a house in Texas; and other meteorites from New Jersey and Massachusetts and Connecticut and Mexico City. A brief survey of article titles from the very sober journal the *English Mechanic* gives a fair picture of Brittania's skies around 1909: "Glorious Midnight Sky," "Smoke-Like Darkness before the Storm," "Aurora," "Nocturnal Glows," "Nocturnal Northern Glows," "Curious Lunar Observation," "Electrical Fireballs," "Unexplained Ringing of House Bells," "Globular Lightning," "Ball Lightning." In May and June, there were scattered reports of a wave of phantom airship sightings—the twentieth century's first "UFOs"—from all over Great Britain. In July and August, thousands of New Zealanders observed zeppelin-type ships, and then in late August, they were sighted on the east coast of Australia.

A million people had watched Wilbur Wright fly a very real air-plane up the Hudson in broad daylight just two months before; air-ships were all the rage, but newspaper editors and reporters—the same ones who fell over themselves getting stories and photographs documenting the latest in aviation news—could without pause dismiss their readers as credulous and attribute all the excitement to an episode of wishful thinking. In 1909, newspapers had already succeeded in undermining the authority of the eyewitness. A steady diet of telegraphed, instantaneous "news" not only erased traditional democratic notions of authority but also fostered a kind of collective amnesia. One needed only glance over newspapers a couple of months old to glean arcana that fleshed out the aerial enigma a bit further. Witnesses clearly heard an unknown language spoken by occupants of the airships, which appeared and disappeared in an instant. There were fireballs and other bright lights and telepathic little men making mischief. It seemed for all the world as if electro-magnetism was driving the modern world right back into the arms of Faerie.

Site #14: Telekinesis, Psychokinesis, and Other Real Magic: Office of Publisher Henry Holt, 34 West Thirty-Third Street, 1914

The publisher Henry Holt was like many New York City publishers, an intensely curious, well-educated, cosmopolitan fellow; after his graduation from Yale (AB, 1862) and Columbia Law School (LLB, 1864), he founded Henry Holt and Company in 1864 with Frederick Leypoldt. He belonged to or was an officer or trustee of some of the city's leading clubs and organizations (New York University Settlement Society; Century, Yale and University Clubs; Sons of the Revolution; the American Geographical Society; American Association for the Advancement of Science; Metropolitan Museum of

Dr. James Henry Hyslop
(*New York Times*, June 24, 1906)

Art; American Museum of Natural History). Author of half a dozen books and essays and reviews on a wide range of subjects, Holt was someone with whom, once you settled into an easy chair at your club, you would be happy to have conversation on most any topic of the day.

Of all the thoughtful, inquisitive, discursive men and women in New York City to take stock of things magical in 1914, why Henry Holt? *On the Cosmic Relations*—his very nearly thousand-page compendium of "Correlated Knowledge" and "Uncorrelated Knowledge" about Body and Soul, the Known and Unknown Universe—is now, a century after he composed it, a very compelling field report on where the prior half century of Spiritualist sports and apports (something brought into the room by a "spirit") left someone still living in the *physical* place called Manhattan. Like so many of his peers (remember that Virginia Woolf would later declare in 1924, "On or about December 1910 human nature changed"), Holt sensed a tectonic shift in "the Cosmic Relations." He put the matter quite directly on the very first page of his mammoth tome:

> There is something more than resemblances of words to make this age of wireless telegraphs, horseless carriages, and tuneless music, an age of lawless laws and creditless creeds. When new things replace old ones, new conceptions must follow; and during the transitions, men's convictions are suspended. Accordingly the comparatively recent realization that the Cosmos is governed by law, uniform, just, and merciless, has dethroned the god whom prayer influences to disturb the order of Nature. With such a god, goes most that such a god implies; and until we assimilate new conceptions of the power behind the universe, we are getting along with a short supply of faiths, and in some respects not getting along at all well. It may not be hard for instance to trace the connection of the lawless laws and creditless creeds with the tuneless music, or with any other art which has parted with inspiration. The old views of our Cosmic Relations being gone, these conditions cry out for new ones.

It was not an easy task by any means. "I cannot envy the man," Holt reflected, "who can write on these vague subjects without painfully mistrusting himself." Professing impartiality as to theory and demonstrating immense good humor in the presentation of such a queer menagerie of phenomena, Holt admitted, "Many of the facts presented are very nebulous, and the guesses are naturally more nebulous still. . . . I don't propose to go to the stake for it, or send anybody else for denying it." What, then, were the facts that necessitated so apologetic a beginning to his inquiry? The facts were a mass of reports on "psychic phenomena"—telepathy, dreams, levitation, controls, spirits, mediums, a suite of outright magic sporting highbrow scientific names: "telekinesis," "autokinesis," "psychokinesis," and "telepsychosis."

Despite these specific epithets for the mysterious phenomena introduced and broadcasted promiscuously by Spiritualism, Holt's exegesis ends up being a very generic "broad" way indeed. Obviously convinced of immortality and of a "Cosmic Soul," the latter becomes his big basket to catch the vast mass of "ideas and impressions of all sorts floating about the universe—picked up in all sorts of ways and in all sorts of combinations, and remodeled into all sorts of new combinations." "Sorts" is the telltale here; Holt can in these thousand pages says almost nothing specific to weave this paranormal jumble into a coherent epistemology, one that accepts rather than denies the reality of magical action but that can do so in a scientific and satisfyingly complex manner. Crying out for a language as rich as that which sprang up in the preceding half century around the technological productions of the age, all Holt can offer is to say that "back of all phenomena the Cosmic Soul, which is sometimes called God, which generates and includes and manifests and intercommunicates all personalities that are, or have been, or are to be, and which, with them, dies not."

Romantic, mystic, rhapsodic optimism alternates irrepressibly in *On the Cosmic Relations* with pages of argumentation, leaving—as was true of every one of the other similar summations available in that decade—a pretty unscientific rhapsody. There were great *stories*—especially for us, who now have a pretty full marquee of the city's quasi-magicians—and these were for the most part *New York stories*. When playing about in the mercurial astral realm, it is always good to have some solid ground truth—indeed, this is the very strategy of *this* book; anchor the "cosmic" and "ethereal" in the good macadam and brick and brownstone of Broadway. One smiles and feels comfortably contextualized when Holt tells how he and his wife one Sunday evening in the early 1870s went unannounced and unknown to see the Salem Seer, Charles Foster, at his boardinghouse on Washington Square, to see what sort of insights about them he might pull out of his magical hat—or inscribe in red letters across his forearm. Holt gives a believable, unsensational account of Foster's telepathic gifts, but even when woven into the fabric of the rest of the book, it tells a reader absolutely nothing at all about "the cosmic relations." In some way, it is like a preview of what will come with the earnest but often cartoonish "science" of parapsychology in the 1930s.

Holt was not alone in the scope and intention of his research. His colleague at the American Society for Psychical Research James Henry Hyslop had served at Columbia University as professor of ethics and logic from 1895 to 1902 and carried on intensive parapsychological research right up until his death in 1920. If such dedicated and honest students of these magical events missed the explanatory mark so egregiously, might anyone on this magic isle come forth with a viable science of magic?

Site #15: The Saint Mark Group of the Anthroposophical Society: Carnegie Hall, 881 Seventh Avenue, Spring 1914

On a fine spring day in April 1914, a detective from the New York City Police Department walked into a luxury suite in the Carnegie Hall Building at Seventh Avenue and Fifty-Fifth Street and arrested Miss Evangeline Adams for fortune-telling. The dozen or so fashionably dressed men and women who waited in the reception room may have included Enrico Caruso or Mary Pickford or Charlie Chaplin, for these and other New York notables were among her clients. Ever since her arrival in Manhattan in March 1899, Evangeline Adams had been a crafty self-promoter whose invented Boston Brahmin roots (she claimed, untruthfully, that she was descended from John Adams) were intended to lend respectability to her profession of astrology.

At nearly the same moment as Evangeline Adams was being arrested, a much younger science—Assyriology, the linguistic, historical, and archaeological study of ancient Mesopotamia and neighboring cultures—was bringing forth discoveries that would eventually lead to a much clearer understanding of astrology's ancient roots in the Near East. In the 1910s and '20s, The *New York Times* regularly

Carnegie Hall
(New-York Historical Society Digital Collections)

carried sensational reports of archaeological finds from Babylon, Ninevah, Nippur, and other ancient cities. Some of the vast number of cuneiform clay tablets that held the long-lost secrets of Babylonian star lore made their way to American museums—including the Metropolitan Museum and J. P. Morgan's private library on Madison Avenue. In 1910, Morgan gave Yale University $100,000 in US Steel stock to found a professorship in Assyriology. Cuneiform-pondering linguists and Indiana Jones–style tablet hunters became popular figures in novels, film, and plays. The word "decipher" showed up frequently in headlines and advertising copy, the quest to penetrate the mysteries of Babylonian culture seizing the national imagination in a way unseen since Champollion's translation of the Rosetta Stone in the 1820s. Americans' enormous interest in the Near East reflected a widespread desire for some affirmation of Old Testament truths in the face of the brash new religion of Darwinism. The clay tablets told epic stories of the gods—Ea, Marduk, Nabu, Inanna—and of a primeval flood and of the movements of the planets against the backdrop of the stars. For the fast and fleeting "flapper" generation, there was the reassurance of cosmic permanence in the simple triangular marks in the clay.

Like the knowledge of the fairy world, which has ever and always been "going away"—vanishing from human sight—while simultaneously coming into view in new forms, astrology has perennially perished in the flood of rationalism, materialism, and scientism (not to mention charlatanry) that has deluged and drowned this ancient arena of human experience. That moment in Manhattan in 1914 is one of countless paradoxical simultaneities down through the centuries, when astrology and other timeless magical sciences seemed to be suffering their death throes at the same moment as they were being born anew.

At the same time as Miss Adams's arrest, in Vienna, Austria, Rudolf Steiner was giving a series of lectures on "the inner nature of man and life between death and rebirth," which described in great detail the panoramic reality of the spiritual worlds encountered by human beings after death. Whenever he spoke of the "star-world" or "star-life," one sensed his intimacy with them; this was a very different sort of astrology than the "Sun Sign" simplification spread by Evangeline Adams. Steiner spoke of the joys and sufferings experienced in the star worlds by souls of different characters, the vision of the "ideal human being" that souls experience, the Cosmic Midnight hour, the deeper causes behind such phenomena as materialism and criminality, the process leading to rebirth in the world of the senses, and why, on Earth, we must lose our direct perception of the spiritual worlds. He also described methods through which direct perception of the worlds of soul and spirit can be developed. Joking asides and small anecdotes alternated with vast, esoteric panoramas to portray the mysterious voyage of the human soul after death, as well as the playing into one life of the deeds and decisions of the previous life, via the records inscribed in the starry world.

Upstairs from where Miss Adams practiced her horoscope readings, in the seventh-floor studio of Herbert Wilber Greene—president of the National Singing Teachers' Association and associate editor of *Étude*—the very first American students of Rudolf Steiner had been meeting since 1910 to discuss his books and lectures about the spiritual world and the methods by which one could attain clairvoyance for that world. Most of the members of this "anthroposophical"—Steiner's alternative term for his *Geisteswissenschaft* (spiritual science)—group were aspiring musicians, singers, and artists, many of them former or current students of Greene's. They took the name "Saint Mark Group" because of Mark's analytical writing style, which they thought was well suited to the American mind.

While forging a wholly modern path of spiritual initiation with anthroposophy, Rudolf Steiner consciously chose to form alliances with older, magical paths—principally Freemasonry and Theosophy. By 1907, he and his students had separated from Theosophy; in 1918, in the wake of the catastrophe of World War I, Steiner chose to end the exclusivity and secrecy of the Esoteric School—a symbolic-ritual path parallel but distinct from Memphis-Misraim Freemasonry, founded by him in 1906—refounding it as the Free High School for Spiritual Science. Anthroposophy was essentially Rosicrucianism brought into the cultural and thought forms of the twentieth century, and like its predecessor groups, it engaged in *theurgic*—aligned with divine will—rather than *personal* magic. The central aspiration of the Saint Mark Group anthroposophists was to cultivate within themselves clairvoyance for Earth's etheric realm, uniting there with Christ.

Fortean Manhattan

1920–1930

Hagstrom's Map of Lower New York:
House Number and Subway Guide, 1921
(New York Public Library)

Remembered as the decade of jazz and flappers and flivvers, the 1920s were also marked by episodes of spectral hauntings and cultural clashes that suggested that despite the best efforts of modern science—which the Mad Manhattan Epistemologist Charles Fort called "exclusionism" or "taboo"—numerous ghosts dwelled restlessly in the rationalist machine of twentieth-century Western civilization. The most noticeable ghost went by the irresistible moniker of "relativity" and was the darling of newspaper reporters and novelists, who made much more hay of its supposedly world-shattering revelations than the physicists who created it could. Darwinism's promise of putting an end to the age of miracles was at the moment seriously shaken by the ghost of neo-Lamarckism, as theories of the inheritance of acquired characteristics (attractive even to Darwin himself) proliferated. More unsettling were the ghosts that floated about outside the scientific realm. In the wake of World War I's carnage, millions of grieving men and women found comfort in the chimeras of Spiritualist séances and automatic-writing sessions. Cambridge and Columbia and Clark and dozens of other well-respected universities saw their boldest thinkers investigate mediums and magic; at just about the same moment as Fort was puzzling over rains of frogs and snakes from the sky, J. B. Rhine invented parapsychology at Duke University. The visionary architect Claude Bragdon played with magic tesseracts as a gateway to the fourth dimension. Sir Arthur Conan Doyle published photographs of supposed fairies from Cottingley and received front-page coverage.

It is rather uncanny that J. K. Rowling intuited 1926 as the year to bring Newt Scamander and his leather valise full of magical creatures to Manhattan. That year emerges for a history of magic as the signal year within a singular decade, and nowhere more dramatically than on this magic isle. In what can only be understood as a truly Fortean encounter, the most famous magician in the world, Harry Houdini, plays the role of archskeptic, while the most famous literary personality in the world, Sir Arthur Conan Doyle, takes the role of archmage, in a magical shootout on Broadway. In 1926, in the wake of scores of reports of strange lights and alien visitations, Fort wrote to the *New York Times* from London to ask why the Martians have "not landed, say in Central Park, and had a big time of it— monstrous parade down Broadway, historic turn-out, eruptions of confetti from skyscrapers?" Instead of ridicule, Fort received a deluge of further reports.

Charles Fort's gift, in an age of home economics, Taylorism, and behaviorism, was, like Barnum, to make the familiar strange. In the 1920s, this task would largely fall to the pop-culture realm of horror and science fiction, to H. P. Lovecraft and Robert E. Howard, *Weird Tales* and *Amazing Stories*. Fort never needed to make anything up; thousands of eyewitnesses the world over merely matter-of-factly spoke about what they had seen. As a pioneering phenomenologist, from the Main Reading Room inside the New York Public Library, Fort single-handedly tackled a century-plus (he drew the limit for his studies at 1800) of reportage of weird and amazing *factual* unnatural history and wrestled mightily with its implications, rather than sweeping it into the "cold case" dustbin of the inexplicable or explaining it away in the manner of the dogmatic scientists. The world is infinitely richer for his bold bricolage of the bizarre, and this magic isle owes him a lusty "Lo!" for keeping an eye on real magic while most of his neighbors were off chasing butterflies.

Site #1: Society of American Magicians Annual Banquet: Egyptian Hall, Formerly the Magical Palace, Thirty-Third Street and Broadway, June 4, 1920

Opened by the most illustrious George Heller, attended by an impressive roster of illustrious compeers that included the stage-magic impresario Francis J. Martinka and John Mulholland, who managed the advertising from his office at 4241 Broadway, the sixteenth annual Society of American Magicians (SAM) banquet at the Hotel

Houdini in handcuffs, 1918

McAlpin was, as usual, *OSTAGAZUZAHUM!* (SAM for "It will be the best ever!"). SAM secretary Oscar J. Teale reported that the English medium-exposer Dr. Henry Irving had met with him to discuss a plan to unify all the magical societies in the world into one grand brotherhood of magic. Compeer Keating inquired if he was violating the rules of the SAM in performing certain feats before the motion-picture camera; the society saw no objection. Applause greeted

Compeer Horace Goldin Merton's magic-lantern-illustrated travelogue from his trip through Egypt, along the Nile and on to Australia, Java, Colombo, and Madras, India, where he was the recipient of a silver wand from the native magicians. Goldin was amused to report that even in far-away India, the Hindu magician was well equipped with Martinka's magical apparatus.

A couple of weeks after the banquet, the society held its first "Ladies Night" at the new Egyptian Hall, and the ladies were treated by Compeer Fitch to new wrinkles on the egg-into-a-bottle trick and an up-to-the-minute adaptation of Robert Houdin's most famous card trick from seventy-five years before. Compeer Gus Vincent, known as the "Boy Magician," presented a number of clever illusions, including one that saw him produce out of thin air a great jar full of candy, which was greedily received by the attending ladies.

Though the SAM president and *Magic, Unity, Might* (SAM's monthly magazine) editor Harry Houdini was present at neither of the events, his influence could be felt this year and every year in the 1920s, up and down Broadway and across the world. The scholarly quest that had driven Houdini to build the world's largest library of books about magic yielded much fruit in *Magic, Unity, Might*: many of the issues featured in-depth historical articles by the world's most famous stage magician. In 1920, Houdini began in earnest his quest to debunk all spirit mediums; in 1921, in New York, after his two-picture stint in Hollywood, he founded his own film production company. His literary output (undoubtedly mostly ghostwritten by others) ranged from stage-magic primers—*Magical Rope Ties and Escapes* (1920), *Houdini's Paper Magic* (1921), a "How I Do My Spirit Tricks" article for *Popular Science* (December 1925), and an article on conjuring for the *Encyclopædia Britannica*'s thirteenth edition in 1926—to exposés such as *Miracle Mongers and Their Methods* (1920) and *A Magician among the Spirits* (1924) to "Imprisoned with the Pharaohs," a 1924 short story ghostwritten by H. P. Lovecraft.

Houdini's grudge match against Spiritualism has been thoroughly documented and recounted by many historians, but all of these accounts take for granted that Houdini was the hero, not the villain—or dupe—in this most glorious episode of skeptical debunking of charlatans and frauds. His disenchantment stands as cipher for the radical skepticism of the Roaring Twenties, whose headlong rush into radio, talkies, and other seemingly magical technologies was a grand sleight-of-hand to distract the decade's denizens from the very obvious but unacknowledged fact that reality kept bending in unexpected and uncanny ways. While Houdini's fans thrilled to witness him escape from padlocks and chains, sealed glass tanks, straitjackets, milk cans, buried boxes, Murderers' Row, and the belly of a whale, few realized that the straitjacketed Houdini and other "fraud busters" were destroying the aptitude of their audience to marvel at and master the world's actual magic.

Site #2: Man in Faded Gray Raincoat and Floppy Hat Mobbed by Twenty Thousand Admirers: Broadway across from City Hall, April 3, 1921

The man standing in the back of the big Model T spoke no English; his hair resembled a pigeon's nest; his cravat and collar were always just a bit crooked. Still, the 1919 Nobel Prize winner was a global star, girls in Geneva mobbing him (one tried to cut off a lock of his hair), town fathers naming telescopes and towers after him, and photographers scrambling to catch his image. At Pier 42 on the Hudson, as he stepped off the steamship *Rotterdam* on April 3, 1921, the paparazzi caught Albert Einstein clutching like a life preserver the violin he would play to help calm down his racing thoughts. The next day, pulling up to City Hall to be given the key to the city by the mayor (after the attempt by an anti-German alderman to bar Einstein's visit), twenty thousand fans lined Broadway to welcome the tousled-haired phenom.

The German physicist had spent fifteen years at work on a theory about which laypersons understood nothing save the fact that it was important. That essence is what also drove the reporters and

Einstein at City Hall, 1921

photographers. The *New York Times* had sent a correspondent to Einstein's home in Berlin, giving the physicist his first opportunity to speak as plainly as possible to the public. The *Times* article on December 3, 1919, closed with the sounding of a clock's chime and the interviewer's wryly ironic (and slightly mocking) observation that "old-fashioned time and space enforced their wonted absolute tyranny over him who had spoken so contemptuously of their existence." Over the next decade, it was largely the *Times* that fashioned Einstein's public image and drove him to stardom. By decade's end, Einstein had become as regular a feature of the newspaper as Babe Ruth, Harry Houdini, and Charlie Chaplin (Chaplin posed with Einstein at the 1931 premiere of Chaplin's *City Lights*). A February 1929 full-page feature in the *Times* headlines, "Einstein Explains His New Discoveries: In a Simplified Discussion of 'Field Theories

Old & New' the Eminent Scientist Shows the Meaning of His Latest Contributions for Gravitation, Electro-Magnetism, and Our Ideas of Time and Space."

As the personification of modernity's wrestling match with existence's intersecting absolutes—time and space—Albert Einstein was bound to be seen through a magical lens, a "wizard" who was the twentieth century's first scientific celebrity. Reportage consistently underscored relativity theory's supposed incomprehensibility. A January 1921 *Times* front-page article discussed the implications of Einstein's theory for the possible measurability of a finite universe; subsequent issues then ran a front-page statement from Einstein, accompanied by an explanation from a Princeton physicist. "Even Einstein's Little Universe Is Big Enough: Prof. Einstein Elucidates (for Those Who Can Understand His Theory That Our Cosmos Has Its Limits)," the *Times* declared in February 1921, on the eve of Einstein's visit. After Einstein's visit with President Warren Harding, the *Times'* front page reported that the theory had puzzled the president.

By the 1920s, magic was a matter not of the hands but strictly of the *head*. Einstein's large head—magnified by his mop of hair—was the perfect icon for the modern view that whatever mysteries remained in the universe, the human brain would solve them.

Site #3: Directing Human Evolution at the American Museum of Natural History, Central Park West and Seventy-Ninth Street, September 25–28, 1921

In honor of, and to welcome and educate, the almost four hundred scientists from all over the world who had come to New York to attend the Second International Congress of Eugenics, the American Museum of Natural History president Henry Fairfield Osborn had overseen the remaking of the first-floor Forestry Hall into the greatest visual display on eugenics the world had ever seen. Entering the hall, straight ahead was a statue of the "composite athlete"—modeled on the fifty strongest men of Harvard. Progressing up the

"Eugenics Is the Self-Direction of Human Evolution"
(*Report of the Second International Congress of Eugenics*, 1923)

right side of the hall, there were exhibits on genetics, breeding of domestic animals, human heredity (with a wide selection of pedigree charts), the family (with an emphasis on mate selection and differential fecundity), aristogenic families (featuring the talented pedigree of Charles Darwin), and cacogenic families (showing a wide range of degenerate pedigrees). Just outside the Eugenics Hall, in the Darwin Hall, Osborn had directed a pair of exhibits contrasting natural and artificial selection. Returning down the left side, the first booth displayed photos of state institutions for the socially inadequate; then followed booths exhibiting the races of man, human migration and immigration, anthropometry (this display drew liberally from the museum's own unparalleled collection of human skulls), mental testing and psychiatry, population and vital statistics, eugenic hygiene, and finally, the geographic aspect of human evolution, centered on a massive poster depicting a cross-section of a giant sequoia whose rings showed the relation between climate change and human migrations.

President Osborn, in his opening address, emphasized that there had never been a moment in world history when "an international conference on race character and betterment has been more important than the present." All present agreed with him, in light of World War I's recent carnage. Not only had Europe lost in part "the heritage of civilization," but the "worst elements of society had gained ascendancy" in some places in Europe. To improve the race, eugenics should encourage aristogenic men and women to put aside their innate individualism and egoism, which tended to result in small family size. The trend toward one- or even zero-child families must be reversed. Just as critical was the initiative—amply illustrated in the hall by sections on eugenic sterilization, marriage restriction, and a review of state legislation on eugenics—to slow the explosive reproduction of the unfit, who were handily characterized by eugenics as the "3 Ds"—the delinquent, defective, and degenerate. Though the distinctly aristocratic Osborn would never have consciously conceived of his Eugenics Hall and Congress as a grand exercise in magic, it was indeed perhaps his age's highest and most Promethean magical aspiration: to biologically refashion the human being, along eugenic—that is, *true*, or *good*, breeding—lines.

The congress benefited immensely from the recent renovation and reopening of Osborn's pride and joy, the Hall of the Age of Man, which definitely echoed the rhetoric of hard-line eugenics voiced in the Eugenics Hall. Its exhibits, most powerfully in Charles Knight's murals of Paleolithic men, conveyed Osborn's conviction that natural humans of old had been racially pure, unlike the unnatural practices of contemporary metropolitan humans, whose mixing was on the verge of causing "race suicide." In Osborn's hands, the museum had become a grand tableau of aristogenic wonders—from the gigantic hornless rhinoceros *Baluchitherium* brought back from the Gobi Desert by Roy Chapman Andrews to his own pioneering work

Charles R. Knight painting of Cro-Magnon cave artists, 1920
(American Museum of Natural History Digital Special Collections)

on the evolution and phylogeny of the Proboscidea—that distinguished order encompassing the one living family of Elephantidae. He had just published a preliminary notice describing the new genus *Miomastodon* and recognizing in *Trilophodon edensis* of California a relative of the South American Andean mastodon. These animals' enormous size, their long muscular trunks, and their priceless ivory tusks made them the ideal taxon for a naturalist obsessed with pedigrees of perfection.

Osborn's collaboration with the museum artist Charles Knight this year had yielded the most gratifying results; of the three new mural panels in the Hall of the Age of Man, one particularly—of Cro-Magnon artists painting on the wall of the Font-de-Gaume cave at Les Eyzies-de-Tayac—had caught the public's attention. Frequently reproduced in newspaper articles and books, it had been Osborn's hope all along that Knight's sensitive portrait (the central character, a tall, graceful, long-limbed young man bore Knight's own countenance) would replace the common, vulgar "Cave Man" popular image with a properly aristocratic one. With the help of the French anthropologist and Paleolithic art expert Henri Breuil,

Osborn and Knight fashioned what they believed to be both a faithful state-of-the-art scientific portrait of a vanished moment in time and a highly artful, almost magical work of art. The mural's play of shadow and light, the intensity of the cave artists' gazes, and the delicate gestures of the hands at work all evoked magical power. The wooly mammoths—Osborn's chosen beasts—being sketched on the cave wall magnified that power.

In *Men of the Old Stone Age: Their Environment, Life, and Art* (1916), Osborn had conveyed his own and his peers' picture of the magical attitudes of these Cro-Magnon men:

> The wonders of nature in their various manifestations begin to arouse in the primitive mind a desire for an explanation of these phenomena, and in which it is attempted to seek such cause in some vague supernatural power underlying these otherwise unaccountable occurrences, a cause to which the primitive human spirit commences to make its appeal. . . . This wonder-working force may either be personal, like the gods of Homer, or impersonal, like the *Mana* of the Melanesian, or the *Manitou* of the North American Indian. It may impress an individual when he is in a proper frame of mind, and through magic or propitiation may be brought into relation with his individual ends. Magic and religion jointly belong to the supernatural as opposed to the every-day world of the savage.

Unbeknownst to Osborn and Knight, the cave painters were actually *enacting* magic—image-based hunting magic—as they laid the pigment on the damp cave wall. Osborn was less interested in the vast gulf in consciousness style that lay between the Paleolithic and his own Jazz Age than in teaching the throngs of museumgoers that all great human talents were precious resources that must, like aristocratic "blood," be conserved and purified. Untethered from any ethical and spiritual tenets, this was a potentially catastrophic black magic, one that the world would soon see escape from the museum's tidy exhibit booths and into the world with unbridled vengeance.

Site #4: Dirigible and Other Dreams: Hugo Gernsback's "Scientifiction," 53 Park Row, February 1922

The prominence in the *New York Times* in the early '20s of headlines trumpeting Spiritualist speculation about surviving death juxtaposed with almost daily reports on the triumphs and tragedies of dirigibles, zeppelins, and other airships suggests another moniker for the Roaring Twenties: the *Flying* Twenties, or perhaps the Lift-Off Age. There was in New York City and around the globe a pronounced proclivity for transcendence, which acutely expressed the continued dilemma for magic in the midst of modernity—with such an accelerated pace of development of technological substitutes for magical powers, why labor to cultivate such powers as capacities of *soul*?

The publisher, inventor, tinkerer, and bon vivant man-about-town Hugo Gernsback's biography neatly captures the transition from "Electric" and "Magnetic" Manhattan to "Radio" and "Rocket" Manhattan. In 1905, at age twenty-one, his first publication was a *Scientific American* description of his invention of a new interrupter for an induction coil. Published under the pen name "Huck," the Luxembourg-born Gernsback had chosen the Mark Twain character as a kind of shortcut for becoming an American native. Gernsback certainly was a "huck"—the nickname carrying the sense of footloose freedom, inventiveness, and perhaps even a whiff of snake-oil salesman.

Over the first two decades of the twentieth century, the dynamic Gernsback moved his various ventures—both manufacturing and selling electrical and radio devices and parts and his multiple publishing ventures (*Electrical Experimenter, Modern Electrics, Radio Amateur News*) back and forth across lower Manhattan—West Broadway, then Fulton Street, then to a series of locations on Park Row. He dined at Delmonico's and went to Victor Herbert musicals and loved to lunch with his chief designer, Frank Paul, and other artists in the basement Automat across from City Hall. More than the

"War of the Future"
(*Science and Invention*, 1922)

New York Times or *Scientific American*, Gernsback's magazines—
*Science and Invention, Wonder Stories, Science Wonder Stories,
Amazing Stories*—catch the metamorphically inventive spirit of the
1920s in Manhattan. "Prophetic Fashion is the Mother of Scientific
Fact" was the motto on *Science and Invention*'s masthead, and it
perfectly voiced Gernsback's conviction that perky, punchy, sharply
delineated stories, illustrated by diagrammatic images, could inspire
any new invention under the sun.

The February 1922 issue's cover illustration of a streamlined space-suited man flying over the ocean powered by his green-ray-projecting jetpack is standard *Science and Invention* fare and but a taste of the futurist visions inside the magazine. From an interview with Nikola Tesla, Frank Paul had rendered Tesla's speculative visions of the future; in an essay titled "10,000 Years Hence," Gernsback exceeded even Tesla's dreams. The artist Howard Brown drew Gernsback's floating hygienic cities kept afloat by solar-powered

Cover of *Science and Invention*, February 1922
(Hathi Trust Digital Library)

rays. The rays shooting from the cover astronaut's jetpack were imagined by Gernsback to be derived from atmospheric static electricity.

Surrounded on lower Broadway by all the innovations of science and technology, Gernsback kept prophetic pace with them. In December 1922, after asking his artists to make images showing the magazine's nine different departments, Gernsback created the first science-fiction magazine cover in history. Eight months later, with the "Science Fiction" number (previously, he had called the genre he was creating "scientifiction") of *Science and Invention* (whose cover bore another "spaceman," this one upside down), Gernsback launched the American science-fiction industry. This virtual space, this "virtual reality," would go forth to cannibalize the American soul, substituting titillating space opera for the rightful indigenous impulse to shepherd a truly spiritual cosmogony, in order to reconnect heaven and Earth.

MANHATTAN AS SITE OF MAGICAL DESTRUCTION

As Gernsback's magazines slipped from science to science fiction, a decidedly apocalyptic tone emerged. In the November 1929 issue of *Science Wonder Stories*, which included articles such as "The Phantom Teleview," "The Stellar Missile," "The Space Dwellers," and "The Green Intelligence," Gernsback launched a short-story contest by offering $300 for the best story written to match Frank R. Paul's cover illustration—of a flying saucer lassoing the Woolworth Building into outer space. Inside, Gernsback coyly taunted his readers, "How the machine did this is not known, whether by gravity nullification or by some unknown rays. When consulted about the cover, and asked what *he* thought the picture describes, Mr. Gernsback assured us that he did not have the remotest idea what it is all about." With that mock profession of ignorance, the dapper publisher launched a trope that would swallow, swamp, vaporize, and

Cover of *Science Wonder Stories*

terrorize fictional Manhattan countless times in the coming century. (Paul's cover illustration is perhaps the first depiction of a "flying saucer.") H. G. Wells may have been the first writer to imagine Martians invading a world city, but New York would leave London far behind for the title of being the most cosmically beleaguered metropolis on Earth.

Some hint at Gernsback's character can be seen in a short story in that issue that he did write. In "The Killing Flash," the narrator uses a telephone to kill a nemesis by long distance. Whether by the latest real technological innovation on Earth or the fictional technologies from other planets, Gernsback's and his many authors' "wonder stories" relied on a sort of magic—unseen, threatening power—to accomplish their ends.

Not all the '20s tales of New York's terrors were strictly technological; with the launch in 1923 of *Weird Tales*—a confluence of supernatural tales, fantasy adventure, and cosmic horror— Manhattan would come to play a premier role as the site of *any* sort of supernatural terror. Seabury Quinn, the magazine's most prolific contributor (he wrote 145 stories and 14 articles for *Weird Tales*), lectured on mortuary jurisprudence at the Renouard Training School for Embalmers, at 381 Fourth Avenue, and edited a trade journal called *Casket and Sunnyside*. The casket side, not the sunny side, was the psychic terrain of his tales; his principal protagonist, Jules de Grandin, a kind of French Sherlock Holmes, was an occult detective whose intimate knowledge of the "Servants of Satan"— black magicians—enabled him to solve crimes.

In light of the nearly complete takeover in our own time by American pop occulture of film, television, and video games, one might say that the metastasis of magic in Manhattan—in the form of this creation of science fiction as a literary genre and as a culture industry—has had profound, and devastating, spiritual consequences. The alchemical, sacrificial, spiritual transformation stewarded and shared by St. Germain and the Rosicrucian Freemasons, Mesmer, Ethan Allen Hitchcock, Blavatsky, and Steiner with every decade became progressively more elusive, while literal dreams of superhuman power increasingly held sway.

Site #5: The Super Sargasso Sea as Source of
Magical Appearances: New York Public Library,
Fifth Avenue and Forty-Second Street, 1923

While the burgeoning industry of supernatural and science-fiction
tales went about *inventing* tales of cosmic terror, a longtime Manhattan resident was *discovering* a nightmare, not, in his friend Booth
Tarkington's words, "on the planetary, but on the constellational
scale." Though the twentieth century's most indefatigable chroni-
cler of all prodigies and wonders, Charles Fort, had for four years
been living in London when his *New Lands* (1923) was published in
New York, he had conducted all of his research over the previous
decade at the New York Public Library. Scrutinizing archival copies of nineteenth- and early twentieth-century newspapers, Fort
scribbled onto thousands of one-and-a-half-by-two-and-a-half-
inch scraps of paper detailed transcriptions of "wonders"—baffling
appearances, disappearances, and metamorphoses reported by
people from all over the globe. Like his previous work *The Book
of the Damned* (1919), *New Lands* was a brilliantly witty critique
of contemporary natural science that doubled as an invitation to
muse on the possibilities of other worlds. It was, in a word, a carnivalesque work of *enchantment*, dropping out of the sky onto a very
disenchanted landscape.

Charles Fort was in 1923 the world's premier diagnostician of
planet Earth's infinite strangeness, gazing relentlessly into that
enigma-producing "Super Sargasso Sea" that he imagined hovering
close at hand, magically, preternaturally fostering and then fledging
from the empty sky all manner of living things. He was interested
in the extrazoological fall from the sky of both vertebrates (fish,
frogs, tadpoles, snakes) and invertebrates (periwinkles, worms, ants,
aphids, bees, beetles, fireflies, hummingbird hawkmoths, ladybirds).
Fort had catalogued and questioned them all, both the reports of
their sudden and unprecedented appearances in particular places
and their notable instances of scarcity. Fort's use of "damned" to

Charles Hoy Fort (1874–1932)

describe the anomalous natural phenomena toward which science turned a blind eye showed considerable epistemological sophistication, for despite his mischievous sense of play, his books were a serious—and still completely unanswered—challenge to the scientific establishment. In a sense, Fort's work anticipated by half a century the philosophical iconoclasm of the philosopher and sociologist of science Thomas Kuhn. While Kuhn and his successors employed dense academic jargon in their critique, Fort goes right for the jugular, and unlike Kuhn, he is unafraid to let his curiosity and skepticism take him absolutely anywhere, including into the Plutonic realm of the truly "damned," in more than just a modern philosophical sense.

In *New Lands*, Fort began with a simple and seductive philosophical premise: "I take for a principle that all being is the infinitely serial, and that whatever has been will, with differences of particulars, be again," and then, like some mad Banshee, he set off to illustrate that just about every once-in-a-lifetime miracle is altogether commonplace and happens with as much regularity as mushrooms coming up after autumnal rains. If the world had kept an eye on Fort's crazy chronicle, it might never have suffered disenchantment at all. Dogmas, not "spirits," were the true phantoms, "clutching at vacancies," coiled around his overwhelming data, all footnoted neatly. Science was really a "serpent of pseudo-thought" that was stifling history itself.

Promiscuously mixed in with Fort's documentation of falling and floating fleshy creatures are eyewitness reports of strange aerial craft. From the book's very first page, airships—spectral ones banished by dogma—haunt *New Lands*. Indeed, the book essentially owes its origin to the fact that from 1874, the year that Fort was born, the Earth's skies had seen a procession of odd vehicles. A half century of civic authority's rejection of the reality of these aerial invaders, combined with astronomy's inability to account for the behavior of certain meteors, planets, and other celestial bodies, had gotten Fort's considerable dander up, and from Neptune right down to the top of the Woolworth Building, he took stock of that Super Sargasso Sea. The great names of astronomy all came in for his lampooning; generation after generation of common folk who faithfully reported what they saw and heard emerge as the heroes of *New Lands*.

As Fort built up his data, so many instances of other, nonplanetary, and noncometary stuff filled the sky that he had to put them in their own book: part 2 of *New Lands*. Skyquakes, mirages, fireballs, ghost lights, stones, luminous disks, auroral glows, then blood, flesh, frogs. Midway through part 2, he circles back to those "damned" (banished from honest consideration) airships, itemizing a cosmopolitan list from the 1880s of inexplicable craft—many inhabited—floating over towns and villages around the world.

In the 1890s, the airships keep coming, until 1897, when, reported on equally in New York and London, they practically filled the sky. In 1913, they keep coming—"serially"—again: 1914, 1915, 1916, 1917, 1918, 1919, 1920, 1921. From the world's leading newspapers, Fort quotes and quotes, but to no avail. The ships keep coming, as fast as the wan explanations from the Fourth Estate. As always, Charles Fort gets the last word, imagining some anonymous everyman processing up Broadway with an impossible—but altogether possible, given the copious documentation that Fort has assembled—entourage.

> There will be a procession. Somebody will throw little black pebbles to the crowds. Over his procession will fly blue-fringed cupids. Later he will be insulted and abused and finally hounded to his death. But, in that procession, he will lead by the nose an outrageous thing that should not be: about ten feet long, short-winged, waddling on webbed feet. Insult and abuse and death—he will snap his fingers under the nose of the outrageous thing. It will be worth a great deal to lead that by the nose and demonstrate that such things had been seen in the sky, though they had been supposed to be angels. It will be a great moment for somebody. He will come back to New York, and march up Broadway with his angel.

There has indeed been a procession, a continual, perennial, universal procession. Not one corner of the planet has escaped it, though most every corner has ignored, mocked, and "damned" it. Parading as "spirits of the dead," the elemental beings were poked, prodded, "tested," in reply to their incessant rappings and knockings. All that attention proved to their liking, as they poured out inane and erroneous and ersatz gospels to an age hungry for the invisible. Nonphysical beings, of the very sort that had universally in earlier ages been the principal agents of magical action and who had birthed the Spiritualist movement, carried on a worldwide campaign of mischief that irked both their immediate targets—the innocent individuals who witnessed the phenomena—and the scientific experts to whom the public turned for explanations. Honest inquiring phenomenologists like Fort were few and far between.

Beginning in exactly the same year as observation balloons began to hover over Earth, the elementals appeared in a new guise, one that mimicked each and every apparatus sent skyward. Balloon, dirigible, zeppelin, airship, airplane, jet, rocket ship—and spacemen and aliens to boot—a vast planetary masquerade in which the little gossamer leprechauns got the upper hand, thanks to the blinders of materialism. They need not go bump in the night anymore, so fully have we populated our noosphere with cinematic and cartoon digital humbugs, gremlins, goonies, pokémon, and all their legion cousins. The "magic" of these lowly invisible infraterrestrial beings is that, as long as we humans give them our attention, they can cross the threshold to become visible, audible, sensible. We have by our fictional creations multiplied their number incalculably and, by continuing to deny their actual existence, give them extraordinary power over us. Taken together, Fort's four books (*Lo!* in 1931 and *Wild Talents* in 1932 extended Fort's inquiry) are the modern, "disenchanted" world's only accurate field report on the doings of the elemental beings of nature. Charles Fort is our modern Goethe, updating the Faust tale's warnings about the dangers of arbitrary magic.

Poltergeist-producing girls had long been a preoccupation of Fort's, and thanks to a pair of such girls, Manhattan puts in an appearance in *Lo!* On the last day of 1842, two French girls had been out picking up leaves near Clavaux when they saw stones falling around them with "uncanny slowness." Returning with their parents, the two girls were suddenly seized and dragged "as if into a vortex." Fortunately, the parents pulled them back. Struck by the odd calculus of this New Year's Eve occurrence of the "taking" of girls for the "giving" of stones, Fort dubbed the phenomenon a "reciprocating current." No such reciprocation had the world known when the Manhattan socialite Dorothy Arnold disappeared while walking through Central Park on December 12 in 1910—until Fort noticed the *New York Sun* report on December 13 that a swan had appeared on the lake near the Seventy-Ninth Street entrance, Miss Arnold's destination. Duly noted, this "now you see it!" prestidigitation took its place as the final word—for the moment—on twentieth-century teleportations of butterflies and girls.

Without ever naming it so, Fort was retrospectively inventorying "signs of the times," at a moment—the turn of the twentieth century—when sightings of "ball lightning" and other luminous phenomena were increasingly giving way to reports of airships bearing bright searchlights, capable of unheard-of speeds, and sometimes even operated by small men speaking in strange tongues. Though Fort died a decade before the first "little green men" and "flying saucers," he was thoroughly acquainted with them; his data give UFOs a history, and it is altogether a *magical* one, where one can discern that all of this weird stuff comes not from "up there" but from down below—the Fire Earth known to alchemists and other magicians. Ultimately as products of the etheric and astral realms, they are directionless, precipitated from out of the cosmic, invisible, but eternally present periphery. And many of them—especially those with the sulphurous smell, the injurious effect, the catastrophic consequence—are quintessentially Mephistophelean murmurings.

Site #6: Manly Palmer Hall, New York Public Library, Fifth Avenue and Forty-Second Street, ca. 1924

Charles Fort's principal years in the Main Reading Room of the New York Public Library scrupulously poring over major metropolitan newspapers, prestigious scientific journals, and obscure meteorological missives were 1914 to 1924, when he moved to London; in 1921, another student of arcane mysteries took up a chair in that wonderful room. Manly Palmer Hall was a Canadian-born author and lecturer on mysticism and occultism who, before founding the Philosophical Research Society in Los Angeles in 1934, spent the

"The Invocation of Mephistopheles," from
Manly Palmer Hall's *The Secret Teachings of All Ages*, 1929

early '20s in New York City. Hall worked at a bank but labored away from 1921 to 1924 at the New York Public Library, researching for a book he hoped to sell via private subscription. By the time he left New York in 1924, *The Secret Teachings of All Ages* (1929) had taken shape in his mind.

If only these two men could have met, perhaps Manhattan's and America's spell of materialism might have been broken. Hall's historical glance went far back to the Greek and Roman and Egyptian mysteries. His book was a vast compendium, superbly organized, beautifully written, and lavishly illustrated. From cover to cover, Hall's magnum opus touches on elementals or nature spirits, the ones evoked by Lenape shamans, conjured by Joseph Smith, summoned originally in Freemasonic lodge rituals, poking and pranking the credulous Spiritualists, and of whose chaotic mischievous behaviors Charles Fort gave the world a report.

Site #7: Bruce Barton's "Brother Rotarian" Jesus, 117 East Fifty-Fifth Street, 1925

Every civilization, whether wittingly or not, creates and cultivates its own idiosyncratic forms of white and black magic. Empires are especially adept at the latter, though their practitioners will deny it. Few recognize them while they practice, for their techniques have become so deeply subsumed by the imperial civilization. When the Aztec priests raised high the blood-soaked organs of their victims before pushing their eviscerated bodies down the Temple of the Sun stairs, one hundred thousand citizens of Tenochtitlan watched and cheered. In the twentieth century, just bring to mind the Nuremberg rallies. Black masses are not always held in the dark.

Our empire, ostensibly run from another American city, has not just deep cultural, political, and social roots in Manhattan but *magical* roots. By 1930, "Madison Avenue" was shorthand for the advertising industry, whose magic, if not entirely black, was at least *gray*. The exertion of one party's will over the will of another lies at the heart of advertising; it is also one definition of black magic. In the 1920s, modern advertising refined and extended its practices, to become the hydra-headed monster it remains today.

Illusion, suggestion, and manipulation—these constitute the core of "Madison Avenue," whose leading firm was for half a century BBDO, which began in 1919 as Barton, Durstine & Osborn. Bruce Barton was the son of a Congregationalist minister, and, as his biographer Richard M. Fried puts it, "the world of the spiritual and the material were never far apart in Barton's professional life." Like

Bruce Barton (1896–1967)
(Library of Congress)

magicians of old, Barton was a master with words; he penned glib
editorials for a dozen different outlets, on an almost daily basis.
During World War I, Barton managed publicity for the United War
Work campaign, which coordinated charitable organizations aiding
US troops. He then went on to market products for Macy's, General
Motors, and US Steel, but his most famous marketing effort came
in 1925 with *The Man Who Nobody Knows: A Discovery of the Real
Jesus*. Barton's Jesus would have been a candidate for Henry Fairfield
Osborn's Eugenic Hall—a virile athlete, rational businessman, and
all-round good fellow who "picked up 12 men from the bottom ranks
of business and forged them into an organization that conquered the
world." Barton's Jesus was, like himself, an adman whose parables
were "the most powerful advertisements of all time."

Just like Knight and Osborn's cavemen, Barton's Jesus was a rugged outdoorsman: "Jesus pushed a plane and swung an adze; he was a successful carpenter. He slept out doors and spent his days walking around his favorite lake. His muscles were so strong that when they drove the money-changers out, nobody tried to oppose him!"

Easily parodied now, Barton was not without critics in his own day. The *New Republic* ridiculed Barton for portraying Jesus as a "Brother Rotarian." But the book's phenomenal sales reflected Barton's successful creation of an everyman Jesus—one that readers could know and love. Barton in a way finished the task begun by Thomas Jefferson with his *The Jefferson Bible; or, The Life and Morals of Jesus of Nazareth* in 1803—Jesus without the miracles.

Of course, there is a good reason that Jesus is the Man Whom Nobody Knows. Age to age, there have been a small number of initiates who have some understanding of the profound mysteries making up Christ's life and work, but as a God become man, the complete story of the life of Jesus of Nazareth will confound many generations to come. Those who came the closest to penetrating the mysteries were in past ages initiates of Christian mystery centers, but since 1933, there are many people who have spontaneously experienced mystical communion with Christ and reported their experiences. Although Manly P. Hall was not one of these, his grasp of the Christian mysteries—the Crucifixion, the Resurrection, and Apocalypse most centrally—is superb and rests on a *magical* foundation. Drawing on Rudolf Steiner, the most intimate companion of Christ, Hall in his *Secret Teachings* was at least partially preserving esoteric knowledge about Christ, at the very same moment, on the very same magic isle, that Bruce Barton was obscuring him.

Site #8: H. P. Lovecraft's Night-Gaunts, 93 Perry Street, August 10–11, 1925

No more haunted soul ever walked Broadway than Howard Phillips Lovecraft. With his "Kalem Club" literary gang or alone, from

H. P. Lovecraft (1890–1937)

his arrival in New York in 1922 until his departure for Providence in April 1926, Lovecraft used Broadway and its parallel north-south avenues as a time machine, throwing himself into all-night tramps to find pockets of antiquarian preservation that might give him a comforting presence of the tidy "colonial" past amid the horrifying pandemonium of present-day New York.

On the night of August 10, 1925, Lovecraft went on a solitary all-night expedition that led to "a little black court at the end of Perry Street" in Greenwich Village. That quotation comes from his short story "He," published in September 1926 in *Weird Tales*. Lovecraft had originally ferreted out that hidden court on August 29, 1924, when, inspired by an article he had seen in the *Evening Post* that day, he had gone in search of it. Its evocative power was strong enough to inexorably draw Lovecraft back a year later; his August 1925 walkabout concluded around seven a.m. on the eleventh, when he boarded a ferry for Elizabeth, New Jersey, where, for ten cents he purchased a composition book, parked himself in Scott Park, and wrote a weird tale about time travel in which a spectral stranger pulls back a magical curtain to reveal not just historical scenes of colonial-era Greenwich Village but a primordial terror endemic to the Mannahatta soil. In "He," Lovecraft pulls back the curtain on his own haunted self.

I need not describe what "He" reveals behind that curtain, for you surely know this monster from any one of a dozen places where it appears: Ridley Scott's *Alien* (1979), John Carpenter's *The Thing* (1980), Sam Raimi's *Evil Dead* series, H. R. Giger's *Necronomicon* paintings, tabletop to smartphone role-playing games, the graphic novels of Neil Gaiman and Mike Mignola, or the horror tales of Clive Barker, Stephen King, and their imitators. Perhaps the "black thing, . . . only a head with eyes, impotently trying to wriggle across the sinking floor . . . and occasionally emitting feeble little spits of immortal malice," has even shown up in your dreams, as it did so often in Lovecraft's. Call that black thing *Azathoth, Cthulhu, Ghatanothoa, Hypnos, Nodens, Nyarlathotep, Shub-Niggurath, Tsathoggua, Yig,* or *Zoog,* it is the perennially appearing "Old Great One" that slithers beneath all human history, ready to swallow up the insignificant creatures—humanity—who dwell unsuspectingly in the sunlit world above it.

Cthulhu was not born out of Lovecraft's sour encounter with New York City—for Lovecraft knew this black thing almost as long as he could remember, back to his Providence cradle—but the phantasmagoric city with its seething hordes of dark-skinned immigrants speaking unintelligible tongues gave the beast new life, new purpose, both historico-literary and autopsychological. Chtulhu and all his brethren monsters were night-gaunts for sure, whose *haunting* of

Lovecraft seemed to intensify in 1898, when he was eight years old. His father, having spent the last five years of his life in an insane asylum, may have bequeathed the thing to him. Who can say whether the monster that hounded his mother to death (in 1921) was the same or merely a related species.

Thanks originally to the admiring fantasies of Kenneth Grant and his *Magickal Revival* (1972), generations of Lovecraft fans and scholars have assumed that he was a mage, but the only magic operative in his tales is wan, third-hand sensationalism. There is an ongoing occult scavenger hunt for Lovecraft's magical sources that uncannily echoes another line from "He": "I had heard of them by vague rumor, and realized that they could not be on any map of today." Most recently, Christopher Knowles, the author of *Our Gods Wear Spandex: The Secret History of Comic Book Heroes* (2007), insists that Alice Bailey's channeled texts are the source for Lovecraft's dark mythos. Lovecraft's biographer S. T. Joshi and a host of Lovecraftians—Jason Colavito, Peter Levenda, W. Scott Poole—may disagree, but to a person, they all share Knowles's materialist take on the pioneer of weird fiction, that he made this stuff up. The scholars have endlessly psychologized Lovecraft's monsters and his monstrous psyche both, all the while oblivious to the Chtulhu that was hiding in plain sight.

Lovecraft knows far too much about these beasts not to have had an intimate, lifelong relationship with them. In "Beyond the Wall of Sleep" (1919)—which goes far in fiction to portray Lovecraft's own somnambulic condition—telepathy is taken for granted, as a mode of communication both between humans and between the netherworld and human beings. In "The Shadow Out of Time" (1936), Nathaniel Wingate Peaslee, a man haunted by the past, develops a strange amnesia that causes him for a time to lose his personality to an alien invader. Lovecraft has the narrator give away his own biographical situation: "I would have it known that there is nothing whatever of the mad or sinister in my heredity and early life. This is a highly important fact in view of the shadow which fell so suddenly upon me from *outside* sources."

At a very early age, Lovecraft experienced night terrors, intensely vivid nightmares that saw giant winged, faceless, bat-like creatures grab him by the stomach, lift him high above the Earth, and then drop him. These nightmares were so terrible that he often avoided sleep as a child. As a teenager, he suffered such strong convulsions that he had to quit school. All his life he had spectacularly realistic dreams, which he could recall in great detail and which invariably were colored with a cosmic unboundedness. "I have been a rider of comets, and a brother to the nebulae," the haunted cosmonaut—whose penchant for astronomy in boyhood led him to plan on becoming an astronomer—once confided in a letter. Dreams as an avenue of invasion and possession are a constant theme in Lovecraft's fiction, as surely as they were in his life. Lovecraft's "magical" abilities to transcend time ("Sometimes it seems that time is running backward, or moving very quickly or slowly") and space ("an individual independence of these laws on my part, whereby I can sail through the varied universes of space-time as an invisible vapour might") suggest not, as so many *Necronomicon* mythographers have assumed, that Lovecraft is a magical "adept" but that he is deeply *mediumistic*, given to hypnotic states that opened him up to elemental invasion.

As an adult, Lovecraft still wrestled with possessing entities, even if—unlike their behavior with both his mother and father, who were driven insane by them—they only took control of him at night. In his 1924 short story "The Shunned House"—like "He," another work of "proto-science fiction"—Lovecraft's New England genealogical/historical obsession, his sensitivity to haunted places, and his personal battle against possession come together in such a way that one can see Lovecraft himself as a microcosm of early twentieth-century America's schizophrenic split between spirit-denying science and the persistence of the supernatural:

Such a thing was surely not a physical or biochemical impossibility in the light of a newer science which includes the theories of relativity and intra-atomic action. One might easily imagine an alien nucleus of substance or energy, formless or otherwise, kept alive by imperceptible or immaterial subtractions from the life-force or bodily tissues and fluids of other and more palpably living things into which it penetrates and with whose fabric it sometimes completely merges itself. It might be actively hostile, or it might be dictated merely by blind motives of self-preservation. In any case such a monster must of necessity be in our scheme of things an anomaly and an intruder, whose extirpation forms a primary duty with every man not an enemy to the world's life, health, and sanity.

What baffled us was our utter ignorance of the aspect in which we might encounter the thing. No sane person had even seen it, and few had ever felt it definitely. It might be pure energy—a form ethereal and outside the realm of substance—or it might be partly material; some unknown and equivocal mass of plasticity, capable of changing at will to nebulous approximations of the solid, liquid, gaseous, or tenuously unparticled states. The anthropomorphic patch of mould on the floor, the form of the yellowish vapour, and the curvature of the tree-roots in some of the old tales, all argued at least a remote and reminiscent connexion with the human shape; but how representative or permanent that similarity might be, none could say with any kind of certainty.

Up and down Broadway and along streets in perhaps every town and village in America, there are today young people who encounter in one iteration or another "Lovecraftian Magick," an avowedly antinomian but deeply conservative archaic virtual reality that all traces itself back to the amoral, infernal entities—the "Night-Gaunts"—that wracked H. P. Lovecraft's soul. The contemporary world's *Necronomicon*–based magic / myth / virtual reality is a weird apotheosis of the Satanic plan, a sad and sophomoric aping of the real, created world. A demon pulled a Satanic prank on a Providence boy with an instinct and aptitude for the stars and succeeded in creating a comic-book pop religion, now the province not just of adolescent males but of adults of both genders. "Serious" creative adults—Joyce Carol Oates, Guillermo del Toro, Ridley Scott—saturate themselves with this black mythos, elevating what should have been one troubled all-night Manhattan walker's crepuscular psychosis to the level of cultural icon.

Embedded within Lovecraft's work, he unconsciously predicted this present predicament. In his 1927 story "The Case of Charles Dexter Ward," Lovecraft portrays a man with no magical training who absentmindedly reads an incantation aloud, thereby setting a train of supernatural events in motion. This unconscious magic works apart from the magical will, the focused intent, or even the *understanding* of the speaker. Think of curses; used routinely, with no actual magical intent, they can still work. The entire corpus of science fiction and horror is like some chthonic cosmic curse unleashed on Earth, fed year to year and moment to moment by Hollywood and its progeny.

Site #9: The Broken Wand: Harry Houdini's Funeral Service at the Elks Club, 108 West Forty-Third Street, November 4, 1926

When J. K. Rowling chose December 6, 1926, as the date for the expelled Hogwarts magizoologist Newt Scamander's arrival in New York City, she intuited something well beyond her writerly ken. In 1926, Gotham's zoologists roamed the globe, in an enterprise to amass the world's most prodigious menagerie of "magical" animals. The American Museum of Natural History mounted thirty-four expeditions in 1926—the greatest number in its fifty-seven-year history. This was more than double the number of the expeditions sponsored by the much-older British Museum of Natural History. Though Newt's compatriot Charles Darwin had in 1859 given the world the organizing principle for all subsequent biological research, by 1926 American life science had superseded Great Britain in the arena of zoological discovery.

THE NEW YORK TIMES, MONDAY, NOVEMBER 1, 1926.

HARRY HOUDINI DIES AFTER OPERATIONS

Continued from Page 1, Column 2.

cause of Houdini's death, for one of the blows caused the appendix to burst, saturating his system with poison.

Streptococcus peritonitis, which developed soon after the operation last Monday, seriously complicated the case. This is a particularly virulent form of poisoning, and few cases are known to the medical profession where persons suffering from it have recovered.

The body will leave Detroit for New York in a special car Monday evening, arrive in New York Tuesday morning about 9 o'clock.

STAGE PAYS ITS TRIBUTES.

Praises Houdini as Magician, Man and Friend.

The stage and the world of magic and magicians joined yesterday in paying tribute to Houdini, not only as the leader in his particular field of entertainment but as a unique figure whose like will probably not be seen again for some time. The following tributes were voiced by persons with whom he had been intimately associated:

B. M. L. ERNST, Vice President of

Sensational escapes from handcuffs at Scotland Yard won him a six months' engagement at the Alhambra. This was the 'first instance of his cleverly obtaining notoriety by a public or semi-public exhibition outside the theatre. No other showman, unless it was Barnum, knew better how to arouse the curiosity and amazement of the public in this manner.

Escaped From Dozens of Prisons.

During a six-year tour of the Continent he escaped from dozens of famous prisons. In the Krupp plant at Essen he met the challenge of the workmen and freed himself from expertly constructed shackles before 10,000 persons. He returned to America to find his fame greatly increased and a newly organized vaudeville ready to pay him many times his old salary. He continued his prison escapes over here and in January, 1907, broke from Cell 2 in the Federal prison at Washington, the cell in which Guiteau, President Garfield's assassin, had been confined.

In 1908 Houdini dropped the handcuff tricks for more dangerous and dramatic escapes, including one from an air-tight galvanized vessel, filled with water, locked in an iron-bound chest. And he would free himself from the so-called torture cell, his own invention. In this he was suspended, head down, in a tank of water. To thrill the general public he would hang from the roof of a skyscraper, bound in a strait-jacket, from which he would wriggle free to the applause of the crowd in the street below. Thrown from a boat or bridge into a river, bound hand and foot and locked and nailed in a box, doomed to certain death by drowning or suffocation, he would emerge in a minute or so.

HARRY HOUDINI,
The Famous Magician, Who Died Yesterday in Detroit.

statement said, "As a showman he was in a class with Barnum, in force of character he resembled Roosevelt."

HOUDINI WORLD FAMOUS.

No Locks Could Hold Him—Foe of Mediums.

how he beguiled the late Theodore Roosevelt and the late Victor Herbert on a voyage to Europe aboard the Imperator. Colonel Roosevelt had just returned from his exploration of the River of Doubt in Brazil.

"I was asked to give an entertainment," Houdini would relate, "and the subject of spirit writing came up. A number of other well-known men were present, all of them having intelligence of a high order. Certainly it was not a credulous audience. I offered to summon the spirits and have them answer any questions that might be asked.

"Roosevelt wanted to know if they could tell him where he had spent Christmas Day. I had a slate with the usual covering and in a few moments brought forth a map, done in a dozen different colors of chalk, which indicated the exact spot where he had been on the famous River of Doubt. That map was an exact duplicate of one that was to appear in his book which had been published. I had never seen the map and, to make my case stronger, the name of W. T. Stead, the English spiritualist and writer who lost his life on the Titanic, was signed below the map in a handwriting which one man present instantly recognized as that of Stead. And I might add that I was unfamiliar with Stead's signature.

Colonel Roosevelt was Dumfounded.
"Roosevelt was dumfounded.

"'Is it really spirit writing?' he asked.

"'Yes,' I replied with a wink."
Of course, Houdini never explained how the trick was done, at least to the public.

The magician tried his hand at the medium business in his early days in Kansas and used to tell in this wise

told friends he was anxious to communicate with and friends who had agreed with acquaintances, numbering first to die was one from the spirit gate from the spirit of reality. Your had died, but not sign, he said.

Anxious for
"One of those people told, "was with W. Sargent, one Palladino in this were most intimate have not heard agreement I met parents. They did heard from them saw my mother believe it was in "Another thing supernatural to death of William and close friend worked together a private telegram messages. We the first who died to communicate his deathbed I had been unconscious. He showed me no turn to conscious mained closed. away I could feel faint pressure up repeated at late recognizing that the

Houdini dies
(*New York Times* Archive)

Newt arrived in New York on December 6, 1926—in the real world, right in the middle of the Clark University Symposium on psychic phenomena. One might reimagine the Clark Symposium—organized by Columbia's own Gardiner Murphy—as a real-life Magical Congress. The symposium, however, presented the views of both "Mags"—those convinced of the reality and efficacy of psychic phenomena (Arthur Conan Doyle, Frederick Bligh Bond, L. R. G. Crandon)—and "No-Mags" antagonistic to this view, Joseph Jastrow and Harry Houdini most prominently. There were also representatives of the middle ground; Hans Driesch, W. F. Prince, and F. S. C. Schiller were convinced of the rarity of the phenomena, while Dr. John Coues and Gardiner Murphy himself were just plain agnostic at that point. The symposium was born out of a December 1925 meeting of William F. MacDougall, Harry Houdini, and Carl Murchison to haggle out the business of the latest round of sensational spirit-medium phenomena—as manifested by Dr. Crandon's wife, "Margery." Clark University sided, unsurprisingly, with the Muggles, and the published volume from the symposium features an excerpt from Harry Houdini's debunking tome *A Magician among the Spirits*.

Sweeping our eye across the entire tableau of the year 1926, we find an astonishing array of "symptoms" of the Mag versus No-Mag struggle in America. The year saw the celebration of Salem's tercentenary, and, as had happened in 1892, there was a renewed conversation about the witchcraft trials. The magically sympathetic writer Montague Summers published his *History of Witchcraft and Demonology* in 1926, and that book sparked a flurry of scholarly and popular debate. In February, Congress held hearings on "fortune-telling" that were really an official referendum on Spiritualist bunkum. That summer, Lovecraft penned his "Call of Chtulhu"; though set in Providence, the tale's protagonist, Professor Angell, might easily be imagined as Professor Gardiner Murphy, and the occult detective Inspector Legrasse as Sir Arthur Conan Doyle. The fallout from the July 1925 Scopes Trial continued throughout 1926, forcing "science" and "religion" into even more polarized corners. The explosion of expeditionary activity that year was a last gasp of the modern era of natural history exploration, which symbolized a palpable decline of the national civilizational life force. This would become most spectacularly seen within the decade, in the creation—just off Broadway on Lafayette Street—of Superman and other pioneering superheroes, who replaced the popular fantasies of virile white explorers conquering nature.

As surely as there is a battle raging in Manhattan in the fictional *Fantastic Beasts* film, there was a battle—usually framed as the "battle between science and religion"—raging in America in 1926. The *New York Times* reported in January that the East Coast magician of surgery Alexis Carrel (the Rockefeller Institute's surgeon was pioneering organ and tissue transplants) disagreed with the West Coast horticultural wizard Luther Burbank's statement, "as a scientist I cannot help but feel that all religions are on a tottering foundation." This philosophical boxing match had no more celebrated antagonists than Harry Houdini and Arthur Conan Doyle. The two men had become friends in the early '20s; performing in England in 1920, Houdini had sent a copy of his book *The Unmasking of Robert*

Houdin (which unmasks Houdini as primordially a researcher rather than a magician) to Doyle. Doyle wrote to thank Houdini and asked whether he thought the Spiritualist mediums the Davenport brothers had real occult powers. Houdini was politely noncommittal in his reply. After the two men met, Doyle was absolutely convinced that Houdini's magic was genuine, not faked. "My dear chap," Doyle wrote to Houdini, "why go around the world seeking a demonstration of the occult when you are giving one all the time?" Doyle further demonstrated his credulity to Houdini when he sent Houdini photographs of fairies supposed to be from a Yorkshire wood. "The fairies are about eight inches high. In one there is a single goblin dancing. In the other four beautiful, luminous creatures. Yes, it is a revelation," Doyle declared.

During Doyle's visit to New York in 1922, at Houdini's Harlem home, Houdini arranged an experiment with slate writing—at that time a popular stage demonstration of both mediums and magicians, in which telepathic thoughts were written with chalk onto a slate board. The elaborate magic trick only convinced Doyle further of Houdini's occult powers, even though Houdini professed it had been done through trickery. Houdini one day told Sir Arthur about an inner voice he heard regularly, which helped him with his escapes. Though Houdini rejected that voice as anything "spiritual," Doyle's interpretation of this inner voice as spiritual help was unwavering. Indeed, most successful magicians have in their invisible employ— even if they have absolutely no belief in them—elemental beings whose capacities for transcending time and space give them insights that the magicians cannot have, unless imparted to them by their "familiar spirit."

In 1925, when Houdini invited Doyle to attend—and address— the annual Society of American Magicians banquet, Doyle came prepared with a trick of his own. After dinner, Doyle darkened the lights for a film he said would show extinct animals; these were, he explained, not "occult" or "supernatural" but "psychic" and "preternatural." Doyle sustained the illusion by stating that he would not answer any questions from the audience or the press. "Whether these pictures were intended by the famous author and champion of spiritism as a joke on the magicians or as a genuine picture like his photographs of fairies was not revealed," the *New York Times* reported. "The audience was left strictly to its own conclusions, whether the sober-faced Englishman was making merry with them or was lifting the veil from mysteries penetrated only by those of his school who know the secret of filming elves and ectoplasm and other things unknown to most minds."

What the magicians and reporters had seen was a few minutes of a test reel of *The Lost World*, Willis O'Brien's feature-length film of Doyle's best-selling 1912 novel. The finished film's first matchup of "prehistoric brutes" would show a stop-motion-animation simulation of *Pteranodon* killing and eating a young *Toxodon*, a Pleistocene mammal; in the brief footage, the magicians saw half a dozen other prehistoric species battling each other. In wedding the new technology of the motion picture to clay models of ancient animals, Willis O'Brien certainly had pulled off an astonishing magic trick; even Houdini himself was baffled by what he saw. O'Brien and Doyle fully believed in the accuracy of their miniature monsters, which were themselves modeled on museum reconstructions. Paleontology even today obscures the degree to which it is a vast imaginative exercise; once animation came along, the public entered into the dream world of the scientists, believing their inventions to be real. Paleontology is really an epic sleight-of-hand, for no paleontologist has ever *seen* a pterodactyl or ichthyosaur or brontosaurus. The illusion of time travel has since Darwin's day been the central conceit of all portraits of the Earth's early history.

No harm was done to the friendship, but the break soon came after Doyle's wife, Bess—who had for years been engaging in mediumism—held a séance with the Houdinis. A "spirit"— mischievous elemental—claimed to be Houdini's beloved mother; Houdini easily saw through the being's superficial communication and was deeply hurt by the incident. The men's friendship now broken by mistrust, the stage was set for the showdown.

Though both men had long been in the public eye, in 1926 they were both at the height of their fame. From this distance, one sees them as twinned "Resurrection Men," Doyle fervently proselytizing for the prospect of spiritual resurrection after death, Houdini using his prestidigitation art to effect bodily resurrection. The magnitude of their fame in the 1920s suggests that resurrection was a preoccupation of the whole world in that decade between two devastating world wars. Houdini was the star of thirty-one *New York Times* articles in 1926; over the summer, at home in New York, he was preparing a bigger-than-ever performance to take on the road that fall. Houdini's act had largely become a grandstand against the humbug of Spiritualism; not only did he expose Spiritualist tricks, but he frequently lectured his audiences about the dangers and deceits of Spiritualism. Crowds booed him, however, when he scoffed at the beliefs of Sir Arthur Conan Doyle.

Doyle published his *History of Spiritualism* in 1926, and *The Lost World* film continued to be a sensation. He was making many public addresses evangelizing for the reality of the spiritual world, but privately he was drawn more deeply into the mediumistic universe being conjured by his wife, Bess, through her "control," a being who called himself "Pheneas." In Doyle's public appearances and in his writings, he routinely invoked as gospel the outlandish prophecies of Bess's spectral adviser. In the summer of 1926, Pheneas predicted that Houdini would not live much longer. In August, when Houdini began to perform his new tricks, they were sensational. On August 5, he appeared to remain in a sealed casket for ninety minutes before being released. But on October 11, onstage at the Capitol Theater in Albany, Houdini was being locked in heavy ankle stocks in preparation to be lowered upside down into the Torture Cell—one of his most dramatic performances. As he was being raised, one of the cables loosened and twisted, causing the stocks to shift and fracture his ankle. With his foot in a brace, he moved on to Schenectady and then Montreal. On the twenty-second, a man named J. Gordon Whitehead visited Houdini backstage, to return some books that he had borrowed. Asking Houdini if it was true that he could withstand blows to his stomach, Whitehead began to pummel him, finally stopping after Houdini said enough.

On October 31, Halloween, in Detroit for another run of performances, Houdini died of acute peritonitis, apparently aggravated by the Montreal assault.

On November 4, the Society of American Magicians held a funeral service for their president at the Elks Club, a block from the Hippodrome, where Houdini had once made a ten-thousand-pound elephant vanish into thin air. Two thousand people attended the service and held their breath as a Society of American Magicians compeer broke Houdini's wand in half over the casket.

There was in 1926 a much more profound magic wand broken: humanity's understanding that it was a wholly magical spiritual creation, momentarily spellbound by materialism. Up Broadway at Columbia University in 1926, professor of medieval history Lynn Thorndike was working on *Science and Thought in the Fifteenth Century*, the third volume of his *A History of Magic and Experimental Science during the First Thirteen Centuries of Our Era*. There would eventually be five more volumes, but this third volume, more than any other, marshaled Thorndike's wide reading in the primary sources of early modern astrology, alchemy, chiromancy, image magic, and other hermetic arts to tell the triumphant story of the Western mind's escape from magical superstition into the light of reason. Thorndike single-handedly, more than J. G. Frazer or Max Weber, drove the final nail into the coffin that was *enchantment*, by "definitively" documenting *disenchantment*.

Or at least he so believed. Outside of perhaps Harry Houdini, whose library of nearly four thousand books documenting the history of magic he bequeathed to the Library of Congress, no Manhattanite ever spent more hours poring over magical *grimoires* than

Lynn Thorndike. His scholarly efforts revolutionized the understanding of Western science's origins, revealing supposed rationalist illuminati from Francis Bacon and René Descartes and Galileo to Kepler, Boyle, and Newton all to be as fully self-conscious magicians as pioneering scientists. The thoroughly modern Professor Thorndike found no enchantment in his own discoveries of the magical proclivities of his subjects; Newton he declared "an unbridled addict" of alchemy, whose manuscripts were "wholly magical and wholly devoid of scientific value."

Thorndike's disdain for magic was an active principle, a conscious choice masquerading as scholarly objectivity; his definition of magic belies his unbelief: "Magic appears as a human art or group of arts employing varied materials in varied rites, often fantastic, to work a great variety of marvelous results, which offer man a release from his physical, social, and intellectual limitations, not by the imaginative and sentimental methods of music, melodrama, and romance, nor by religion's spiritual experience, but by operations supposed to be efficacious here in the world of external reality." There is no reason to disqualify modern science from this definition, but Thorndike assumed a sharp divide between the two realms and never wavered from his commitment to science—or scientism—as the ultimate arbiter of truth. Understanding science as a form of magic would wait another half a century or so before gaining a foothold in academe, which still largely commits itself to the epistemological distancing voiced in Professor Thorndike's not-so-subtle "supposed."

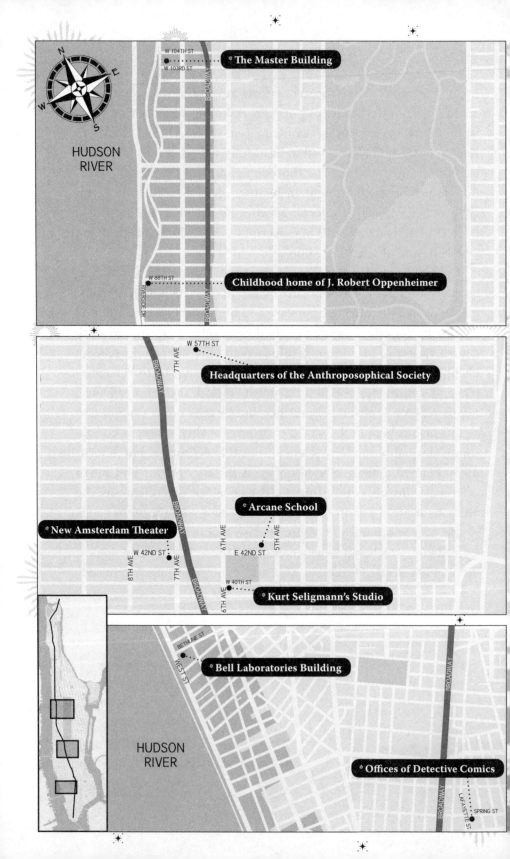

N

HUDSON
RIVER

W 104TH ST
W 103RD ST
* The Master Building

BROADWAY

W 88TH ST
Childhood home of J. Robert Oppenheimer

RIVERSIDE DR

BROADWAY

W 57TH ST
7TH AVE
BROADWAY

Headquarters of the Anthroposophical Society

* Arcane School

5TH AVE

* New Amsterdam Theater

8TH AVE

W 42ND ST

7TH AVE

6TH AVE

E 42ND ST

BROADWAY

W 40TH ST

6TH AVE

* Kurt Seligmann's Studio

BETHUNE ST

WEST ST

* Bell Laboratories Building

BROADWAY

HUDSON
RIVER

* Offices of Detective Comics

BROADWAY

LAFAYETTE ST

SPRING ST

6

Apocalyptic Manhattan

1933–1948

Samuel Freedman's *Supervue of New York City,* 1937
(Library of Congress)

Over the course of the twentieth century, dozens of groups drew inspiration from the belief that the end of the Kali Yuga (the ancient Hindu mythology's conception of a five-thousand-year age of spiritual darkness) in 1899 heralded an incipient dawning of the "New Age," whose hallmark was most often believed to be the appearance of new soul powers. At the same moment, through the new broadcast media, "Supermen" of varying magical powers were proliferating in popular culture. The vast expansion of technological powers at midcentury both offered a mechanical substitute for magical power and simultaneously *was* a magical power, in the hands of certain individuals and institutions. In retrospect, one can fairly call these developments "apocalyptic," since they both "uncovered" or revealed formerly unseen currents and proved massively destructive. Expanded powers always mean the potential for both good and evil, and along Broadway, we find bold imperial projects that often sought to stay subterranean, even as they unleashed themselves on the rest of the world.

The occult brotherhoods, as well as the spiritual beings conspiring with them, made use of other women for their designs after the death of Blavatsky. Helena Roerich's and Alice Bailey's teachings emanated from Manhattan, and both of the arcane schools they founded continue here. Quite self-consciously opposed to those magical schools, the American branch of Rudolf Steiner's Anthroposophical Society continued to bring forward a spiritual science that aimed to transform magic, religion, and science. The magical knowledge fostered by these opposing spiritual streams lays open a vast metahistorical drama, a magical space opera fit for the Broadway stage.

Site #1: Meeting the Christ Rhythm:
Headquarters of the Anthroposophical Society,
144 West Fifty-Seventh Street, July 1933

Of the tens of thousands of commuters who passed across the floor of the Grand Concourse of Grand Central Terminal, on July 8, 1933, there was one eccentric little knot of friends who—before boarding the train out to Spring Valley in Rockland County—took special note of the zodiac mural on the ceiling above. It was not so much that they were aware that the zodiac's rendering was backward or even that they possessed the arcane knowledge that due to precession of the equinoxes, the vernal equinox—depicted in the great mural as the place, in the constellation Pisces, where the plane of the ecliptic and the celestial equator crossed—was no longer in the position shown. These friends, who were on their way to the first Summer Conference of the Anthroposophical Society in America, were poignantly aware that a great cosmic rhythm was unfolding in 1933, one altogether "apocalyptic," in both the ancient and modern sense of that word. Delighted to be leaving the city for a week of study and recreation, still they held their breaths a bit, for their teacher, Rudolf Steiner, had repeatedly identified the year 1933 as a turning point for humanity.

The art student Charlotte Parker had first come to know the *New York Herald-Tribune* journalist Ralph Courtney at an Adirondack summer camp during the terribly hot summer of 1922. Courtney had put up a sign outside his cabin: "Lectures by Rudolf Steiner read here every evening." Only one person usually attended the readings; Courtney fully understood the lukewarm response, for though he had moved to England as a child, he had been born in Texas and retained a Texan sensibility about the world as an impressively physical place, with no need for occult ideas to help explain it. But after he had met Steiner's work while in Paris to cover the Versailles Conference as the *Herald-Tribune*'s chief European correspondent, Courtney had become one of Steiner's most enthusiastic students. There

Threefold Vegetarian Restaurant
(Threefold Foundation Archive)

were very few; in 1927, the Anthroposophical Society in America could claim no more than 177 members. Courtney, whose passion centered on Steiner's philosophy of social threefolding—which aims to foster human rights and equality in political life, freedom in cultural life (art, science, religion, education, the media), and associative cooperation in economic life—founded the Threefold Group out of those Adirondack meetings.

In 1923, when Courtney leased an apartment building at the corner of Sixth Avenue and Fifty-Sixth Street, just a block below Carnegie Hall—the center of the Saint Mark Group started in 1910 (see Site #15 in chapter 4)—he began by renting rooms to members and friends. Before long, they had expanded into a second building, and Courtney talked Charlotte Parker (who had never cooked before in her life) and the piano students Louise Bybee and Gladys Barnett into preparing an evening communal meal for the tenants. Courtney also instituted afternoon teatime. By January 1924, the dinner group outgrew its room and began renting the building's basement space to open the Threefold Vegetarian Restaurant—the first in New York

City. The small grocery store in front of the restaurant sold products from Weleda, an anthroposophically inspired pharmaceutical company; distinctive anthroposophical artwork graced the restaurant's walls; and the wooden chairs and tables built by community members were sculpted to give expression to the cosmic formative forces. In 1926, the community bought a farm in Spring Valley, where, practicing Rudolf Steiner's alchemical methods, they intended to grow "biodynamic" produce to supply the restaurant.

In a large circus tent set up in the oak grove beyond the Threefold Farm garden and barns, thirty-three-year-old Ehrenfried Pfeiffer delivered his first American lecture: "Making Visible the Formative-Forces in Nature." His teacher, mentor, and friend Rudolf Steiner had groomed him for this very task from an early age; Steiner advised Pfeiffer on his course of college study and, for the last five years of Steiner's life, closely collaborated with Pfeiffer on his research. Pfeiffer began his address by condemning contemporary natural science's relentless endeavor to turn Natura into a corpse and society's reckless use of the subearthly forces of nature—electricity, magnetism, and gravity. In 1933—the very year for which Rudolf Steiner had prophesied the return of Christ in the etheric realm, in service for which he had labored his entire life—only a handful of human beings over the entire Earth possessed sufficiently fluid etheric bodies to achieve supersensible perception. Conscientious anthroposophists who had not achieved etheric clairvoyance consoled themselves with the knowledge that even the active attempt to understand the reality of the spiritual world was a step on the path to gaining direct knowledge of it.

When, in 1920, the young engineer Ehrenfried Pfeiffer had asked Rudolf Steiner if there might be some way of using the constructive, synthetic forces as the foundation of a new altruistic technics that would have within itself the impulse of life rather than death, Steiner had first set his student the task of demonstrating the etheric forces in visible form, by developing a substance that would react with the *Bildekräfte* (etheric formative forces) in plants and human blood.

Pfeiffer made the formative forces visible through the process of sensitive crystallization—added to a glass petri dish holding a copper chloride solution, both blood and plant sap produced grayish-blue patterns like frost on a windowpane. He attributed this serendipitous success to having followed Rudolf Steiner's advice to make the laboratory a place where the elemental beings of nature would feel comfortable, through a spiritual atmosphere of prayer and meditation.

A meditative state was also required to interpret the crystallization images, which to the untrained eye of the flesh appeared as little more than crystalline Rorschach blots. Pfeiffer's inner eye distinguished subtle differences in the crystallizations, but when he reported his results to Steiner, Steiner interpreted them as indicating that the time was not yet right for humanity to make use of the etheric forces; that time would come about only when the Threefold Social Order had been established in at least a few regions on Earth. Until then, no experiments toward an etheric technology should be conducted. Already by 1933, when Pfeiffer addressed the very group of anthroposophists who had pioneered American efforts in founding social threefolding in New York City and then at Threefold Farm, he doubted that he would see the advent of the necessary conditions in his own lifetime and felt sure that he would go to his grave keeping secret the little knowledge he had gained about the application of the etheric forces.

This was a decade before the most deadly subearthly force was discovered, with the splitting of the atom. Atomic fission was the destructive counterimage of the Rosicrucian ideal of turning the Earth into a sun, by conscious cultivation of the resurrection forces within the human heart. In one of Pfeiffer's Threefold Farm lectures, he revealed that occult brotherhoods were so determined to keep to themselves the secret of the fifth chamber of the heart that they had poisoned Rudolf Steiner.

The New York City anthroposophists shared with Ehrenfried Pfeiffer the understanding that Rudolf Steiner was a high Christian initiate whose own living master had been Christian Rosenkreutz.

As Rosicrucian initiates who were working far into the future in their spiritual scientific research and activity, both Steiner and Pfeiffer worked within what they called the "Cain Stream" of individualities who had for millennia brought insight and innovation to humanity in the realm of science and technology. In a single lecture in 1952, Pfeiffer touched on numerous researches suggested by Steiner: working with absolute-zero temperatures to realize "warmth energy"; the study of plant ashes versus mineralized ashes, in relationship to a study of the etheric light emitted by the eye; "peptonization," the creation of remedies by experimenting with day and night rhythms (Pfeiffer said that he believed one hundred PhD theses could be written on this subject!); and superimposing ultraviolet on infrared light. In this same talk, Pfeiffer touched on the subject of the "Keely Motor," a controversial attempt to devise an engine that magically operated solely from the forces of the human operator. Pfeiffer warned that society was not yet prepared for this technology; three and a half centuries after Elizabethan-era alchemists cautioned about making esoteric knowledge public, this principle still held, not because of the potential for public derision but because of the absence of the necessary social crucible into which this knowledge might be received.

During all of the years that Dr. Pfeiffer was laboring to penetrate the physical world with new spiritual perceptions, Ralph Courtney indefatigably attempted to penetrate the even-deeper secret of how to found and foster the Threefold Commonwealth. From his efforts in the 1930s to introduce an alternative currency in the local economy to his long-running newsletter calling for the decentralization of society, Courtney engaged fully with the deep mystery of American destiny. Thanks largely to the seeds planted that summer of 1933 by Ehrenfried Pfeiffer, the Biodynamic Farming and Gardening Association was founded by Courtney, Parker, and other members of the Threefold Group, at the Anthroposophical Society's headquarters at 144 West Fifty-Seventh Street, on January 8, 1938.

The spiritual science that Rudolf Steiner taught from 1900 until his death in 1925 and that Ehrenfried Pfeiffer and the Threefold Group sought to practice and develop further was essentially alchemy for the twentieth century—a truly *spiritual* scientific practice that rested on recognition of and collaboration with the elemental beings of nature: the salamanders, sylphs, undines, and gnomes of Paracelsus, whose existence was denied by modern materialistic science. For anthroposophists, the ultimate goal and impetus for their efforts to create a new alchemy was to prepare for the event prophesied by Rudolf Steiner to occur in 1933: Christ's uniting of his etheric body with the etheric body of the Earth.

Site #2: Alice A. Bailey's "New Age" and Djwal Khul's
Rules for Magic: Salmon Tower Building,
11 West Forty-Second Street, August 1934

By 1933, it was a commonplace in America to speak of (1) an incipient "New Age," generally characterized by progress in human spiritual development; (2) the link between this epoch's inauguration and the passage of the vernal equinox into the constellation of Aquarius; and (3) the connection of these developments to some iteration of "Christ's return." Though we may now trace the roots of these cultural commonplaces back to Madame Blavatsky, by 1933 "Theosophical" thought and principles had fractured into dozens of doctrinal variants—often as bitterly sectarian as their Christian counterparts. If one commonality could be found within these "New Age" groups, it would be something they shared with HPB's Theosophy; they usually had at their center a highly mediumistic woman who "channeled" prophetic, millenarian texts from elusive beings who claimed superior spiritual status. Mediumism had become so normalized in America by 1933 that no one ever cited Blavatsky's own strenuous objections to mediumism and its dangers. The unconscious, hypnotically controlled transmission of "revelations" became routinized in parallel with the "medium" of radio and its handmaiden, modern broadcast advertising. At the moment when a nation of avid magical practitioners was singing the anthem of a New Age of individual consciousness expansion, human beings were succumbing to spectacular contractions of consciousness in the form of mass electronic and print propaganda.

New York City, as the national center for both radio and advertising, was clearly the epicenter of exoteric "mediumism"; it was also the center of *esoteric* mediumism. By 1933, the leading voice of apocalyptic New Age-ism was Alice A. Bailey and her "Arcane School." Founded in April 1923 on her channeled texts—*Initiation, Human and Solar*; *Letters on Occult Meditation*; and *The Consciousness of the Atom*—the Arcane School had as its initial impulse a desire for magic, just as had George Felt's "Miracle Club" that had led to Blavatsky and Olcott's founding of the Theosophical Society. Bailey's Lucifer Publishing Company was located at 135 Broadway; in 1928, the Arcane School and its publishing program (renamed Lucis Publishing) moved to the new Salmon Tower Building, across from Bryant Park.

Library Journal ad for Alice Bailey's books, 1922

In August 1934, for the first time, the anonymous "Tibetan" who dictated Alice Bailey's Arcane School teachings came out to speak and write directly—but still anonymously. (His identity as "Djwhal Khul" [DK] was revealed *accidentally* by Bailey in a 1943 article; by that time, Bailey's books had reached millions of people, in sixteen different languages, and some thirty thousand people had come to visit the Arcane School in New York City.) In *A Treatise on White*

Magic; or, The Way of the Disciple (1934), Djwhal Khul—a "brother of yours who has traveled a little longer upon the Path than has the average student"—gave fifteen "Rules for Magic," promising to "elucidate the problem of the supernormal powers, and give the rules for their safe and useful development." White-magical workers were "invariably, and through the very nature of things, advanced human beings." Djwhal Khul's treatise was perfectly tailored for the twentieth-century urban American mind, promising vague superpowers as surely they were promised by a hundred modern nostrums and comic-book fantasies. It was filled with so many narcissistic tautologies that anyone reading it would assume that *they* were among the "advanced human beings" who would usher in the New Age. The text itself had a hypnotic effect, one that facilitated the penetration of the "Solar Angel" into the reader's consciousness. *A Treatise on White Magic* was indeed a magical text, a *black-magical agent* for disseminating DK's gospel of occult materialism.

Even a cursory reading of Bailey's—that is, "Djwhal Khul's"— books makes it clear that the Arcane School was a sustained, planned preemption of genuine twentieth-century Rosicrucian paths of soul development. The language is quite explicit: DK says that the Arcane School's aim is "to train those disciples who can implement the Plan and thus prepare for the reappearance of the Christ." To his advanced pupils, DK intimated that they were in "the senior ranks of the New Group of World Servers" and as such had the responsibility "of preparation for the reappearance of the Christ." "The world must be flooded with the information," DK claimed, information that rested on two materialist, wholly anti-Christian, and Satanic principles: that this preparation was for a second coming of Christ *in a physical body* and that the Christ is equal to the Buddha and the Buddha to Christ.

Another DK / Alice Bailey text published in 1934 shows how the occult materialism of the Arcane School had very specific— and, in retrospect, shocking—social and political perspectives on the first steps of humanity into the "New Age." In *The Next Three*

Years (1934–1935–1936), the telepathic communications pronounce on science: spirit photography will help prove survival of bodily death, and radio will be used "by those who have passed over." The predictions were invariably "hopeful," in the sense of ushering in magical powers:

> Certain happenings in 1936 will do more to annihilate the veil between the seen and the unseen than any other line of activity hitherto initiated. About that time an illumination will be set up and a radiance revealed which will result in a tremendous stimulation of mankind and bring about an awakening of a new order. Man will be keyed up to a perception and to a contact which will enable him to *see through*, which will reveal the nature of the fourth dimension, and blend the subjective and objective together into a new world. Death will lose its terrors and the fear of death will come to an end between the years 1936 and 1945.

As in earlier episodes involving seemingly prophetic foreknowledge, *The Next Three Years* was a promiscuous mix of fairly innocuous readings of the signs of the times with disturbingly casual assessments of the things to come:

> The next three years, and in a lesser degree the succeeding nine years, mark a happening of such profound and widespread consequences that the present era in which we now live will come to be looked upon as the dark ages. Science will penetrate deeper into the realm of the intangible, and work in media and with apparatus hitherto unknown. The release of the potencies in an atom will mark a revolutionary era, and science will have much to discard and much to give as it works with energies and forms of life hitherto unrecognized. The spiritualists will make a discovery whereby the means of contact with those who function out of the physical body will be greatly facilitated, and a group of mediums will begin to act as intermediaries for a number of scientists on the inner side of life and those who are still in physical

bodies. Through the activity of the real esoteric schools, a technique of training will be instituted which will develop the new powers that will substantiate the old truth and turn men's beliefs into certainties. Through the stimulating and important work of the department of religions, men will come to new knowledge and awareness, and will arrive at an uplift that will bring mankind to the Mount of Transfiguration. Through the work of the department of government, men will come to an understanding of those ideas which are needed to carry the nations the next step forward to mutual help.

Here was full-blown twentieth-century occult Prometheanism, as brazen and unapologetic as would soon explode in the colored panels of a *Superman* comic. Bailey's rhetoric of the Superman—"Yet the ideal of the superman is a true ideal, and it needs upholding before the world"—was an almost exact caricature of the Rosicrucian path for the redemption of the elemental beings of nature:

> Let us attempt to express, at this time, the deepest objective of the Brotherhood, so that we can understand and cooperate. Humanity is intended to act as a powerhouse through which certain types of divine energy can flow to the various types of life found in the subhuman kingdoms. This flow of life must be intelligently apprehended and intelligently directed, and thus will be brought to an end conditions of decay and of death now prevalent everywhere. Mankind can thus link the higher and the lower manifestations of Life, but this will only be possible when men have themselves (within themselves) linked their higher and lower aspects. This is, and should be, one of the objectives of all esoteric training. Men are intended to acquire the facility to function freely in either direction, and so with ease contact the life of God as it flows through forms we call superhuman, and those which are subhuman. Such is the emerging goal.

Though both books were published in 1934, many of the "transmissions" in *A Treatise on White Magic* and *The Next Three Years* were given by DK in 1932, before the Reichstag fire and Hitler's seizure of power in Germany. In these and subsequent works, Bailey noted political developments in both Stalinist Russia and Nazi Germany quite approvingly, to the degree that they advanced the "Superman."

In September 1939, Bailey wrote, "The men who inspired the French revolution; the great conqueror Napoleon; Bismarck, the creator of a nation; Mussolini, the regenerator of his people; Hitler, who lifted a distressed people upon his shoulders; Lenin, the idealist, Stalin and Franco" were "great and outstanding personalities who were peculiarly sensitive to the will-to-power and the will-to-change." All of these cruel and antihuman monsters, according to Alice A. Bailey's inspirer, were "expressions of the Shamballa force" who "emphasized increasingly the wider human values."

"Shamballa" in this Satanic concoction was the magical kingdom from which Bailey's secret inspirer claimed to utter his visions, and in keeping with the rest of Bailey's teachings, it was a place of raw, materialistic, *physical* power. Bearing the hallmark of being a complete inversion of Christian esoteric understanding of Shambhala as an entirely *etheric* realm accessible only through a Rosicrucian path of moral sacrifice, Bailey's Shamballa joined a roster of Satanic inversions—"darkness is pure spirit"; "the true communistic platform is sound . . . and does not run counter to the spirit of Christ"; World War II "with all its unspeakable horrors, its cruelties, and its cataclysmic disasters, was but the broom of the Father of all, sweeping away obstructions in the path of His returning Son"; "the atomic bomb emerged from a first ray Ashram, working in conjunction with a fifth ray group; from the long range point of view, its intent was and is purely beneficent." Bailey embraced an occult program of eugenics; "certain physical restrictions should be imposed, because it is now evident that *beyond a certain point the planet cannot support humanity.*" As sure as the burgeoning science-fiction literature encouraged the human being to leave Earth for some cold physical planet, Bailey's antihuman agenda discouraged humanity from staying and redeeming its home planet.

In the 1960s, in the music of Van Morrison, Lou Reed and the Velvet Underground, Jonathan Richman, and others, Alice Bailey and her inspirer, DK, were given a whole new audience for breathless intimations of this Luciferic nightmarish world: "Beautiful Visions" of the "Dweller on the Threshold," "Astral Weeks," "Sister Ray," and "White Light." "Let the great illusion drown," sang Van Morrison in 1982, but the fact that these Satanically inspired platitudes continued to drift uncontextualized and unquestioned through American pop culture suggests just how deeply Bailey's DK-inspired magical illusions are still with us.

Site #3: Nicholas and Helena Roerich's Agni Yoga: The Master Building, 310 Riverside Drive, Fall 1935

However nonmaterial magical forces may be, they can raise immense, dense, even titanic material monuments. When, in March 1929, five hundred persons assembled on a site at the junction of Riverside Drive and 103rd Street, for the cornerstone laying of a new twenty-nine-story apartment building, the architect Harvey Wiley Corbett called the planned structure "a living thing" that would be "the first living home of art, where art and human beings will grow side by side." Though the edifice's name—the Master Building—was said to refer to the Russian esotericists Nicholas and Helena Roerich's invisible Tibetan Mahatma master, "Morya," its financier, the investment banker Louis Horch, equally conceived of the name as referring to *his* master—Nicholas Roerich himself.

Albert Einstein and Rabindrath Tagore had sent congratulatory wishes; Professor of Law Dr. Alfredo Colmo of Argentina compared Roerich to Dante, Goethe, and Michelangelo. New York City Assistant Commissioner of Education James Sullivan in his welcoming address attacked American bigotry and intolerance, especially toward Asia and Buddhism, praising Roerich's efforts to build cultural bridges across the Himalayas. At the moment when Horch placed a four-hundred-year-old Rajput casket—containing

Nicholas Roerich (*front row, second from right*) and New York City mayor
James Walker (*to Roerich's right*) on the steps of City Hall, at a June 1929
reception given by Mayor Walker (Nicholas Roerich Museum)

photographs and other objects from a four-year expedition by the
Roerichs to Central Asia—inside the cornerstone, the Roerichs were
far off in Mongolia; but, especially for a small inner circle of followers, this was yet another sign that that the "Great Plan" was coming
to fruition.

One object *not* inside the casket was the "Treasure of the World"—
known variously as the Chintamani Stone, *Norbu-rinpoche* (Precious
Jewel), *Lapis Exillis*, and even "the Holy Grail"—since its mysterious delivery to the Roerichs in Paris in September 1923. A powerful
"psychomagnet" believed by the Roerichs to be imbued with a rare
astral substance called *moryi*, whose emanations could affect the
fate not only of its possessors but of entire nations, it was alleged
to have fallen to Earth from Orion. A series of messages channeled
by Helena Roerich from "Master Morya" in April to October 1923

had made the half-dollar-sized object out to be the world's most occult talisman. Its former possessors supposedly included Moses, King Solomon, Alexander of Macedonia, the Mogul Emperor Akbar, Tamerlane, Napoleon, and even the Roerichs themselves in their thirteenth-century incarnations as the Naumburg princess Margravine Uta and her consort, Ekkehard. Given such an august magical heritage, Roerich was unfazed when, through his wife's channeled communication from Morya, he learned that when the stone was held in the right hand, one could pronounce an enemy's name three times, and that person would drop dead, and a "whirlwind will sweep him away." Morya also said that the stone would permit Nicholas Roerich to command hordes of Mongol warriors in the "Battle of Shambhala."

On this four-year Asiatic diplomatic (and, secretly, intelligence) expedition, the Roerichs had carried the little sliver of black stone with one further magical and apocalyptic goal: to reunite it with its larger parent "Treasure of the World" safeguarded within the citadel of the Great White Brotherhood in Shambhala. The megalomaniacal Roerich expected that this act would "complete the victory" of the Great Plan—to create a pan-Buddhist, transnational new religious state, spanning from Tibet to southern Siberia.

That a magic magnetic stone should play such a seminal role in the destiny of the Roerichs is strange when considered against the content of Morya's/Helena's Agni Yoga teachings, which consistently denigrated *all* magical activity and routinely characterized even the mildest opposition to the Roerichs' various pan-Asian initiatives as infernal black magic carried out by evil secret brotherhoods. But obsession can blind even the most perspicacious to all contradictions. In April 1935, just two weeks after representatives from twenty-one American states met at the White House with proponents Henry A. Wallace, the secretary of commerce, and President Franklin Delano Roosevelt to sign the "Roerich Pact" (officially the *Treaty on the Protection of Artistic and Scientific Institutions and Historic Monuments*), Helena Roerich—who since 1922 had engaged

Nicholas Roerich's *Treasure of the World*, 1924
(Nicholas Roerich Museum)

in *daily* trance-induced automatic-writing sessions—channeled a lengthy letter from Morya that gave a capsule cultural history of magic. In it, she declared that magic inevitably "ends up in the darkest manifestations." Advising the "abolition of magic"—"let it be left to the dark necromancers"—Morya railed against the invocation of the "lower entities," saying the abolition of magic would be "a white stone on the path of the world":

To study and to cognize the marvelous approaches to the Subtle World and to the Fiery World will not be magic. Prayer of the heart is not magic. Aspiration of the spirit toward Light is not magic. One must guard against all forms of ignorance, for it is a source of falsehood, and falsehood is the entrance way to darkness. Be able to find in your heart the truth of turning to the one Light. Terror fills the world. Do not follow the pathway of terror. One may be fortified by examples of former times. The saints themselves were in contact with the Fiery World through the heart, the same heart which has been given to everyone. Ability to hear the voice of the heart already leads to truth.

Like Alice Bailey's DK, Helena Roerich's Morya was downright glib with such platitudinous pronouncements, while simultaneously violating in plain sight the very tenets he espoused. Morya's long-running apocalyptic manifesto in 1935 morphed in the direction of destruction, favorably speaking of the "New Epoch" as an era when the "Cosmic Magnet" would bring down deadly purification on the path to the Fiery World. Thanks to the boldness and coldness of the Roerichs' apocalyptic elitism, a few of the Roerichs' staunchest allies were in 1935 finally abandoning them; in February, just as Nicholas—called by Morya *Fuyama* (Helena was *Urusvati*; the other seven members of the Agni Yoga inner circle all had similarly obscure but "royal"-sounding names)—prepared to implement the "Grand Plan" in Mongolia, Louis Horch began preparing a lawsuit to regain legal control of the Roerich-inspired institutions housed in the Master Building, as well as to recover $200,000 in loans he had made to Roerich. Henry Wallace, who had proved so useful in providing the Roerichs access to President Roosevelt, also began to wake up. Having cavalierly provoked both the Russian and Chinese governments by conducting an US-financed (and armed), White Russian–led escapade in a region that was in the middle of an anti-Communist Mongolian uprising, the Soviets assumed that Roerich was seeking to provoke a Buddhist holy war against Communist rule in Outer Mongolia. When Louis Horch informed Secretary Wallace that Roerich guaranteed US support for a Mongolian insurrection, Wallace ordered Roerich to surrender his credentials and end the expedition.

"I think all the time about Kansas," Fuyama wrote to "Galahad" (Morya's and the Roerichs' moniker for Wallace, whom, in one communication, they intimated would succeed Roosevelt as president). "Kansas" was their code word for the pan-Buddhist utopian fantasy that drove all the Roerichs' manic initiatives, and perhaps—given Yip Harburg's rendering of "Kansas" as a symbol for the state of bourgeois normality in *The Wizard of Oz*—we can pause to cipher the deeper implications of this Manhattan-to-Mongolia magical extravaganza, whose monuments (the Master Building and the Roerich Museum a few blocks away on 107th Street) are still very much present, even if their phantasmagoric inspirations have passed away. There are tangible, traceable, telling *arcana* embedded within this minor episode of the "Great Game" of imperial struggle between East and West.

"The Stone cometh"; "It is a most grievous error to deny the Stone"; "Await the Stone!" pronounced Morya in the summer of 1923. On September 10, 1923, Helena Roerich wrote in her diary, "The greatest hope of humanity pinned on the Stone is being revived." This dark stone was like some materialistic crystallization of all the twisted mythos manufactured by Morya—of a *physical* Shamballa, where a *physical* Great White Brotherhood labored in sacrifice for humanity's progressive evolution, preparing for a *physical* manifestation of the "Maitreya," Buddhism's prophesied future benefactor of humankind. Each of these images of occult materialism was an inversion of very specific revelations almost simultaneously being given by a true servant of the Holy Grail, Rudolf Steiner—not from some cryptic remote Himalayan fastness but from the simple Swiss village of Dornach, where Steiner, with an international cadre of men and women, had in the midst of World War I built the Goetheanum, a temple for the cultivation of a new alchemy, spiritual science. In the hall of the Goetheanum, in December 1923, Steiner proclaimed the advent of a *supersensible stone*, not physical but *etheric*, a double dodecahedron of love, manifesting in the Earth's subtle body in a divinely sanctioned and appointed revelation of the true Shambhala: the etheric realm in the center of the Earth.

The path of Agni Yoga—the "Yoga of Fire"—incubated and promulgated by the Roerichs and their followers (all of their inner circle's members lived in Manhattan) was and is, point by point, doctrine by doctrine, arcanum by arcanum, a black-magical attack on the true mystery of the Holy Grail, which is in the twentieth century the mystery of Christ's appearance and activity within the etheric realm of the Earth.

In Russia, Helena Roerich's books are widely read, and new spiritual movements echoing the Roerichs' materialist conception of Russia as the site of the incipient "Sixth Race" continue to pop up every decade. Up at the Roerich Museum, visitors who are unacquainted with the full history of Agni Yoga move from room to room, admiring Nicholas Roerich's dark, stony canvases. Fed by *Da Vinci Code*–style myths about Wallace's, FDR's, and Roerich's role in the All-Seeing Eye atop the pyramid on the obverse of the dollar bill and possible connections to the "Holy Grail," pilgrims regularly make their way to the black cornerstone at the base of the Master Building, to muse on whether the magic stone is inside.

Site #4: Orson Welles's *The Shadow*: New Amsterdam Theater, 214 West Forty-Second Street, September 26, 1937

Having begun fictional life as the mysterious narrator of *The Detective Story Hour* in 1930, "The Shadow" had then become a full-fledged literary character—"an Old Testament avenger, a ruthless slayer of the wicked, very befitting the Depression decade of his greatest strength," according to his creator, the writer Walter B. Gibson. In September 1937, voiced by the twenty-two-year-old actor Orson Welles, The Shadow had inevitably picked up a magical power beyond mere Sherlock Holmesian ratiocination. While living in the Orient (of course!), The Shadow (aka Lamont Cranston) had acquired the power to cloud men's minds, to make himself invisible, and also to telepathically see what others saw.

Listening to "Death House Rescue," the very first episode of *The Shadow*, one can feel Cranston's metropolitan elegance and independence, and whether he is invading the criminal's or the innocent's

Orson Welles (1915–1985)

mind, one feels Cranston somehow has the right to break in. But Welles himself felt no such permission or authority as a creative artist, even if he may have used his own natural hypnotic abilities—and skills as a stage magician—to fashion himself into one of the twentieth century's greatest actors and directors. Maturing as an artist in the 1930s, when fascism threatened from all directions, Welles recognized that fascism was simply the specter of a hypnotized mass public and that stage and film directors as much as political dictators dabbled in a realm that operated on magic principles. That his first radio drama performance should center on a wizard citizen sleuth with immense hypnotic powers was a reflection of the era's fascination with the mysteries of hypnosis; but it also was a kind of bellwether of his biography, for over the course of his artistic career, he passionately warned about and subverted fascism, championing in its stead the democratic promise of a people's theater.

Lamont Cranston: "I'm going to think, with your mind. Just do as I tell you. Make mental pictures; I'll see what you see. Like mental telepathy, mind reading, hypnotism."

In 1937, enchanted New York had become in some strange fashion a reflection or echo of Welles's *Citizen Kane* (1941) or *Black Magic* (1949), narrating again and again the tragedy of the misuse of special powers. The fictional Lamont Cranston—the name dripping with mere social, rather than magical, prestige and privilege—may be the closest to a benign Count Cagliostro that we have met in these pages since the magnetic healer LaRoy Sutherland back in chapter 3. Whether 1937 or today, we should know that for every Cagliostro or Charles Foster Kane or Nicholas Roerich or Alice Bailey, there were along Broadway innumerable practitioners of "natural, true magic." Voicing Lamont Cranston, Orson Welles once proclaimed, "Why do you think I've devoted countless hours to investigating electrical and chemical phenomena? Why do you think I went to India, to Egypt, to China? What do you think I studied in London, Paris, and Vienna? Except to learn the *old* mysteries that modern science has not yet rediscovered, the *natural true magic* modern psychology is beginning to understand. . . . I studied and learned, for a purpose, my dear."

The two words most often used to describe Welles—"mesmerizing" and "charisma"—were hardly hyperbole, for he indeed possessed the "natural true magic" of the most gifted performers. Amid a maelstrom of Madison Avenue's and Broadway's and Wall Street's misuse of power to subconsciously influence the masses, Welles employed both his natural charm and his acute theatrical skills to a white-magical end: to wake up his fellow citizens.

Site #5: *Superman*: Offices of Detective Comics, 225 Lafayette Street, June 1938

The writer Jerry Siegel and the illustrator Joe Shuster had tried since 1933 to find a publisher for their Superman character—originally a bald madman who used his telepathic abilities to wreak havoc on humanity. Reinventing him for the June 1938 debut of *Action Comics* as a force for good instead of evil, Siegel and Shuster unleashed

"The Reign of the Superman," short story by Jerry Siegel,
illustrated by Joe Shuster, 1933

a hydra-headed magical force into American—and soon world—
culture. Though it may be difficult to find "Supermen"—actual New
Yorkers possessed of supernormal powers who used them for benevolent purposes—along Broadway, after the imaginative birth of
Superman, fictional superheroes would see a population explosion.
Indeed, just months after *Superman #1*—the first comic devoted to
a single character—hit the newsstands in the spring of 1939, Batman
(whose alter ego, Bruce Wayne, owed much to Lamont Cranston)
made his debut in *Detective Comics #27*.

Shuster—who grew up in Cleveland—said that he modeled the
original Metropolis on Toronto, but by the fall of 1939, "Metropolis" was surely New York City; in *Superman #2*, Clark Kent sends a
telegram to George Taylor, the editor of the *Daily Star* (the precur-
sor to the *Daily Planet*), addressed to "Metropolis, N.Y." In the 1940s
Superman cartoons produced by Paramount Pictures and Fleischer

Studios, Superman lives on the island of Manhattan, where, in the seventh cartoon of the series, "Electric Earthquake," a Native American mad scientist, claims that his people are the rightful owners of the island. Though Superman comes from a distant planet "destroyed by old age," grows up as an orphan, and outruns trains and lifts automobiles, along with hurdling twenty-story buildings, he is The Shadow with a cape and tights; he is a champion of the underdog and oppressed and often, just like The Shadow, simultaneously frees the innocent while convicting the guilty. That these magical superpowers must come from some exotic place, that they must be wrapped in a cloak of secrecy, and that they only truly shine when opposed by equally supernaturally endowed villains suggests that the appetite for enchantment expressed by the twentieth-century creators of comic-book supermen, and their eager audiences, grew out of a particular species of historical disenchantment.

The advent of atomic science intersecting with the creation of the first American superhero set the stage for a battle of invisible magical powers. In February 1940, the *Adventures of Superman* radio drama—almost two full years before the United States entered World War II and a number of years before the Manhattan Project began—depicted a Superman foe called The Yellow Mask procuring steel tubes for his city-destroying "Atomic Beam" weapon. Once the United States entered the war, Superman's creators, at government insistence, steered clear of tales of atomic power; in January 1946, a story titled "The Battle of the Atoms" appeared in DC Comics' *Superman #38*, in which Superman's archenemy, Lex Luthor, launches an attack with what he calls an "atomic bomb." Though Luthor's "atomic bomb" in no way resembled an actual atomic bomb, the War Department in 1945 had demanded that the story's publication be delayed.

Site #6: The Manhattan Project: Childhood Home of
J. Robert Oppenheimer, 155 Riverside Drive, October 1942

It is completely fitting that the Manhattan Project, arguably the culmination of the wedding of US science and state power and the first
scientific project of truly global reach, should be christened with a
name that identifies it with this magic isle. As an endeavor of Promethean scope, its geographic extent in Manhattan is also large, taking in three-fourths of Broadway's length. From 25 Broadway (the
Cunard Building, which was in 1942 the home of the African Metals Corporation) and 233 Broadway (the Woolworth Building, whose
tenant the Kellex Corporation was the front company for the project's gas diffusion plant at Oak Ridge, Tennessee) north to Columbia
University's Pupin Hall (home to the university's Physics Department, where Enrico Fermi's initial experiments leading to the Manhattan Project were conducted in the basement) and 3310 Broadway
(the Nash Garage Building, where Columbia physicists produced
critical equipment for the Manhattan Project), Broadway was in-
arguably the backbone of the theoretical and practical engineering
and financial infrastructure that built the world's first atomic bomb.
In September 1942, under the direction of General Leslie Groves,
270 Broadway quietly became the original headquarters of the Manhattan Project; a staff of thousands on floors 11, 12, and 14 worked
unwittingly in support of the Columbia University physicists who
met here to develop the process for separating uranium isotopes.

There are other important Manhattan Project locations scattered
across the island: 261 Fifth Avenue, the second Manhattan Project
headquarters and home of raw-materials processing operations; and
30 East Forty-Second Street, where Union Carbide and Carbon Corporation discovered new sources of uranium ore and where General Groves, Columbia physicists, and Kellex Corporation staff met
in early 1943 to plan the Oak Ridge plant. Most importantly, there
is 155 Riverside Drive, up at the junction with Eighty-Eighth Street,
where in 1911, one could have looked through the gracious building's

J. Robert Oppenheimer

windows to watch the intense concentration of a seven-year-old boy there, as he sorted and labeled his rock and mineral collection. When he was not at his rocks, he was building elaborate structures with wooden blocks or reading and writing poetry. By age twelve, he would use the family typewriter to query American Museum of Natural History geologists about the bedrock of Central Park; one unsuspecting correspondent nominated him for membership in the New York Mineralogical Club, where the boy was soon invited to lecture. After the boy's proud parents introduced their son as "J. Robert Oppenheimer," the shy, awkward twelve-year-old read his prepared remarks and, according to Oppenheimer biographers Kai Bird and Martin Sherwin, "was given a hearty round of applause."

As Oppenheimer reflected on his boyhood in a 1963 interview, he said that he had no interest in the geological origins of the rocks but was fascinated by the structure of crystals and polarized light. His childhood and then his celebrated and complicated adulthood bear the unmistakable gesture of someone seeking to cross the threshold of matter, to work into the deep structure of the universe. Since we continue to live in the apocalyptic shadow of the weapon he built, we might consider that this American Prometheus is a modern magician, seeking to control deep forces of nature that had remained secret and guarded for millennia. Close study of his biography, like any biography, reveals a life poised between the highest ideals for social good and the most challenging dilemmas of compromise and capitulation. But for all the supernormal powers surveyed within these pages, it is only with J. Robert Oppenheimer and the Manhattan Project that we arrive at a truly world-destroying power, immortalized in Oppenheimer's quotation of Vishnu's remark to the Prince in the *Bhagavad Gita*: "Now I am become Death, the destroyer of worlds."

In the post-Hiroshima photographs of Oppenheimer, we can clearly see that death haunts him, hollowing out his cheekbones, furrowing his brow, turning his eyes into cold, lifeless pools that recognize and are stupefied by human monstrosity. Walk, if you will, along Riverside Drive from Eighty-Eighth Street to 105th Street, to the statue of Shinran Shonin, the founder in the twelfth century of a school of Buddhism. On August 6, 1945, this statue stood at the entrance to a temple in Hiroshima that was only a mile and a half from the center of the atomic blast that leveled 70 percent of the city's buildings and murdered 150,000 people. When the dust cleared, the statue stood unscathed before the burning remains of the temple. In 1955, the sculptor, Hirose Seiichi, a devout Jodo Shinshu Buddhist, had the bronze statue dismantled and shipped to New York.

By 1955, Robert Oppenheimer had withstood half a dozen years of harassment by the FBI (which had had him under close surveillance since 1941), Senator Joseph McCarthy's House Un-American Activities Committee, and the US Justice Department, all of which were uneasy with his sympathy with the Communist Party. Like tens of thousands of other Americans, Oppenheimer's misgivings about capitalism led him to explore socialist ideas. His misgivings about the ability of the state to morally wield massive technological power and the tendency of the state to interfere with scientific inquiry put him beyond the pale for the amoral technocrats—men like J. Edgar Hoover, Roy Cohn, John Foster Dulles and Allen Dulles, Lewis Strauss, and a host of others who played roles in persecuting Oppenheimer and so many other American liberals—who had gained the upper hand on US state power. Their deeds of secrecy, deception, and subterfuge unmistakably mark them out as the blackest of modern magicians, fascist by both the exoteric yardstick of wedding corporate to state power and the esoteric measure that their manipulations were *binding*, permitting no freedom of individuals to seek the highest individual good but enslaving them to the mass, mechanical magic of Mammon.

Site #7: Surrealism in New York: Beaux Arts Studios Building, 80 West Fortieth Street, May 8, 1948

Just six weeks before the Bell Labs transistor announcement and the publication of the first section of Claude Shannon's revolutionary paper on information theory, the Surrealist artist, printmaker, designer, and scholar of magic Kurt Seligmann emceed "An Evening of Magic" at his studio in the Beaux Arts Studios Building at 80 West Fortieth Street, fronting on Bryant Park. One of the first things he had done when he took the studio in 1939 upon his arrival from Switzerland was to install a nineteenth-century letterpress; in the next eight years, a steady flow of hermetic, alchemical, and other mantic images would flow from that press. On this evening of May 8,

Kurt Seligmann and Enrico Donati at "A Magic Evening" in Seligmann's studio, 1948 (Seligmann Center at the Orange County Citizens Foundation)

1948, Seligmann was celebrating the launch of his book *The Mirror of Magic*—which was crammed full of 250 woodcuts, diagrams, circles, seals, and other magical images from that press—by throwing an elegant, magically themed party in his Bryant Park studio. The celebrity guest list included the artist Enrico Donati, the painter Julio de Diego, the ceramist Carol Janeway, and the photographers Milton Gendel and Bernard Hoffman—Hoffman was a *Life* magazine photographer who was planning a photo-essay about the event.

In one of Hoffman's photographs, Seligmann stands with Donati in the center of a magic circle inscribed in white chalk with Archangelic names: Michael, Dardiel, and Hurapatal. Taking their tableau's inspiration directly from John Dee's *A True and Faithful Relation of What Passed for Many Years between Dr. Dee and Some Spirits* (1659), the two men—Seligmann playing the spirit medium Edward Kelley as he reads an incantation, Donati playing the role of the necromancer Dee, holding a torch—mock-enacted a summoning-of-the-dead ritual described in Seligmann's book. Donati's *Fist* (1946) sculpture, with its fingers clutched around an evil eye, a Chinese tripod incense vessel, candles, and a human skull decorate the outer ring of the magic circle. In another Hoffman photograph, Seligmann demonstrates a popular seventeenth-century divination practice, marking moles onto Carol Janeway's face and shoulder. In another photograph, Julio de Diego, wearing a bearded and owl-bedecked paper mask and holding a prayer book, approaches the magic circle while bending over in supplication.

The linguist and classical scholar Harry Wedeck, in his review of *The Mirror of Magic* for the *New York Times*, described Seligmann's lifelong quest to discover the rationale behind magic: "It is magic that, far from being a mere accumulation of unique phenomena illustrative of the persistence of human aberrations, is an attempt on man's part, recurrent in every age, to synthesize all human knowledge." Perhaps this generous—and wholly uncharacteristic—equanimity on the part of the *New York Times* was a result of the previous decade of magical celebration brought to New York by the Surrealists. Seligmann was both the first to arrive from Europe (Basel, Switzerland—Paracelsus's old stomping grounds) and, as wave upon wave of Surrealist refugees from Europe arrived in New York, their answer man about magic. Seligmann held both within his astonishing library and more importantly within his voluminous library of mental images a treasure house of arcana.

One of the favorite magical image repositories (and generators) of the Surrealists was the Tarot. André Breton, Marcel Duchamp, Seligmann, and other Surrealists returned to it repeatedly for inspiration and guidance. In 1940, while stranded for months with other

Surrealist Tarot cards, 1940
(Cornell University Library, Rare and Manuscript Collections)

writers and intellectuals in Marseilles as they attempted to escape
Nazi-occupied Europe (the Surrealists came in for especially intense
persecution, having been labeled "decadent" by Hitler), Breton imagined a collective revisioning of the classical Tarot deck, featuring
such magical modern personalities as the German idealist philosopher G. F. Hegel ("Genius") and the nineteenth-century psychic and
automatic writer Hélène Smith ("Mermaid").

One could as easily assemble a complete Tarot deck of Major and Minor Arcana out of the extraordinary cast of characters, both natives and exiles, who found each other in New York City during World War II. Those snapshots from Seligmann's 1948 Magical Evening could be multiplied to illustrate the entire decade: Kurt Seligmann's sets and costumes for *The Golden Fleece*, a ballet about alchemy, at the Mansfield Theater on West Forty-Seventh Street, in March 1941; the spectacular "Artists in Exile" photo taken at Peggy Guggenheim's Beekman Place mansion in 1942; the magical window display advertising Denis de Rougemont's *Le part du diable*, created in January 1943 by Seligman, Breton, and Duchamp for Brentano's; Maya Deren's photographs of the "Lazy Hardware" display at the Gotham Book Mart in April 1945, for Breton's *Arcane 17*; Anaïs Nin's March 1946 diary snapshot of the film shoot, with Nin, the young Gore Vidal (her current lover), and the dancers Rita Christiani and Frank Westbrook at Maya Deren's Morton Street loft.

"Snapshots" of course, will hardly do, as this was a mercurially metamorphic assemblage of artists, thrown together in Greenwich Village at what was perhaps the darkest moment in human history. Their intense impulse toward magic was part of a larger impulse to substitute art for religion, as a way of heightening reality, life, and the meaning of the human being. Film was now part of the artistic repertoire, and only cinema could possibly capture the dynamism of this Surrealist-stewarded reexamination of reality that transpired on this magic isle in the 1940s. It is possible through the magic of the internet to call up Maya Deren's 1946 film *Ritual in Transfigured Time* and experience something of the splendor and wonder of that coven of young artists. The "now you see it, now you don't" ballet between Deren and Christiani, the slow-motion choreography of the cocktail-party collisions, and the stop-motion freezing of Frank Westbrook's lithe, ever-reaching form in midair bring to us across time some frisson of recognition, that we too yearn to transfigure time, to ritually insert ourselves between the interstices we intuit there.

Site #8: The Birth of the Information Age: Bell Laboratories Building, 463 West Street, June 30, 1948

"We have called it the Transistor," the Bell Labs spokesman Ralph Bown began, slowly spelling out the name for the assembled reporters, "because it is a resistor or semiconductor device which can amplify electrical signals as they are transferred through it." Compared to the bulky vacuum tubes inside radios, phonographs, and telephones, the transistor could accomplish the very same amplification and do it much better, wasting far less power. Editors at the *New York Times* were intrigued enough to mention the invention in the next day's issue, but they buried the story on page 46: "In the shape of a small metal cylinder about a half-inch long, the transistor contains no vacuum, grid, plate or glass envelope to keep the air away. Its action is instantaneous, there being no warm-up delay since no heat is developed as in a vacuum tube."

The building where the press conference was held had already seen a remarkable series of technological breakthroughs: the first vacuum tube (1912), condenser microphone (1913), cross-continental phone service (1915), radar (1919), high-fidelity sound recording (1925), sound motion pictures (1926), television transmissions (1927), the digital computer (1938). These were the technologies that so frightened Orson Welles, as potential handmaidens of fascist political states. The transistor set the stage for the closest thing to vanishing a lady or an elephant: miniaturization, a development completed in 1954 here at Bell Labs with the invention of the silicon solar cell, that is, the silicon chip.

There was one missing ingredient to transform the transistor-powered and miniaturized electronic brain into the modern supercomputer: some way of turning information into digital signals. That same summer of 1948, in a tiny office in the same massive Bell Labs complex on West Street, the mathematician, electrical engineer, and cryptographer (as well as stage magician/juggler) Claude Shannon finished a paper titled "A Mathematical Theory of Communication."

Bell Labs inventors of the transistor (*from left*) John Bardeen,
William Shockley, and Walter Brattain, 1948

The paper opened by asserting that "the fundamental problem of communication is that of reproducing at one point, either exactly or approximately, a message selected at another point." Embedded within Shannon's paper were the ideas of information entropy, the redundancy of a source, channel capacity, and the bit—a new way of seeing the most fundamental unit of information.

Perhaps some future cultural historian looking back on the geographic—even *etheric geographic*—dimension of the invention of the personal computer will make a pilgrimage to Westbeth (the dynamic residential artists community that reinhabited Bell Labs beginning in the late 1960s) and the surrounding streets of the West Village, juggling the information that in the early '40s, when Claude Shannon was working on information theory, his downstairs neighbor at 51 West Eleventh Street was the anthropologist Claude Lévi-Strauss, whose ideas about the shaping of human culture had curious points of intersection with Shannon's work. Was it only *chance* that saw the composer John Cage in 1943–1944 living at 550 Hudson Street, just a few blocks from Westbeth, tossing the *I Ching* eighty to one hundred times before going to sleep, so as to arise the next morning with his compositional program laid out for him? Another six blocks south, at 61 Morton Street, the filmmaker Maya Deren was playing chess regularly with Marcel Duchamp and integrating into her 1943 *Witch's Cradle* the sort of magical string figures that so fascinated him and Lévi-Strauss.

The dense, delicate, often ephemeral network of friendship and collegiality that permeated the West Village in the 1940s and '50s was like one of those string figures, passed from hand to hand, alternately tightening and loosening as it went, shifting configurations seemingly magically—as Maya Deren so exquisitely captured with her films. All of these sensitive, creative souls were performing a very time-specific alchemy, digesting old forms and birthing new ones, at the cusp of the "Information Age." Their fascination for juggling, the *I Ching*, chess, string figures, children's street games, and dozens of other divinatory systems seems an expression of a kind of intuitive counterimpulse to the shrinking of the Cosmos that the technicians at Bell Labs were effecting. With every analytical step the engineers made toward compressing data into transistors and silicon chips, these artists were making synthetic countermoves in the direction of the unseen, opening up new spaces of movement, where the human body and mind might magically stretch and leap like the dancers in Deren's cinematic dreams.

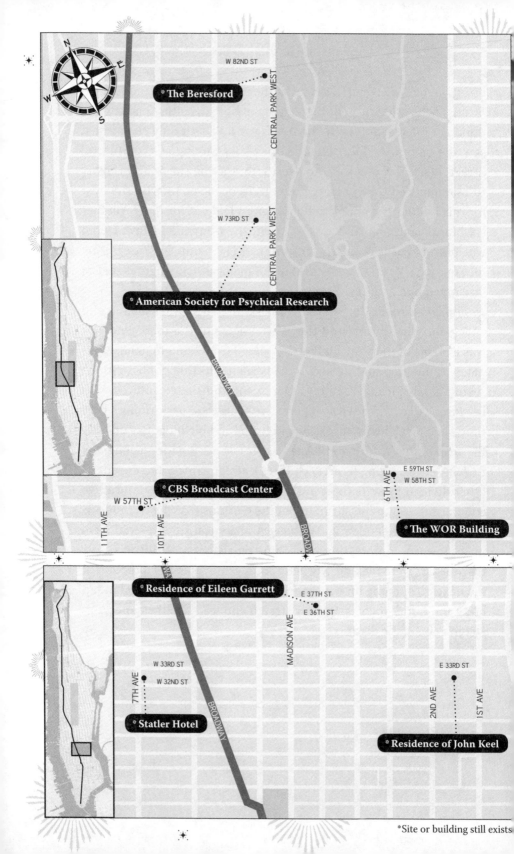

*Site or building still exists

Sinister Manhattan

1952–1981

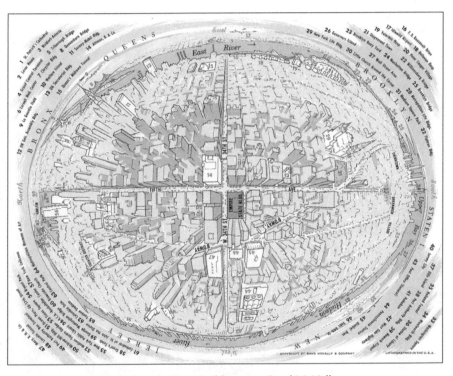

Atop the Empire State Building map, Rand McNally, 1952
(David Rumsey Map Collection)

In the 1950s, both historians and cultural critics employed the German sociologist Max Weber's terms "enchantment" and "disenchantment" to help understand the twentieth century; an alchemist might instead espy clear signs of *coagula* (solidification) and *solve* (dissolution). Twentieth-century science and technology—epitomized by the invention and use of the atomic bomb and atomic power—carried the nineteenth century's penetration of the subearthly forces of electricity and magnetism to even greater depths, as its models (or "idols") of matter colonized the popular consciousness. Computing, statistics, transistorization, and mass adoption of electronic appliances democratized mechanical modes of production and *solidified* all dimensions of human existence. Simultaneously these same developments and others—psychoanalysis, radioactivity, parapsychology—fostered a distinct trend of *dissolution*. From a magico-alchemical and metahistorical point of view, humanity, most spectacularly in its cosmopolitan urban-industrial centers, had clearly entered the last phase of the Kali Yuga, a stepwise stasis of matter and spirit at the conclusion of the Iron Age. The great cosmic rhythms standing behind time demanded an antipodal impulse of *solve*, to free up the forces and potentialities momentarily frozen in the *coagula* of modern materialism.

One can retrospectively recognize this dynamic tension between *coagula* and *solve* in the opposed but parallel productions of the Manhattan Project and the Greenwich Village Surrealists. In 1953, a book appeared—René Guénon's *The Reign of Quantity and the Signs of the Times*—that despite its own cautions about the dangers and deceptiveness of "prophecies," uncannily prophesied the proliferation of similarly opposed but complementary magical currents in the second half of the twentieth century. Written by Guénon in 1949, two years before his death, the first English edition of *Le règne de la quantité et les signes des temps* was published in London, translated by the farmer, philosopher, writer, and Olympic Gold Medal rower Walter James, Lord Northbourne (1896–1982). The coiner of the term "organic farming" and its first promoter in the English-speaking world, Northbourne recognized Guénon's prophetic cultural diagnosis as supportive of his initiative to replace industrialized chemical agriculture with a life-enhancing *alchemical* agriculture. Guénon's magnum opus took as axiomatic that "the lowest reality is the least stable," and hence the dense, petrified, coagulated world of midcentury would soon see an explosion of dissolution in the wake of its utter exhaustion. Guénon saw this simultaneous solidification and dissolution of matter and spirit as ushering in an unprecedented unleashing of diabolic entities and forces, through the "fissures" in reality opened up by Promethean twentieth-century civilization. Via an insistent distinction between the psychic and the spiritual and unconscious versus conscious magic, a recognition of the incipient convergence of occultism and science, and most prophetically the prediction of an unleashing of Satanic forms, Guénon's work—founded in traditional metaphysics—offers a profound philosophical position from which to assess and understand the culmination of *coagula* and *solve* along Broadway in the late twentieth century.

Somewhat arbitrarily isolated here as discrete moments and locations where both the "reign of quantity" and the "signs of the times" can be glimpsed, these episodes might best be arranged as interpenetrating mandalas or hyperlinked planes of action. The stunning but mostly sinister—in its sense of a left-hand magical path—intersections and overlaps of parapsychology, covert state operations, pharmaceutical millenarianism, criminal activity, and mass media are best comprehended as what Guénon soberly called them: "the end of the world," the tragic but necessary exhaustion of culture at the end of a cosmic cycle.

Site #1: Adventures in the Supernormal: Residence of
Eileen Garrett, 220 Madison Avenue, February 16, 1952

When the Irish psychic medium Eileen Garrett arrived in New York
City in 1940, she was renowned in Great Britain for having received
from the craft's deceased captain very specific—and correct—
technical information about the crash of a British dirigible in 1930.
Psychic since childhood, she became a trance medium in 1926 while
attending a séance in London, when suddenly an invisible entity calling itself "Uvani" began to speak through her, inviting the séance participants to communicate with their dead loved ones through him.
Uvani said that he was an Arabian soldier from the fourteenth century; soon he was joined by another spectral visitor—"Abdul Latif"—
who, identifying himself as a seventeenth-century Persian physician,
manifested for healing purposes. Garrett herself was always unsure
if either of these "spirits" were who they claimed to be, believing
instead that they were more like the fays whom she had known since
she was a young child. To test whether these were really independent
beings or fragments of Garrett's subconscious, the American para-
psychologist Hereward Carrington in 1931 administered personality
tests. While Garrett listed "generous, honest, forgiving, and conscientious" as her most positive traits, Uvani gave "honesty, physique,
vigor and swordsmanship." For negative traits, Garrett gave "indif-
ferent, too sensitive, unsocial and over-critical," Uvani "irresponsi-
ble, desire for bloodshed, desire to rule his household, inability to
forgive and forget easily." When Carrington interviewed Uvani about
his nature and methods, he explained that since Garrett's childhood,
he was able to "impress himself upon her underconsciousness" the
moment she entered sleep or trance.

Along with possessing a whole suite of psychic abilities, Eileen
Garrett was an irresistible personality who by 1952 had gathered
around herself New York City's most devoted students, practitioners, and spectators of occult phenomena. As seems to be true in
every historical era, this magic-seeking social circle included many

Eileen Garrett

of Manhattan's social, cultural, and financial elite. Garrett's pent-
house apartment at the John Murray House across Madison Avenue from the Morgan Library was often the meeting ground for
this crowd, which had a prodigious appetite for "adventures in the
supernormal"—the title of Garrett's 1949 memoir, published by
her Creative Age Press. Having sold this very successful publishing
house to Farrar, Straus and Young in 1951, she founded the Parapsychology Foundation and turned from being the subject of study by
the world's leading parapsychologists to stewarding, funding, and
promoting others' work. At a party at her home on February 16, 1952,
the guests gathered around the trance medium Dr. D. G. Vinod, a
professor of philosophy and psychology from the University of
Poona, and Dr. Andrija Puharich, who was conducting research in
"experimental electrobiology" that depended heavily on the use of

trance mediums. Holding the middle joint of Puharich's right ring finger, Vinod entered a trance and then recited Puharich's biography in breathtaking detail, going beyond the past to *future* events. The two men would within the year meet again at Puharich's "laboratory" in Maine, where they unleashed an entity that called itself "The Nine," which would end up as a spectral player in everything from the CIA's MK-ULTRA program to the JFK assassination, archaeological digs in Egypt, the spoon-bending psychic Uri Geller, and *Star Trek*. One of The Nine later told Geller that they were behind the worldwide explosion of UFOs, beginning with Kenneth Arnold's 1947 "flying saucer" encounter.

Eileen Garrett's magazine *Tomorrow*, begun in 1941, covered topics—Atlantis, poltergeists, ghosts, fairies, witches, vampires, and a host of Fortean phenomena—that even the parapsychological journals would not touch. Like the *siddhi*—the Hindu term for magical powers—that Garrett and a growing number of individuals exhibited, these phenomena were not supernormal but *subnormal*; that is, they all depended on the activity of beings below the human. Though Garrett herself performed a number of exorcisms of possessed people—including the socialite Jane Kendall Mason Gingrich, fictionalized by Martin Ebon in *The Devil's Bride: Exorcism, Past and Present* (1974)—and places, she never entertained that her own familiar spirits may have been of a similar nature, that is, elemental beings of the etheric realm. Garret was a gifted healer thanks to her own qualities, and her elementals were always a blessing to others and herself. She could not guarantee that similar benevolence would attend Puharich, Vinod, or others who pursued the parapsychological path of magic.

Site #2: MK-ULTRA Subproject 8: Statler Hotel, 401 Seventh Avenue, June 8, 1953

Nine months after Andrija Puharich had his life history psychically read by Dr. Vinod, he gave a talk to Pentagon officials titled "An

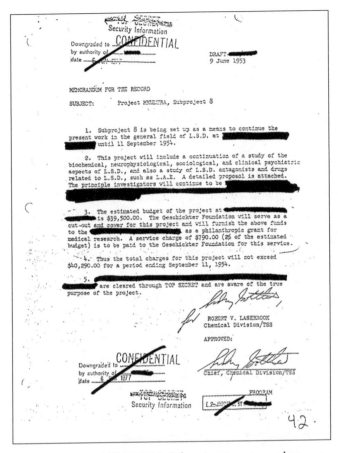

CIA Project MK-ULTRA, Subproject 8 memorandum

Evaluation of the Possible Usefulness of Extrasensory Perception in Psychological Warfare." The very next day, Puharich—whose medical education had been funded by the Army Medical Corps—was redrafted into the Army and then assigned to the Army Chemical Center in Edgewood, Maryland. The next decade would see Puharich evangelizing within the intelligence and military establishment in favor of the use of parapsychology as a weapon, as well as conducting CIA- and Army-funded research on hallucinogens, hypnosis, and psychic spying techniques.

On June 8, 1953, the federal narcotics agents George White, Vance Newman, and Arthur Guiliani, the Narcotics Bureau "special agent" Pierre Lafitte, and the CIA officers Sidney Gottlieb, Robert Lashbrook, Henry Bortner, and Ray Treichler met in a third-floor conference room of the Statler Hotel to be taught sleight-of-hand magic techniques by America's most famous magician, John Mulholland, who had recently been hired to produce a manual on such magic for the CIA. Its working title was *Some Operational Applications of the Art of Deception*. The meeting was the first of eight instructional sessions, concentrating on techniques for surreptitiously administering doses of LSD and other hallucinogens at close quarters. With the enthusiastic support of the former Wall Street banker Allen Dulles, director of the CIA, his clubfooted chemist confederate Dr. Sidney Gottlieb—known also as "Merlin," the "Black Sorcerer," and the "Dirty Trickster"—was about to embark on a vast expansion of the government's psychological warfare program. The day after the Statler Hotel tutorial with the magician Mulholland, Gottlieb signed a memo authorizing $40,000 for Subproject 8 of the top-secret MK-ULTRA program, accelerating the existing program of weaponizing LSD.

The CIA's appetite for "MK"—code for "mind control"—had been fed for a decade by parapsychology's demonstrations of telepathy, ESP, and other clairvoyance, which were all seen as potentially useful avenues for espionage, torture, and assassination. The tens of thousands of drab redacted documents like the memo seen in the illustration accompanying this site description portray a vast bureaucratic banalization of evil that was ultimately founded on the desire for magical powers. Mulholland's manual, Subproject 4, received continued CIA support in Subprojects 19 and 34, "More Support to Magic." In Subproject 121, the McGill University transcultural psychiatrist Dr. Raymond Prince conducted research on witch doctors; Subproject 136 funded ESP research. In Subproject 13, George White rented an apartment at 81 Bedford Street in Greenwich Village, where he instructed a group of young women in Mulholland's techniques to give unsuspecting johns LSD, to study its effectiveness both as a "truth serum" and for the creation of a mind-controlled "Manchurian Candidate." Those who took part in the deception called Subproject 13 "Operation Midnight Climax."

While keen to monopolize every imaginable occult power, Dulles, Gottlieb, and many of the other men running MK-ULTRA did not necessarily believe in magic. The archskeptic Mulholland—who both continued Houdini's magical-debunking career and presaged James Randi—was on occasion sent to oversee Puharich's experiments to see if he could detect any sleight-of-hand deception. Mulholland and Puharich detested each other, the stage magician because he was unsure if Puharich was a charlatan or an actual wizard, the psychic sorcerer because Mulholland profaned his black parapsychological art with his cynical unbelief.

In November 1953, another of Puharich's skeptical foes within the MK-ULTRA mind-control complex—Frank Olson, a Camp Detrick chemist whose specialty was formulating methods to aerosolize anthrax and other biological weapons (George White in 1950 had actually detonated an aerosol device to release vaporized LSD in a New York City subway car)—came to New York City with Gottlieb's deputy Robert Lashbrook to visit Dr. Harold Abramson at his 133 East Fifty-Eighth Street office. Olson and Abramson had known each other for ten years, having first worked together on a classified Army research project involving chemotherapeutic aerosols. What began as research to protect American soldiers from aerial gas attacks had by 1950 morphed into a massive program to develop deadly biologi- cal warfare agents. Olson and Abramson had also often attended meetings in New York to develop "truth drugs" to be used in inter- rogation. In the months leading up to Olson's visit to Abramson, he had begun to question the morality of his work, and the CIA was concerned that he was spilling dark secrets—like the CIA's August 1951 mass poisoning of the French village of Pont-St.-Esprit by aero- solized LSD. Olson had been the head of the CIA's Special Opera- tions Division at the time and was probably involved in the planning and execution of this "experiment," which killed five people. At Gottlieb's instruction, Lashbrook had taken Olson to see his old colleague in hopes of learning whether Olson intended to make public any of the secret CIA programs. Just nine days before their New York City trip, Olson and others had been unwittingly given a massive dose of LSD in hopes that it might cause Olson to reveal his state of mind and possible whistleblowing plans.

Following the call on Abramson, Lashbrook and Olson checked into room 1018A of the Statler Hotel and after dinner and cocktails watched TV in their room until about 11:00 p.m.. At 2:30 a.m., as a Statler doorman was rounding the corner of Thirty-Third Street and Seventh Avenue, he saw something falling. It was a man, twisting and grabbing at the air as he fell before striking a construction awning and landing on the sidewalk in front of the hotel's entrance. The man was Frank Olson, who had been hit on the head and then thrown through the tenth-floor window of his hotel room by Pierre Lafitte and François Spirito, French gangsters who had met in the Marseille drug trade in 1939. Lafitte was masquerading as the Statler doorman "Jean Martin" in 1953; he was George White's principal operative in running drugs, shaking down informants, and other criminal escapades.

Only five months had passed since Lafitte, Lashbrook, Gottlieb, and White had come for their training with Mulholland at the Statler. Each played a key role in murdering Frank Olson; but it would be fifty years for that truth to come out, and all the conspirators were already dead. To keep secret that the US government conducted biological warfare with Earth's deadliest poisons, experimented with hallucinogens and other chemicals on tens of thousands of innocent service members, prisoners, asylum patients, and even children, and murdered anyone who might divulge any information about the many illegal, amoral, and unethical "subprojects" of MK-ULTRA, the CIA merely doubled down on its wholly Satanic program. Killing Frank Olson ensured that no one might challenge the Cold War United States' black-magical mobilization of cutting-edge science, parapsychology, psychedelics, and even stage magic to fortify its empire.

Site #3: Contactees on the Long John Nebel Radio Show: The WOR Building, 1440 Avenue of the Americas, June 21, 1957

Perhaps one could say about white magic what Jackie Gleason once said about his friend Long John Nebel, that he "opens your mind and tells you the world is bigger than you thought it was." In a decade that saw the fear-driven panic of McCarthyism, Cold War secrecy and paranoia, and a national wave of conformity and conservatism, Nebel's all-night radio show on WOR broke rules, violated boundaries, and laughed at itself as much as at others, opening up a welcome space of freedom amid a time of claustrophobic constraint. Nebel was himself an expanded world, the perfect foil and rudder for the dizzying vortex of tales about voodoo, witchcraft, parapsychology, hypnotism, conspiracy theories, ghosts, and flying saucers that he broadcast out into the night. The archskeptic Nebel was a classic magus, igniting the imaginations of a nation by permitting and cultivating free discourse that always entertained the possibility of other dimensions of existence. Given the straightjacket of 1950s cultural containment, it is no wonder that Long John Nebel and his audience longed for contact with other worlds as a release from this one.

"Contactee" was still a new word in 1956, when the former salesman and auctioneer John Nebel took over Jean Shepherd's all-night show, but Nebel's free-wheeling repartee with contactees became the show's hallmark. On June 21, 1957, he hosted in the studio Hans Stefan Santeson, editor of *Fantastic Universe*; Morris K. Jessup, author of *The Expanding Case for UFOs* (1957); Dan Fry, arguably America's first postwar contactee, who claimed that a spaceship picked him up from the White Sands Proving Ground and flew to New York City and back in thirty-two minutes; and George Van Tassell, who, after having met the occupants of a space ship from

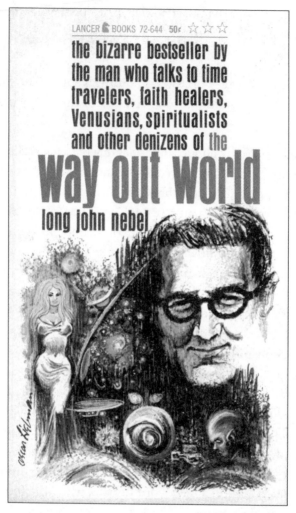

LANCER BOOKS 72-644 50¢ ☆ ☆ ☆

the bizarre bestseller by
the man who talks to time
travelers, faith healers,
Venusians, spiritualists
and other denizens of the

way out world

long john nebel

Cover of Long John Nebel's *Way Out World*, 1961

Venus, was telepathically given plans for a machine to rejuvenate the human body, after they had demonstrated it by disintegrating and then restoring the crushed head of a desert lizard.

The skeptical Santeson opened the show by reading a passage from a recent article in his magazine: "UFOs themselves may be alive. This is to say they may be a life form either equivalent to, but not specifically, animal, vegetable, or virus that may dwell in the upper atmosphere of this or all planets or live in space itself." Santeson challenged the contactees to state whether they agreed or disagreed with this theory, and George Van Tassel soberly replied that in his experience, the craft were mechanical objects that moved by levitation. Inside were creatures shaped like an electric lightbulb or, more exactly, "like the comic strip *Shmoo*, except they have thirty-two eyes in a ring completely around their head, and a field around their body that can ward off our machine gun bullets."

Invariably, after the contactees' fantastic reports, Nebel would respectfully ask the most down-to-earth questions—what language do they speak? what do they eat?—or admit, "I'm still a little confused," and permit the contactee to elaborate. To listen to the archival recordings of these multihour conversations now, one is struck by their innocence and equanimity (Nebel and his guests often preface their replies with "In all fairness . . ."). The far-away, nasal, deadpan banter between Nebel and his contactees, broken by the occasional news report about the Korean Armistice Agreement or an irresistible Long John sales pitch for a sponsor's product, only underscores that in spite of all the earnest conversation conducted six nights a week over nearly two decades, no consensus ever emerged about the nature of the alien visitors or the ghosts, vampires, and other paranormal phenomena that titillated the fancies of Nebel's enormous audience.

An inveterate, adept prankster, Long John Nebel was at first suspected to be staging a prank when, shortly after marrying the former pinup girl and model Candy Jones in December 1972, he claimed to have discovered that she had spent a dozen years as a CIA mind-controlled courier. Under hypnosis conducted by Nebel, his wife revealed an altogether terrifying episode of "contact." Not only had CIA hypnotists tortured her to test the effectiveness of the alternate personality they created, but fearful that she was—like Frank Olson— about to reveal their identities and deeds, they had programmed her to throw herself off a cliff in the Bahamas. The marriage to Nebel saved her life.

Like so many of the arcane topics discussed in the wee hours by Long John Nebel and his guests, the workings of destiny are invisible and thus appear to us as inexplicable magic. The most salient lesson that anyone might draw from the contactees, hypnotists, and ghost hunters is that all human beings draw to themselves their own menagerie of invisible beings, good and bad—including the higher selves of other human beings. Whether by conscious ceremonial magic or by unconscious focusing of our attention (even by the seemingly innocuous act of listening to late-night talk radio), crossing the threshold of the physical world into the psychic/astral realm attracts and engenders invisible forces and beings. Every time we think, we are already in the "other world"—the spiritual world—and so the quality of that world shall always be consonant with those thoughts. That the skeptical prankster should by his love save his beloved's life is the ultimate contact, touching into a magic that will always prevail over any other.

Site #4: *UFOs: Friends, Foes, or Fantasy*: CBS Broadcast Center, 524 West Fifty-Seventh Street, May 10, 1966

Manhattanites have had unsettling encounters with elemental beings ever since Henry Hudson sailed the *Haeve Maen* up Mahicantuk and spied Lenape villages along the shore. But in the perpetual daylight of electrified, neonized mid-twentieth-century Broadway, spectral encounters of the third kind were relatively rare. In the timeless tradition of city slickers looking down on the eccentric ways of rural folk, the parade of contactees of the 1950s and '60s—almost without exception from isolated village outposts—was embarrassing to the enlightened readers of the *New York Times* and the *Wall Street Journal*. This sophisticated superiority ended in November 1965, when, during the largest electrical blackout in American history, thousands of people saw UFOs practically scrape their enigmatic bellies on the

COMMONLY REPORTED UFO TYPES

These basic shapes, generalized from hundreds of UFO reports, represent with reasonable accuracy virtually all UFOs that have been reliably described in detail. Extraneous details (portholes, projections, body lights, etc.) have been eliminated. Examples of each type appear in left-hand column.

This information and the chart reprinted from
The UFO Evidence, with permission of NICAP

UFO SHAPE	BOTTOM VIEW	BOTTOM ANGLE	SIDE VIEW
1. FLAT DISC A. 10-54 Cox 7-2-52 Newhouse B. 7-9-47 Johnson 7-14-52 Nash	oval	A B	A *lens-shaped* B *coin-like*
2. DOMED DISC A. 9-21-58 Fitzgerald 4-24-62 Gasslein B. 5-11-50 Trent 8-7-52 Jansen		A *hat-shaped* B	A *World War I helmet* B
3. SATURN DISC (Double dome) A. 10-4-54 Selandia 1-16-58 Trindade 10-2-61 Harris B. 8-20-56 Moore	A B elliptical or *winged oval*	A *diamond-shaped*	A *Saturn-shaped* B
4. HEMISPHERICAL DISC 9-24-59 Redmond 1-21-61 Pullian 2-7-61 Malloy		*parachute*	*mushroom* *half moon*
5. FLATTENED SPHERE 10-1-48 Gorman 4-27-50 Adickes 10-9-51 C.A.A.			sometimes with peak
6. SPHERICAL (Circular from all angles) 3-45 Delarof 1-20-52 Buller 10-12-61 Edwards metallic-appearing ball	A	B ball of glowing light	
7. ELLIPTICAL 12-20-58 Arbereon 11-2-57 Levelland 8-13-60 Carson	*football* *egg-shaped*		
8. TRIANGULAR 5-7-56 G.O.C. 5-22-60 Majorca			*tear-drop*
9. CYLINDRICAL (Rocket-like) 8-1-46 Puckett 7-23-48 Chiles	*cigar-shaped*	10. LIGHT SOURCE ONLY *star-like* or *planet-like*	

Chart of UFO shapes from 1967 Dell Publishing Company's
Flying Saucers: UFO Reports (CIA Reading Room,
https://www.cia.gov/library/readingroom/docs/
CIA-RDP81R00560R000100010002-9.pdf)

city's skyscrapers. Twenty minutes after the blackout began, a group of Time-Life employees saw a large luminous object hovering outside their building on Sixth Avenue. A *Time* photographer snapped a photo of the object, and the magazine published it in its next issue. Though officials attributed the blackout to a "broken relay," speculation was rampant that the UFOs had knocked out the city's—and much of the Northeast's—power. The Associated Press picked up the story, which was so widely reprinted that the whole world heard about the spaceships over Gotham. In March 1966, House Minority Leader Gerald Ford called for a congressional inquiry on UFOs, largely irked at the derision aimed by government officials and big-city papers at some of his UFO-witnessing rural-Michigan constituents, during that state's own recent "flap"—the term used by ufologists for significant sightings of extraterrestrial craft.

Skeptical keepers of the cultural order were now forced to pay attention. In May 1966, IBM sponsored the *CBS Reports* documentary *UFOS: Friend, Foe, or Fantasy*. Firmly anchored in quotidian reality by the always reassuring presence of the narrator Walter Cronkite, embracing a visual and audio rhetoric of realism in its focus on the scientific via a procession of interviews with astronomers and military officials, Cronkite's report unambiguously framed the UFO enigma within the last of its three alternative explanations. As the film opens, Cronkite sits calmly in a chair while the Milky Way galaxy spins behind him. He asks, "How thin is the line between science and science fiction? Is there anyone out there, and are they headed our way?"

The film's longest segment—the penultimate moment before Cronkite authoritatively pronounces, "While fantasy improves science fiction, science is more often served by *facts*"—features the astronomers Thornton Page of the University of Chicago (who had served in 1952 on a CIA panel investigating UFOs) and Carl Sagan of Cornell, sitting together on a couch to share their scientific wisdom. Page—smiling somewhat ambiguously so one does not know whether he is fibbing or just uncomfortable discussing the subject so publicly—reports that his panel's findings were negative, but as Sagan follows his opening, "There's not a single verified report that is at all connectable with the possibility of extraterrestrial life," with the qualifier, "That isn't to say I don't think extraterrestrial life is impossible," Page becomes visibly uncomfortable, lighting up his pipe as Sagan rhapsodizes about the likelihood of vastly advanced technical civilizations in outer space.

Watching it now, Sagan's four-minute soliloquy looks like the opening gambit for his and Frank Drake's hieroglyphic extraterrestrial message affixed to a gold-anodized aluminum plaque on the *Pioneer* spacecraft in 1972. Like George Van Tassel and other contactees and the wider American public, the great allure of extraterrestrial beings for Sagan was their magical abilities—whether telepathy or advanced technology. As Sagan would soon demonstrate with his popular books and *Cosmos* PBS series, the scientifically scrutinized cosmos could still be *sublime* and harbor the promise of magic.

Site #5: Operation Trojan Horse: Residence of John Keel, 330 East Thirty-Third Street, December 15, 1967

On December 15, 1967, the New York City writer John Keel and a friend were in Keel's Murray Hill apartment watching the televised White House Christmas-tree-lighting ceremony. It was for Keel a moment of welcome calm after nearly a year and a half of intermittent but incessant pandemonium. The public fascination for UFOs in the wake of the *Time* (then *Life, Look, Reader's Digest, Saturday Evening Post,* and *Popular Science*) article had prompted *Playboy* to commission a feature article from Keel, and due to his usual manic thoroughness, the piece had grown to eighty-six manuscript pages before the magazine eventually killed it. Shortly after he had begun his research, a tidal wave of weird events far beyond the mere appearance of UFOs had enveloped him. Keel felt that the phenomenon—which he had dubbed "Operation Trojan Horse," to highlight its devilishly deceptive scope—had "zeroed in" on him:

Luminous aerial objects seemed to follow me around like faithful dogs. The objects seemed to know where I was going and where I had been. I would check into a motel chosen at random only to find that someone had made a reservation in my name and had even left a string of nonsensical phone messages for me. I was plagued by impossible coincidences, and some of my closest friends in New York . . . began to report strange experiences of their own—poltergeists erupted in their apartments, ugly smells of hydrogen sulphide haunted them. One girl of my acquaintance suffered an inexplicable two-hour mental blackout while sitting under a hair dryer alone in her own apartment. More than once I woke up in the middle of the night to find myself unable to move, with a huge dark apparition standing over me.

By May 1966, Keel expected an imminent invasion of aliens, whom he believed had plans to drop chemicals into reservoirs all over the Earth that would then trigger a conversion of the atmosphere to ammonia and methane—the gases he thought the creatures breathed. Keel had purchased a couple of gas masks, but these would be of little use protecting against nuclear radiation; he was certain that the thirty atomic bomb tests conducted in the past six months were preparation by the US government for total war with the aliens.

The sightings in West Virginia of the Garuda—Keel's name (borrowed from Hindu mythology) for the red-eyed, muscular flying monster with the ten-foot wingspan—had begun in November 1966, and Keel within the month had begun going out to West Virginia periodically to investigate. This started up a whole new cycle of inexplicable, topsy-turvy, yet altogether mundane events both for him and for a wide circle of his associates. "Things are terribly complicated now," he had written on November 3, 1967, to his Point Pleasant friend Mary Hyre, a reporter at the local paper who had both chronicled the monster's exploits and had her own run-ins with the "Men in Black" who had accompanied the UFO/Garuda (aka Mothman) outbreak. Keel confessed to Hyre that he expected a disaster—"a plant along the Ohio River may either blow up or burn down"—to occur soon in the Point Pleasant area. "There are weird and frightening days ahead for all of us," Keel told her, before advising her to "wear the gold cross all the time."

On that December 15 evening, Keel had tuned in to the Christmas-tree-ceremony broadcast because his "mysterious friends"—the spectral ones who called him so often on the phone—had repeatedly

Operation Trojan Horse

AN EXHAUSTIVE STUDY OF UNIDENTIFIED
FLYING OBJECTS - REVEALING THEIR
SOURCE AND THE FORCES THAT
CONTROL THEM

by John A. Keel

For my good friend Håkan Blomqvist—
The secret To The UFOs is on
page 321.

John A. Keel
Oct. 18, 1976

London SOUVENIR PRESS LTD.

Title page of John Keel's *Operation Trojan Horse*,
with Keel's inscription to the Swedish ufologist
Håkan Blomqvist; the book ends on page 320
(Håkan Blomqvist)

told him to tune in and that something important would happen. Keel—who well knew the electromagnetic nature of the creatures and their propensity both to communicate through and to wreak havoc on any electrical devices—suspected a big blackout the moment the president threw the switch and so heaved a sigh of relief when nothing happened. A moment later, the program was interrupted by a news flash. The Ohio River bridge that he had in the past year often traveled over from Gallipolis, Ohio, to Point Pleasant, West Virginia, had just collapsed, killing forty-six people—the deadliest bridge disaster in US history. The "friends" had made a whole series of other accurate predictions for events—plane crashes, an earthquake in Turkey, a blizzard on the Hopi and Navajo reservations—both leading up to the bridge collapse and after, including the disappearance of the Australian prime minister (just hours after the bridge tragedy) and a series of explosions in Moscow.

In 1970, when Keel attempted in his book *Operation Trojan Horse* to make sense of both his own and the world's unprecedented experience of spectral attacks, he called the criminal culprits behind them both "ultraterrestrials" and "elementals" and even admitted that he had been "catapulted into the dreamlike fantasy world of demonology." In the book, he divulged that when he had begun his research on UFOs, he had been an atheist; now he seriously entertained the Bible's warnings about wonders in the sky and false prophets during the "last days." Keel knew that he had dodged a very deadly bullet by riding out the Trojan Horse much further than most did. Along with the contactee cults, which slavishly gave themselves over to their invisible masters' pretensions, Keel felt there were "thousands, perhaps millions, of people all over this planet" who had been directly and adversely affected by the ultraterrestrials. "I have," he said, "watched helplessly as witnesses fell into hopeless personality deterioration and went insane or even committed suicide."

Keel titled his final chapter of *Operation Trojan Horse* "You Can't Tell the Players without a Scorecard," and his journalistic journey through the quixotic realm of the ultraterrestrials gave America that scorecard. He had come very close to being a mark, a hapless victim of the amoral and often cruel elementals' twisted games. For over a year, he had played the game on the demons' terms, believing it was the only avenue to find out just what the game was. A playful, alert intelligence had ultimately kept him from succumbing to the literalness of the UFO cults and parapsychologists and the CIA, which, like the Spiritualists had before them, had been determined to drag the spiritual world into the cause-and-effect arena of the physical, so it could be controlled.

"The game seems to be headed for some kind of grand climax," Keel warned, fifty years ago. Will we bar the gates the next time the Trojan Horse—in the guise of UFOs, angels, Mothman, or some new and as yet unknown entity—appears?

Site #6: Superpowers of the Biomind: Offices of the American Society for Psychical Research, 5 West Seventy-Third Street, December 8, 1971

In a hypersensitive quest for scientific respectability, American parapsychology had from its early twentieth-century inception dedicated itself to quantification, repeatability, and thus to mechanical instrumentation. The third floor of the American Society for Psychical Research's (ASPR's) gracious Beaux Arts mansion (originally the Louis Strasberger residence; the physicist and inventor of the Xerox machine Chester Carlson had helped the ASPR purchase the building in 1966) across from the north side of the Dakota was a Rube Goldberg–esque maze of electronic recording devices enabling the researchers Dr. Karl Osis and Dr. Gertrude Schmeidler to conduct experiments on ESP, psychokinesis, and other phenomena. On this snowy day in 1971, Dr. Osis's assistant Janet Lee Mitchell had hooked up the New York City artist Ingo Swann to a Beckman Dynograph, which monitored and recorded brain activity. Half a dozen electrodes attached to his scalp, a blood-pressure instrument attached to his finger, Swann could barely move without generating some "artifact" in the instrumentation.

Suspended from the ceiling above the electrode-laced chair were a number of trays in which the researchers placed objects—"targets"—for their subjects to attempt to view by projecting themselves out of their bodies. Swann had on his first attempt a couple of weeks before shown great promise, but quickly his descriptions—spoken into the microphone of a large reel-to-reel tape recorder, so

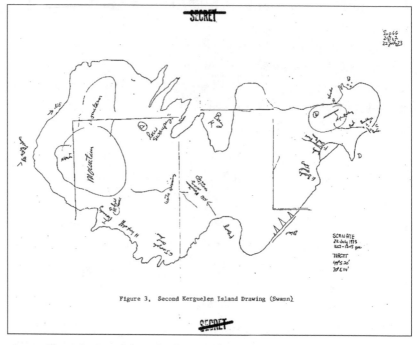

Figure 3. Second Kerguelen Island Drawing (Swann)

Sketch by Ingo Swann for CIA SCANATE remote viewing program
(CIA)

that the parapsychologists could later analyze them—had become vague and confused. Swann had diagnosed the problem as having to switch from visualizing to verbalizing; when he began to speak, the images would vanish. Requesting a sketchpad, he had quite quickly achieved spectacular results by silently drawing what he saw in the trays above his head.

During Swann's last session, while waiting for Mitchell to adjust the Dynograph, Swann suddenly saw—from his out-of-body consciousness—a woman going by on the sidewalk outside, dressed in a bright-orange coat that struck him as inappropriate for the cold, snowy day. He tore off the electrodes, grabbed Mitchell, and dashed down the stairs into the street, just in time to see an orange coat turning the corner onto Central Park West. This "out-of-body" experience was hardly new, for countless people throughout history had experienced spontaneous projection of their astral body to distant locations (see, for example, the account of Loraina Brackett in chapter 3). In the annals of the very young science of parapsychology, however, it was unprecedented. Ingo Swann's consciousness had jumped out of the confines of the laboratory; he had followed, and now he had an open invitation to continue following, to new horizons. He and Mitchell came up with an experiment in which she would be handed an envelope with a location; she would read it out, Ingo would describe the weather conditions at that place, and then Mitchell would telephone the local weather bureau to find out the conditions.

When Mitchell said, "The target is Tucson, Arizona," Swann got a picture of hot desert, and then in an instant he was *there*. "Am over a wet highway, buildings nearby and in the distance. The wind is blowing. It's cold. And it is raining hard." Mitchell dialed the weather service, which told her that Tucson was in the midst of an unexpected thunderstorm and that the weather was freezing. Needing a name for the experiment, Swann suggested "remote viewing." But Swann had actually *felt* the weather in Tucson, not just saw it. Before Ingo Swann, parapsychology posited that all extrasensory perception was a function exclusively of the mind, not of the body. The laboratory experiments had been restricted to artificial situations, and the participants sat still and were expected to produce results mentally, not bodily. Swann liked the term "biomind" as a way to emphasize a more holistic, whole-body orientation for psi capacities—which he saw as a universal human potential.

Around this same time, Swann had conducted a number of experiments with Cleve Backster at the Backster School of Lie Detection on West Forty-Sixth Street. Backster—who had been an interrogation specialist with the CIA—had used his polygraph instruments to test if plants showed a galvanic response to watering. When he found that they did, he tested them for other responses, and the polygraph showed that they would respond to his mental images of harming them and even to the death of brine shrimp in the next room. Backster asked Swann to telepathically influence gases, metals, and graphite sealed in glass vials. When the CIA learned from Backster of Swann's ability to move a small amount of graphite with his thoughts, they put an end to the ASPR experiments and, giving Swann top security clearance, brought him to Stanford Research Institute, where the CIA had a thriving parapsychological research program going under the direction of Hal Puthoff. Before long, Swann was instructing Army personnel in his remote viewing techniques, to create a cadre of "psychic spies" to strike at targets in the Soviet Union and other places. Originally titled SCANATE, the program was eventually called STAR GATE.

The ten-year collaboration between Swann and Puthoff produced a mind-boggling array of "supernormal"—and in every way *magical*—experiences and events, far from Manhattan and so beyond the scope of this book. What has often gone unspoken in the many histories of modern remote viewing is that Puthoff and Swann were Scientologists and that "remote viewing" was identical with "exteriorization with full projection," Scientology founder L. Ron Hubbard's term for astral projection. By the early 1950s, Hubbard got the centerpiece of his "religion"—actually a modern path of left-handed or black-magical initiation—from his association with Jack Parsons, a full-blown black magician who was instrumental in the dissemination of Aleister Crowley's "Thelema."

Ingo Swann's relationship with Scientology had begun in 1960, when he read Hubbard's "Dianetics" essay in a 1950 number of *Astounding Science Fiction.* In 1962, he began active training in Scientology and, by 1969, had become Clear #2231, "clear" being Hubbard's term for a person free from the influence of unwanted emotions and memories of trauma. The next stage, "Operating Thetan," promised godlike control over "matter, energy, space and time" (known in Scientology as MEST); Swann had reached OT Level VII (the penultimate level before full godhood) by the time he began the ASPR experiments in 1971. In a 1973 interview, Swann stated that his ability to leave his body and to mentally influence matter is solely the result of Scientology's occult training process. Both Backster's lie-detector machine and the ASPR's Dynograph would have been quite familiar to him, for Scientology's "auditing" process had as its central technological prosthesis Hubbard's "E-meter," essentially a slightly modified galvanometer, that is, lie detector.

It is quite possible to look at both Scientology's "exteriorization with full projection" and the CIA's "remote viewing" protocol as Satanic inversions of the central and sacred rite of Christian initiation practices. In the modern Rosicrucian path of initiation developed and taught by Rudolf Steiner, the ancient maxim of three steps in moral development for each step in occult development is central; a gradual path of simple exercises to strengthen and purify the soul is undertaken before any attempt to enter the spiritual world. In Rosicrucian instruction and practice, this training prepares one to meet the Lesser Guardian of the Threshold, who protects all human beings from the dangers of unlawful entry to the spiritual world. Scientology is essentially an elaborate, technocentric system to destroy the Lesser Guardian of the Threshold in order to "storm heaven," that is, to forcibly gain clairvoyant perception of the spiritual world. Seen either as modern demonstrations of the *Faust* drama, realizations of René Guénon's prophecy of the end of the world, or an expression of Thomas Hobbes's "war of all against all," the tragic history of both Scientology—from the tellingly high rate of psychoses, suicides, and strange deaths suffered by OT-initiated Scientologists to the administrative hierarchy's vengeful and often criminal attacks against perceived enemies—and the CIA (a kind of parallel history carried out as a state operation rather than a "religion") explicitly portrays the danger of magic as a spiritual path.

Site #7: *A Course in Miracles*? The Beresford,
211 Central Park West, June 22, 1976

"This is a course in miracles. Please take notes," the Voice began, on October 18, 1965. Having been in constant inner communication with the Voice for the previous three months, Helen Schucman, associate professor of medical psychology at the Columbia University College of Physicians and Surgeons, took up her pen and did just that. Along with the Voice, Schucman had been experiencing waking visions and strange dreams, which, as almost invariably occurs when momentous personal visions arrive, had come in a wave of three episodes of three portentous dreams. In the final one, in midsummer, she saw herself drifting along a Venice canal in a gondola, wondering if there might be treasure in the water below. Seeing a fishing pole at her feet, she dropped the line, pulled up a treasure chest, to find nothing inside but a large black thesis binder—the very one that she would later use to hold the typed transcribed pages of her stenographic notes of *A Course in Miracles* (*ACIM*).

During these same months, Schucman had a series of precognitive and telepathic experiences, seeing both far into the past and ahead into the near future. Writing up a research report with her Columbia colleague Bill Thetford one day, she suddenly sensed that a friend of his was contemplating suicide, and she urged him to telephone the friend, who had indeed been thinking of taking his own life. When Thetford left for summer vacation on Fire Island, she sent him a mental image of a gold pin that she was keen to have as a present, and he returned with exactly the one she had pictured. These sorts of experiences were unsettling to Schucman, an atheist Jew who, unlike Thetford—who eagerly pursued contact with the paranormal—was fearful of anything that resembled psychic powers. Each time one of these episodes transpired, Schucman had a distinct evil foreboding, a sense of danger, but also, increasingly, fantasies of power and prestige. She came to conceive of all this unbidden activity as *magic*, and indeed, as the Voice began to dictate the fundamental principles of

A Course in Miracles, it frequently referred to magic, always warning strenuously against it: "#14. Miracles attest to truth. They are convincing because they arise from conviction. Without conviction, they deteriorate into magic, which is mindless, and therefore destructive, or rather, the uncreative use of Mind"; "Illness is a form of magic. It might be better to say it is a form of magical SOLUTION"; "'Casting spells' merely means 'affirming error,' and error is lack of love."

The Voice identified itself as "Jesus Christ of Nazareth," and for years, Schucman and Thetford and a very small circle of friends quietly circulated photocopies of the dictated material among themselves for discussion and study. Among the most enthusiastic admirers were Robert and Judy Skutch, longtime ASPR members at whose home on Central Park West the *ACIM* study group often met to continue conversation with the Voice, which urged hardcover publication of the material. On June 22, 1976, the Skutches' Foundation for Inner Peace released five thousand copies of the first three-volume edition of *A Course in Miracles.* In 1992, after Marianne Williamson discussed the book on *The Oprah Winfrey Show,* over two million copies were sold. Half a century after its emergence, it is still popularly known as "the New Age Bible."

Though *ACIM*'s "Jesus" admonished against magic, it was entirely a magical production, its genesis undeniably rooted in Helen Schucman's soul and psyche, her complicated relationship with her colleague Bill Thetford, and even in the dense psychic atmosphere of Freudian, Adlerian, Rogerian professional psychology of Manhattan circa 1967. The entire history of twentieth-century psychology is populated with ghosts and specters and poltergeists—often ones that the professional students of the human soul had themselves conjured or invoked by their own intensely emotional astral activity. The crack in the wall of twentieth-century reality was opened so wide to the underworld of subphysical elemental beings that they poured into the Earth's atmosphere as UFOs, aliens, Mothmen, and other monsters, to be worshiped by cultists, glamorized by media, and feared by governments; infiltrated deep into the national security state via the black sciences plied by the CIA and its sub-contractors; and spawned countless channeled heresies claiming salvific power for twentieth-century human civilization. The psychic plane's chameleonesque denizens even waltzed right into the plush prestigious homes and offices of Upper East and West Side sophisti-cates, passing themselves off as cosmic psychotherapists, their call-ing cards weak and mendacious metaphysics wrapped around the promise of magical personality transformation.

That Helen Schucman's "Voice"—which may or may not have been the same elemental being who planted the series of phantasma-goric visions and effected the eruption of her psychic powers—called itself "Jesus" strikes admiring devotees as largely irrelevant and agnostic scholars as banal Christian camp. Only a handful—most of them fundamentalist Christians—who have perused its pages con-sider Schucman's "Jesus" to be a magically invoked demon, intent on the destruction of both God and humanity. For all of the book's sac-charine prose and sophomoric and often trite philosophy, *A Course in Miracles* is a sophisticated and devilish half truth exquisitely tai-lored to the late twentieth-century religion-adverse but otherworld-hungry soul. It is also an altogether *indigenous* talisman from this magic isle, hatched from a suite of very local circumstances and then unleashed like Pandora's box on an unsuspecting planet.

Two centuries of false gospels peddled by invisible adversaries of the human being have clearly not taught us to "test the spirits." While L. Ron Hubbard's Scientology centered its black-magical double-bind invitation to demonic possession explicitly and un-ambiguously on the ersatz exorcism of demons ("body thetans," in Scientological parlance), *A Course in Miracles* glibly psychologizes demons, stating in one chapter that possession merely means that one's body has been taken over by one's thoughts. Though the psy-chic plane is admittedly populated by countless entities produced by unhealthy human thinking, it is also a realm of dangerous, cunning creatures who were not created by our thoughts but are sustained and fed by them.

Earlier generations of demonologists made a sharply delineated distinction between *possession* and *obsession*. "Obsession" is a demonological distinction that helps make sense of how Helen Schucman and Ingo Swann and John Keel and so many others who trafficked with beings of the psychic plane could remain independent enough not to succumb to full demonic possession—and consequent psychosis, suicide, or death. Still, Schucman clearly paid a price for her communion with the Voice. Her friend Father Benedict Groeschel, who met Schucman while a graduate student in psychology at Columbia at the time she was channeling *ACIM* and had at first thought of it as "religious poetry," witnessed "the black hole of rage and depression" that Schucman fell into during the last two years of her life. At her bedside in her final days, the priest was terrified to hear her utter the vilest curses against all things spiritual, particularly "that book, that goddamn book," saying it was the worst thing that ever happened to her.

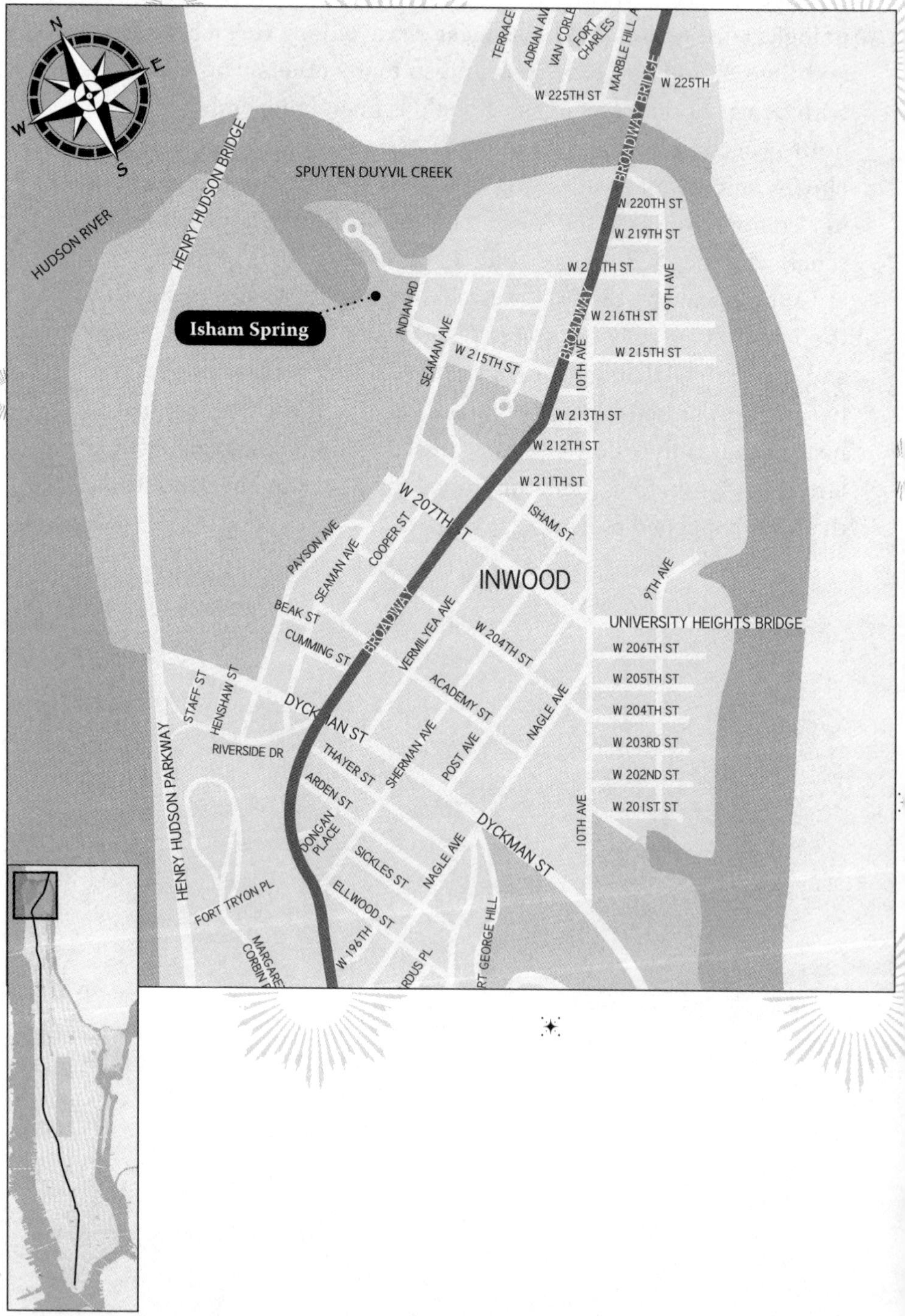
N
E
S
W
HUDSON RIVER
HENRY HUDSON BRIDGE
SPUYTEN DUYVIL CREEK
TERRACE
FORT CHARLES
W 225TH ST
W 225TH
BROADWAY BRIDGE
W 220TH ST
W 219TH ST
W 216TH ST
W 215TH ST
9TH AVE
Isham Spring
INDIAN RD
SEAMAN AVE
W 215TH ST
10TH AVE
BROADWAY
W 213TH ST
W 212TH ST
W 211TH ST
ISHAM ST
COOPER ST
PAYSON AVE
SEAMAN AVE
INWOOD
9TH AVE
UNIVERSITY HEIGHTS BRIDGE
W 206TH ST
W 205TH ST
W 204TH ST
W 203RD ST
W 202ND ST
W 201ST ST
BEAK ST
CUMMING ST
BROADWAY
VERMILYEA AVE
W 204TH ST
ACADEMY ST
NAGLE AVE
STAFF ST
HENSHAW ST
DYCKMAN ST
RIVERSIDE DR
THAYER ST
SHERMAN AVE
POST AVE
ARDEN ST
DONGAN PLACE
SICKLES ST
NAGLE AVE
DYCKMAN ST
10TH AVE
HENRY HUDSON PARKWAY
FORT TRYON PL
ELLWOOD ST
W 196TH

Conclusion

Manhattan's Magical Future

The "miracles" itemized both by the entity who employed Helen Schucman to channel *A Course in Miracles* and by the many readers of the books are almost exclusively limited to the realm of personal synchronicities—which have taken on a sacred significance in the New Age pantheon. The unexpurgated *ür*-text dictated to Schucman is replete with parenthetical asides giving pregnant interpretations about trivial incidents in the lives of Schucman, Thetford, and their friends. In the wake of the summer of paranormal fireworks around Schucman, she and her circle were caught up in a cascade of just the same sort of magical thinking in which the "Voice" indulges.

History is full of examples of civilizations whose sacred religious mysteries have degenerated into a catastrophic eruption of magical practices. Mature contemplation of Manhattan's magical future demands reflection on the distinction between personal, arbitrary magic of the kind whose history has been traced here and *sacred magic*, which includes actual miracles. Personal magic employs fallen, subearthly forces and beings—whether in exoteric science and technology, parapsychological investigation and experiment, or ceremonial magic. Sacred magic works directly with the agent of growth, that realm in which God and his servants act. This Tree of Life, the divine creative realm, is protected from personal human will and is thus the arena of miracles. Miracles, though untouched by human will, are shot through with the moral qualities of those beings—both human and otherwise—who either effect or experience them. Neither science nor personal magic can perform miracles.

Just before crossing Dyckman Street up in Inwood, Broadway makes its most dramatic turn, bending east away from the rocky ramparts of the Fort Tryon ridge. Looking down from the heights there stands Manhattan's most breathtaking bricolage of magical objects: the Cloisters, the Metropolitan's twentieth-century master-piece assemblage of a trio of medieval sanctuaries. From the moment one enters the Late Gothic Hall, one is surrounded by numinous treasures: a fifteenth-century *Palmesel*, an intricately carved red-robed Christ astride a donkey, all atop a rude wooden-wheeled cart; a half-sized sculptural assemblage of the Three Kings attend-ing the infant Jesus; a human-sized Archangel Michael with his foot on the neck of the dragon, hovering above the whole hall. The pol-ished oak of Michael's breastplate shines like actual steel armor, and the sculpted wooden monster seems alive. A full five centuries ago, some anonymous Castilian carver gave life to the archangel whose regency—and magically charged mission—would not begin until 1879 and would leap into its most spectacular world-historical relief here on Manhattan island.

A dozen paces south and then west brings you into the great room displaying the famous *Unicorn Tapestries*, whose otherworldly alchemical journey is brought starkly down to Earth by the alabas-ter narwhal tusk flanking the hall's great hearth. Even five hundred years ago, when the weavers were at work on these fine silver and gilded wool and silk threads, the most educated European intellects were passing through the Scylla and Charybdis of reason and hence banishing the imaginal—and a host of spiritual beings with it. Clair-voyant understanding of the unicorn as an image of a spiritual being would give way to scholarly debate about the actual existence of a *physical* unicorn—and end in tortured natural history construing the unicorn as nothing but a narwhal.

The *Nine Heroes Tapestries* in the next hall depict Hebrew heroes, Joshua, David, Judas Maccabeus; then pagan heroes, Hector, Alex-ander the Great, and Julius Caesar; and finally the Christian heroes, King Arthur, Godfrey of Bouillon, and Charlemagne. Each and every one lived out his biography in an altogether magical milieu and was credited with magical deeds. So it was for the knight who created amid the chalky canyons of Provence the cloister that constitutes the building's north side. Known variously as Guilhem, Guillaume le Court Nez, William of Orange, Count of Toulouse, and Saint Guillaume d'Aquitaine, this grandson of Charles Martel and principal paladin of Charlemagne was the very same knight described by Wolfram von Eschenbach in his epic *Willehalm*, composed in the early thirteenth century. A fearless aristocrat who followed the Christian creed and who, thanks to his unfailing faith and courage, drove the Saracens from the heart of Christendom, Guilhem in AD 804 retired to the secluded valley of the Hérault, where he founded a monastery—known today as Saint-Guilhem-le-Désert. Magical heroic tales are still told of Saint Guilhem's exploits, though most miss the esoteric significance of this Grail knight's biography.

Surrounding the intimate skylight-illuminated courtyard of the Saint Guilhem Cloister are a suite of carved limestone columns faced with sinuous zigzags or waves, topped by a fantastic assortment of sculptured scenes, many depicting gruesome, threatening demons. Atop the courtyard's northwest-corner column, over a band of decorative acanthus leaves, a pair of lions flanks a seated man. Mustached and goateed, the figure is dressed in a cloak held by a large clasp at the left shoulder. His nose seems to be cut off—a spectacular telltale that this is indeed Guillaume le Court Nez, who lost the tip of his nose to a Saracen's scimitar.

When I have visited this courtyard, that column seems to radiate waves of subtle energy; the whole room seems to breathe. Something profound echoes there and in many of the quiet spaces within the Cloisters, as if the sleeping magicians of centuries past awake. The Cloisters are a fantastic reminder that even the stones are alive, that no matter how much we have traded medieval fleshy, sensuous, sympathetic magic for the silicon-based digital sorcery of our modern simulacrum, the bones and stones and old oak carvings forget nothing. Each and every sacred relic here at the Cloisters is

Saint Guilhem sculpture from Cloisters column
(author photo)

potentially "apocalyptic"—in its original sense of meaning to reveal, to uncover. Sacred magic requires both *gnosis* and *mysticism*, and this tranquil ridgetop, imbued with the prayers of half a millennium of pilgrims, is undeniably *holy*.

Manhattan is clearly a modern mystery center, and like all ancient mystery centers, it has about it a magical aura. As the preeminent mystery center of the Kali Yuga—the Dark Age—New York City necessarily expresses titanic mechanizing and rationalizing currents, rooted in our era's soul-deadening materialism, paired with misguided flights of mediumistically inspired New Age apocalypticism, which now has culminated in a weird sacralization of modernity, worshiping idols of "freedom" (usually merely fetishistic capitalism), science, and technology. The bird's-eye-view map of this Manhattan Kali Yuga mystery center resolves as an altar of chrome and stainless steel and glass towers sporting corporate logos, at whose feet—as always, particularly along Broadway—are equally apocalyptically expressive yoga centers, Reiki institutes, virtual-reality parlors, flotation-tank chambers, and personal-development salons and spas. As churches, synagogues, and mosques have emptied, a ubiquitous landscape of postmodern magics has sprung up around them. The New Age magical millenarianism of the '60s and '70s has given way to a kind of routinization of the occult and magical as lifestyle politics and leisure.

I have been surprised recently to hear people say, "It's the granite, the crystals underneath the skyscrapers; they are what makes New York such a dynamic, magical place." No matter that the closest granite is up in Westchester County and that the Cambrian schist that is the principal bedrock of this magic isle has an altogether different structure, geochemistry, and geological history than granite. It is much more important to invite reflection on the possibility that, granite or schist, silica or iron, the human being is endowed with the capacity to alchemically transmute these substances and will do so in the far future. As the Threefold folk up by Carnegie Hall in the '30s were doing, we will do so by working consciously and gratefully with the elemental beings of the island, who have waited patiently for us to pass through this dark age of materialism. Manhattan's magical future will surely continue to see some ebb and flow of *coagula* and *solve*, one that hopefully will find a renewed recognition of the sacred magic of Rosicrucian alchemy.

"If there is magic on this planet, it is contained in water," said the uncanny star-throwing naturalist Loren Eiseley. Coming upon running water anywhere on Manhattan's relentlessly rip-rapped surface today truly feels like magic, but once upon a time not so very long ago, this well-watered isle still had springs, seeps, wells, and other watery expressions to delight the palate and cool one's brow. At the turn of the twentieth century, an eccentric Gotham vagabond made it his business to discover and document the surviving springs and wells of Manhattan and the Bronx. Between 1893 and 1902, at the very moment when Broadway saw gigantic new buildings scrape the sky, James Reuel Smith (1852–1935) pedaled his sturdy Columbia bicycle right past them, his eyes fixed on the ground as he hunted for clues at the base of stone walls, along the edge of sidewalks, even out in the middle of the street. His Hawk-Eye box camera fixed to his handlebars, ever on the lookout for truant boys and girls who would share with him the location of their secret springs, Smith sought out the last artesian and riparian refuges of this watery island, from the Battery to Spuyten Duyvil.

Poring over Smith's field journals at the New-York Historical Society, one can follow him and his passion, as surely as his notes follow and document the island's northward urbanization. Below Fourteenth Street is almost bone dry, then it is macadamized riparian desert until Central Park, where he and his bicycle delight in dozens of discoveries. Then, with each bike ride northward, the damps and seeps proliferate: Sixty-First to 110th Street, 110th to 119th, and ten-block section by ten-block section all the way up to Inwood Hill and Isham Park—the island's last rural vestige, where horses and cattle still grazed on the floodplain of the channelized (to make a navigable canal through from the Hudson to the Harlem River) Spuyten Duyvil Creek. Smith's sites map out the subterranean riparian landscape that could once again be brought to life and also reveal an altogether overlooked episode of Gotham's closing of the commons.

Up in Inwood, in June 1898, Smith visited and photographed half a dozen springs and wells, but one—the Isham Spring—stands out. "It bubbles up freely like champagne at the southwestern end of a small ledge of rock that crops out from nearly the lowest level of the marshy meadow," he wrote in his field journal. "The water is cold and nice, although it is completely open to the sun. There is a

Isham meadow spring, June 1898
(James Reuel Smith Springs and Wells Photograph Collection,
The New-York Historical Society)

frog in the spring." We can follow him there, by turning off Broadway at West 218th Street and walking down to the intersection with Indian Road, where a pair of paths lead out over the floodplain on the south side of Spuyten Duyvil Creek. Looking west toward the Hudson River from here, you will see a scene surprisingly similar to the one Smith photographed. The spring is now covered, the grove of four fruit trees—two apple trees, a plum tree, and a peach tree—that Smith described is gone, but the broad riparian meadow still stretches west toward the opening between the Inwood Hill cliff and Spuyten Duyvil, to the Palisades on the opposite side of the Hudson.

Concomitant with that eccentric quest to document Manhattan's last wells and springs, James Reuel Smith made an exhaustive scholarly study of the magical water sources described in ancient Greek poetry, mythology, and history. Human consciousness at that time was still capable of perceiving the elemental beings of the watery realm; Greek poets and historians alike employed an exhaustive taxonomy for the Naiades, freshwater elemental beings: Pegiai, the spirits of springs; Krinaiai, of fountains; Potameides, of rivers and streams; Limnades, of lakes; and Eleionomai, of marshes. As we inhabitants of this enchanted isle seek to live more consciously and harmoniously with the Earth, and our formerly physically enchanted technologies and ideologies give way to etheric ones, we will again meet, converse with, and learn from the beings who have ever and everywhere been the principal agents of magical action. Following the path of magic, perhaps Manhattan's future shall see this prodigious island once again sport healing springs and wells from out of its dark bedrock.

NOTES

CHAPTER 1. AN ENCHANTED INAUGURATION

George Washington quoted from his first inaugural address. *Fenno's Gazette* quoted in Rufus Wilmot Griswold, *The Republican Court; or, American Society in the Days of Washington* (New York: Appleton, 1856), 146. Lafayette's letter to Washington is in *Memoirs, Correspondence, and Manuscripts of General Lafayette* (New York: Saunders and Otley). Mesmer's letter to Lafayette can be seen at Founders Online, https://founders.archives.gov (accessed February 1, 2020). Helena Petrovna Blavatsky quotations from *Isis Unveiled: A Master-Key to the Mysteries of Ancient and Modern Science and Theology* (New York: J. W. Bouton, 1877). New York Legislature quoted from John A. Dunlap, *The New-York Justice; or, A Digest of the Law Relative to Justices of the Peace in the State of New-York* (New York: Isaac Riley, 1815), 89. On the African Burial Ground, see Andrea E. Frohne, *The African Burial Ground in New York City: Memory, Spirituality, and Space* (Syracuse, NY: Syracuse University Press, 2015); and also Joyce Hansen and Gary McGowan, *Breaking Ground, Breaking Silence: The Story of New York's African Burial Ground* (New York: Holt, 1998). David Grim quotations from "Notes on the City of New York," n.d. [1819], David Grim Papers, New-York Historical Society. Grim's *A Plan of the City and Environs of New York as They Were in the Years 1742–1743 and 1744* may be viewed at the New York Public Library Digital Collections website: https://digitalcollections.nypl .org (accessed February 1, 2020). The German sociologist Max Weber first used the phrase "Die Entzauberung der Welt" (disenchantment of the world) in the 1913 essay "Ueber einige Kategorien der verstehenden Soziologie" (Some categories of interpretive sociology). See Weber, *Gesammelte Aufsätze zur Wissenschaftlehre* (Tübingen: Mohr, 1922), 409. Both the history and historiography of disenchantment are labyrinthine problems; for a detailed, wide-ranging academic (but itself "disenchanted"—that is, lacking magical understanding) study of the "disenchantment" thesis, see Jason A. Jesperson-Storm, *The Myth of Disenchantment: Magic, Modernity, and the Birth of the Human* (Chicago: University of Chicago Press, 2018). Egil Asprem's *The Problem of Disenchantment: Scientific Naturalism and Esoteric Discourse, 1900–1939* (Albany: SUNY Press, 2014) identifies and critiques contemporary academic "reenchantment" programs.

CHAPTER 2. MASONIC MANHATTAN

John Greenleaf Whittier quoted from his *The Supernaturalism of New England* (London: Wiley and Putnam, 1847), 11.

Site #1: St. John's Lodge #1

Quotation about the higher degrees of Freemasonry from Henry Ward Dana, *Free Masonry: Its Pretensions Exposed in Faithful Extracts of Its Standard Authors* (New York, 1828), 285. Quotation about "the science of the Cabalistic Rosicrucian" from Abbé Barruel, *Memoirs Illustrating the History of Jacobinism* (New York: Cornelius Davis, 1799), 183. For the description of the cornerstone-laying ceremony, see James Hardie, *The New Free-mason's Monitor; or, Masonic Guide, for the Direction of Members of That Ancient and Honourable Fraternity, as Well as for the Information of Those, Who May Be Desirous of Becoming Acquainted with Its Principles* (New York: George Long, 1818). The ritual texts are drawn from Malcolm C. Duncan, *Duncan's Masonic Ritual and Monitor* (New York: Dick and Fitzgerald, 1866). For insight into the original esoteric magical impulses behind Freemasonic rituals, see Rudolf Steiner, *Freemasonry and Ritual Work: The Misraim Service: Letters, Documents, Rituals, and Lectures from the Cognitive-Ritual Section of the Esoteric School: 1904–1919* (Hudson, NY: Anthroposophic Press, 2007).

Site #2: The House of Thomas Paine

Thomas Paine quoted from his *The Age of Reason: Being an Investigation of True and of Fabulous Theology* (London: H. D. Symonds, 1794). For Tom Miller's superb little essay on his detective work to discover the "lost house," see "The Lost Thomas Paine House—No. 309 Bleecker Street," *Daytonian in Manhattan* (blog), November 12, 2012, http://daytoninmanhattan.blogspot.com.

Site #3: DeWitt Clinton House

Morris quotation and quotation about the Erie Canal from Peter L. Bernstein, *Wedding of the Waters: The Erie Canal and the Making of a Great Nation* (New York: Norton, 2010), 325. Henry Quitman quoted from his *A Treatise on Magic; or, On the Intercourse between Spirits and Men* (Albany, NY: Balance, 1810), 3, 71. *Medical Repository* review quoted from Samuel Latham Mitchill, "Quitman on the Popular Prevalence of Magical Notions," *Medical Repository* 3, no. 2 (1811): 183. See also David Low Dodge, *A Religious Conference, in Four Dialogues, between Lorenzo and Evander* (New York: Collins and Perkins, 1808). For Clinton's diary, see "Private Canal Journal, 1810," in *The Life and Writings of De Witt Clinton* (New York: Baker and Scribner, 1849).

Site #4: Devotional Somnium

Primary sources for the Rachel Baker case include Charles Mais, *The Surprising Case of Rachel Baker, Who Prays and Preaches in Her Sleep, with Specimens of Her Extraordinary Performances Taken Down Accurately in Short Hand at the Time, and Showing the Unparalleled Powers She Possesses to Pray, Exhort, and Answer Questions, during Her Unconscious State, the Whole Authenticated by the Most Respectable Testimony of Living Witnesses* (New York: S. Marks, 1814); Samuel L. Mitchill,

Devotional Somnium; or, A Collection of Prayers and Exhortations Uttered by Miss Rachel Baker, in the City of New-York in the Winter of 1815 during Her Abstracted and Unconscious State (Sangerfield, NY: Tenny and Miller, 1815); Mitchill, preface to *Medical Repository* 4 (1818): iv. Quotation about Mitchill from John W. Francis, *Old New York; or, Reminiscences of the Past Sixty Years* (New York: Charles Roe, 1858), 57. On the Friendly Club, see Bryan Waterman, *Republic of Intellect: The Friendly Club of New York City and the Making of American Literature* (Baltimore: John Hopkins University Press, 2007).

Site #5: William Gowans's Bookshop
If you were to pursue for yourself a single historical trail from within these pages, you can do no better than to go to the Brooklyn Historical Society and sit in its extraordinary reading room to peruse Gabriel Furman's journals. For the online finding aid for the Garbriel Furman Papers, see http://brooklynhistory.org.

Site #6: College of Physicians and Surgeons
See Stanley B. Kimball, "The Anthon Transcript: People, Primary Sources, and Problems," *BYU Studies* 10, no. 3 (Spring 1970): 325–352. On Mormonism and folk magic, see D. Michael Quinn, *Early Mormonism and the Magic World View* (Salt Lake City: Signature Books, 1998).

Site #7: Baldwin Gardiner Store
See William Leete Stone, *Matthias and His Impostures; or, The Progress of Fanaticism, Illustrated in the Extraordinary Case of Robert Matthews, and Some of His Forerunners and Disciples* (New York: Harper, 1835); and Paul E. Johnson and Sean Wilentz, *The Kingdom of Matthias: A Story of Sex and Salvation in 19th-Century America* (New York: Oxford University Press, 2012).

Site #8: Colonel Stone on Masonry and Anti-Masonry
William Leete Stone quoted from his *Letters on Masonry and Anti-Masonry: Addressed to the Hon. John Quincy Adams* (New York: O. Halsted, 1832).

CHAPTER 3. MAGNETIC MANHATTAN

Site #1: The Iron Fence, Bowling Green
William Leete Stone quoted from his *Letter to Doctor A. Brigham, on Animal Magnetism: Being an Account of a Remarkable Interview between the Author and Miss L. Brackett, While in a State of Somnambulism* (New York: George Dearborn, 1837).

Site #2: Varick House
See Charles Ferson Durant, *Exposition; or, A New Theory of Animal Magnetism, with a Key to the Mysteries: Demonstrated by the Most Celebrated Somnambulists in America* (New York: Wiley and Putnam, 1837).

Site #3: Samuel F. B. Morse's Daguerreotype Studio

Quotations about making money and Daguerre from Samuel Irenaeus Prime, *Life of Samuel F. B. Morse* (New York: Appleton, 1875), 132, 401. Southworth quoted in Peter Bacon Hales, *Silver Cities: Photographing American Urbanization, 1839–1939* (Albuquerque: University of New Mexico Press, 2005), 12. Samuel Morse is both an irresistible character study for the intersection of art, science, and technology—all magical terrains—in antebellum New York and America and also a still unfathomable mystery. For a superb biographical study, see Kenneth Silverman, *Lightning Man: The Accursed Life of Samuel F. B. Morse* (New York: Knopf Doubleday, 2010). In focusing on Samuel Morse, I have unfairly given short shrift to his partner in photographic experimentation, John William Draper; for a detailed description of this collaboration, see Howard McManus, "Into the Light: John William Draper and the Earliest American Photographic Portraits," History Broker, accessed February 1, 2020, www.historybroker.com.

Site #4: Peale's Museum

David Meredith Reese quoted from his *Humbugs of New-York: Being a Remonstrance against Popular Delusion, Whether in Science, Philosophy, or Religion* (New York: J. S. Taylor, 1838). On Collyer, see *The History and Philosophy of Animal Magnetism, with Practical Instructions for the Exercise of This Power* (Boston: J. N. Bradley, 1843).

Site #5: The Fowler Brothers' Phrenological Cabinet

Emerson quoted from *Journals of Ralph Waldo Emerson, 1820–1872*, vol. 8 (Boston: Houghton Mifflin, 1909), 574. The Fowler Brothers published an immense number of tracts; for the heart of their phrenological philosophy, see Orson Squire Fowler and Lorenzo Niles Fowler, *Phrenology Proved, Illustrated and Applied* (New York: W. H. Colyer, 1836). Some of the text for this site draws on a section of my book *Expect Great Things: The Life and Search of Henry David Thoreau* (New York: Tarcher Perigree, 2017).

Site #6: Astor House

For Buchanan's account of the psychometric experiments with Henry Inman, see Joseph Rodes Buchanan, *Manual of Psychometry: The Dawn of a New Civilization* (Roxbury, MA: Holman Brothers, 1885).

Site #7: Barnum's American Museum

Chapin quoted in A. H. Saxon, *P. T. Barnum: The Legend and the Man* (New York: Columbia University Press, 1989), 122. P. T. Barnum left a large enough thumbprint on nineteenth-century America that there are, in addition to his own writings, many biographies; the gold standard continues to be Neil Harris, *Humbug: The Art of P. T. Barnum* (Chicago: University of Chicago Press, 1981).

The Feejee Mermaid and Magizoology; "The Sea Serpent Caught at Last!"

Benjamin Silliman, "A Sea Serpent," *American Journal of Science* 28 (1835): 373; "The Sea Serpent," *Zoologist* 5 (1847): 1604. I wish that I could claim having coined the word "Magizoology"; the honor of course belongs to J. K. Rowling. My discussion here draws on research I did for *Expect Great Things: The Life and Search of Henry David Thoreau* (New York: Tarcher Perigree, 2017).

Site #8: Offices of LaRoy Sunderland's *Magnet*

The first issue of La Roy Sunderland's *Magnet* can be seen online at Google Books. Sunderland quoted from his *Book of Psychology: Pathetism, Historical, Philosophical, Practical; Giving the Rationale of Every Possible Form of Nervous or Mental Phenomena Known under the Technics of Amulets, Charms, Enchantment, Spells, Fascination, Incantation, Magic, Mesmerism, Philters, Talisman, Relics, Witchcraft, Ecstacy, Hallucination, Spectres, Trance, Illusions, Apparitions, Clairvoyance, Somnambulism, Miracles, Sympathy, etc.: Showing How These Results May Be Induced, the Theory of Mind Which They Demonstrate, and the Benevolent Uses to Which This Knowledge Should Be Applied* (New York: Stearns, 1853), which is also available for viewing online through Google Books. Sunderland's comment about sympathetic communication is quoted in Richard Harte, *Hypnotism and the Doctors*, vol. 2 (New York: Fowler, 1903), 205.

Site #9: Andrew Jackson Davis's *Principles of Nature*

Quotations from Andrew Jackson Davis, *The Principles of Nature, Her Divine Revelations, and a Voice to Mankind* (Boston: Colby & Rich, Banner, 1847); George Bush, *Mesmer and Swedenborg; or, The Relation of the Developments of Mesmerism to the Doctrines and Disclosures of Swedenborg* (New York: J. Allen, 1847); and Sunderland, *Book of Psychology*.

Site #10: Morse's Magnetic Telegraph Company Office

Morse's declaration to Captain Pell is quoted in Alfred Vail, *The American Electro Magnetic Telegraph: With the Reports of Congress, and a Description of All Telegraphs Known, Employing Electricity or Galvanism* (Philadelphia: Lea and Blanchard, 1845), 153. The bird's-eye view of Trinity Church can be viewed at the Library of Congress's site: www.loc.gov/resource/cph.3a04367/.

Site #11: Barnum's Howard Hotel

My account of both the Fox sisters' appearance in New York and the Stratford poltergeist draws from Emma Hardinge Britten, *Modern American Spiritualism: A Twenty Years' Record of the Communion between Earth and the World of Spirits* (New York: published by the author, 1872).

Site #12: Brittan and Partridge Publishing Office

Quotations from Thomas Lake Harris, *An Epic of the Starry Heaven* (New York: Partridge and Brittan, 1854); Harris, *Song of Satan: A Series of Poems Originating with a Society of Infernal Spirits, and Received, during Temptation-Combats* (New York: New Church, 1858); and Harris, *Songs of Fairyland* (Fountain Grove, CA: published by the author, 1878). "Demagnetise" from Edwin Markham Papers, Wagner College.

Site #13: Clinton Hall

Quotations from Paschal Beverly Randolph, *The Unveiling; or, What I Think of Spiritualism [with] Medicinal Formulas* (Newburyport, MA: William H. Huse, 1860); and John Patrick Deveney, *Paschal Beverly Randolph: A Nineteenth-Century Black American Spiritualist, Rosicrucian, and Sex Magician* (Albany: SUNY Press, 1997). For a thorough biographical study, supplemented by many Randolph texts, see Deveney, *Paschal Beverly Randolph.*

Site #14: Bangs, Merwin and Co.

Quotations from Ethan Allen Hitchcock, *Fifty Years in Camp and Field*, ed. William Croffut (New York: G. P. Putnam's Sons, 1909); I. Bernard Cohen, "Ethan Allen Hitchcock, Soldier-Humanitarian-Scholar Discoverer of the 'True Subject' of the Hermetic Art," *Proceedings of the American Antiquarian Society*, April 1951, 29–136; and Hitchcock, *De Obfuscastionibus; or, A Glimmering Light on Mesmerism* (New York: Charles S. Francis, 1845).

Site # 15: Great Hall of Cooper Union

Quotations from John Tyndall, *Six Lectures on Light: Delivered in America in 1872–1873* (London: Longmans, Green, 1875); and "What Is Planchette?," *Scientific American* 19, no. 2 (July 8, 1868): 15–18.

The Planchette Mystery

Quotations from Samuel Wells, "The Planchette Mystery," *American Phrenological Journal* 49 (1869): 149–151; and Wells, *History of Salem Witchcraft* (New York: Samuel Wells, 1872). See Brandon Hodge's fantastic bit of material culture archaeology at "Kirby & Co.," Mysterious Planchette, accessed February 1, 2020, www.mysteriousplanchette.com.

Site #16: Oregon Wilson's Studio

George C. Bartlett quoted from his *The Salem Seer: Reminiscences of Charles H. Foster* (New York: United States Book Company, 1891), 113.

CHAPTER 4. OCCULT MANHATTAN

Site #1: Offices of the *Liberal Christian*

Quotations from *New York Times*, January 11, 1876, 4; and Rev. James Henry Wiggin, "Rosicrucianism in New York," *Liberal Christian*, September 4, 1875, 4.

Site #2: Apartment of Madame Blavatsky

See Henry Steel Olcott, *Old Diary Leaves: 1874–1878* (New York: Putnam, 1895).

Site #3: Apartment of Madame Blavatsky and Colonel Olcott

See Olcott, *Old Diary Leaves*, for accounts of John King with Blavatsky. Blavatsky quoted from *The Letters of H. P. Blavatsky*, vol. 1, *1861–1879* (Wheaton, IL: Quest Books, 2003), 309. K. Paul Johnson's *The Masters Revealed: Madame Blavatsky and the Myth of the Great White Lodge* (Albany: SUNY Press, 1994) is a superb, wide-ranging, and politically astute study of the "elusive teachers" of HPB. Recent research by Richard Cloud points toward the highest Rosicrucian adept as the identity of the original "John King" who inspired *Isis Unveiled*; see Cloud, "The Secret Rosicrucian Adept Alois Mailander," Rosicrucian Tradition, August 24, 2018, http://pansophers.com.

Site #4: Mott Memorial Hall

For Olcott's address, see *Theosophist* 28, no. 5 (1907): 321–327.

Site #5: Residence of Emma Britten

The original edition of the anonymous *Art Magic; or, Mundane, Sub-Mundane, and Super-Mundane Spiritism* (New York: published by the author, 1876) is difficult to find; an online version of a 1909 edition can be found at the Emma Hardinge Britten Archive online: www.ehbritten.org. Also see E. H. Britten's *Ghost Land: Researches into the Mysteries of Occultism* (New York: published for the author, 1876), which is available on Google Books. For the account of HPB's production of the spirit photograph of "Louis," see Olcott, *Old Diary Leaves*, 194–199. Mark Demarest's Emma Hardinge Britten Archive is online at www.ehbritten.org.

Site #6: The Lamasery

Blavatsky quoted from her "A Few Questions to 'Hiraf,'" *Spiritual Scientist* (1875): 217; "The Science of Magic," *Spiritual Scientist* (1875): 64; "Huxley and Slade," *Banner Light* 40 (1876): 11; "The Knout, as Wielded by the Great Russian Spiritualist," *Religio-Philosophical Journal* (1878): 1. Olcott's *Old Diary Leaves* and *People from the Other World* (New York: American, 1875) have great descriptions of the Lamasery. A number of websites have collected a wide range of HPB's articles; see, for example, "H.P. Blavatsky: Collected Writings Online," comp. Boris de Zirkoff, Katinka Hesselink's website, accessed February 1, 2020, www.katinkahesselink.net.

Site #7: J. W. Bouton Bookseller

Blavatsky quoted from *Letters of H. P. Blavatsky*, vol. 1, 290. See also Helena P. Blavatsky, *Isis Unveiled: A Master-Key to the Mysteries of Ancient and Modern Science and Theology* (New York: J. W. Bouton, 1877).

The Hidden Hand

See C. G. Harrison, *The Transcendental Universe: Six Lectures on Occult Science, Theosophy, and the Catholic Faith: Delivered before the Berean Society* (Great Barrington, MA: Steiner Books, 1993). Christopher Bamford's introduction is a tour de force, as is T. H. Meyer's afterword. Harrison's lectures themselves deserve repeated reading, bearing in mind these editorial caveats about the limits of his insider knowledge about the whole "Affair Blavatsky." See also Rudolf Steiner, *Spiritualism, Madame Blavatsky and Theosophy: An Eyewitness View of Occult History: Lectures* (Great Barrington, MA: Steiner Books, 2002). Again, Christopher Bamford's introduction is a treasure and provides helpful background for a deeper understanding of the "occult battle" still being waged.

Site #9: Offices of *The Path*

Thomas Burgoyne quoted from his *The Light of Egypt; or, The Science of the Soul and Stars* (London: George Redway, 1889), 121, 115. On the Hermetic Brotherhood of Luxor, see Joscelyn Godwin, *The Hermetic Brotherhood of Luxor: Initiatic and Historical Documents of an Order of Practical Occultism* (York, ME: Weiser Books, 1995); and also John Patrick Deveney, *Paschal Beverly Randolph: A Nineteenth-Century Black American Spiritualist, Rosicrucian, and Sex Magician* (Albany: SUNY Press, 1997). For the Hermetic Brotherhood of Luxor ad, see William Q. Judge, *The Path: A Magazine Devoted to the Brotherhood of Humanity, Theosophy in America, and the Study of Occult Science, Philosophy, and Aryan Literature*, August 1890.

The Columbian

The Columbian—the Columbia University yearbook—can be viewed online at "Yearbooks," Columbia University Archives, accessed February 1, 2020, http://library.columbia.edu. For a superb look at the ritual dimension of fraternal orders in America, see Mark Christopher Carnes, *Secret Ritual and Manhood in Victorian America* (New Haven, CT: Yale University Press, 1989).

Site #10: Heydenfeldt's Residence

Solomon Heydenfeldt Jr. quoted from his *The Unison of the Conscious Force* (New York: J. J. Little, 1891). Mike Jay's *The Air Loom Gang: The Strange and True Story of James Tilly Matthews and His Visionary Madness* (New York: Four Walls Eight Windows, 2003) is a perfect example of how an inadequate grasp of "magnetic influence"—that is, of magical manipulation of consciousness—can completely distort historical understanding. Absent this understanding, black and gray magical use of similar techniques can—and does—continue to go on undetected.

Site #12: Residence of "Father" Thomas Lake Harris

Harris's architectural blueprints for the New York City Fountaingrove are in the Edwin Markham Papers at Wagner College; there is in the collection a brief newspaper article by Gaye LeBaron, in the *Press Democrat*, December 9, 1979, about the plans. Thomas Lake Harris quoted from his *Wisdom of the Adepts: Esoteric Science in Human History* (Fountaingrove, CA: privately printed, 1884). For a very thorough academic study of Harris's relationship with a prominent acolyte—the British author and adventurer Laurance Oliphant—see Herbert Wallace Schneider and George Lawton's *A Prophet and a Pilgrim: Being the Incredible History of Thomas Lake Harris and Laurence Oliphant; Their Sexual Mysticisms and Utopian Communities Amply Documented to Confound the Skeptic* (New York: Columbia University Press, 1942). Primary documents deposited by Schneider and Lawton are at Columbia University's Rare Book and Manuscript Library Collections.

Site #13: Astor Library
Carl Henry Andrew Bjerregaard quoted from his *The Great Mother: A Gospel of the Eternally-Feminine; Occult and Scientific Studies and Experiences in the Sacred and Secret Life* (New York: Inner Life, 1913), 201; and "The Elementals, the Elementary Spirits, and the Relationship between Them and Human Beings," reprinted in *Lectures on Mysticism and Nature Worship* (Chicago: M. R. Kent, 1897), 326.

Manhattan's First UFOs?
Marconi quoted in *New York Times*, September 27, 1909, 9. The descriptions from the Hudson-Fulton celebration are drawn from my *A Short Story of American Destiny: 1909–2009* (San Rafael, CA: Fortunatus, 2009). On the 1909 airship flap, see Alfred M. Goilin, "England Is No Longer an Island: The Phantom Airship Scare of 1909," *Albion: A Quarterly Journal Concerned with British Studies* 13, no. 1 (Spring 1981): 43–57. The last paragraph is an open invitation to all sky watchers to consider that these visitors are not "extraterrestrial" but *infraterrestrial*. For superb guidance along these lines, see Charles Upton, *Cracks in the Great Wall: UFOs and Traditional Metaphysics* (San Rafael, CA: Sophia Perennis, 2005); and Father Seraphim Rose, *Orthodoxy and the Religion of the Future* (Platina, CA: St. Herman of Alaska Brotherhood, 1975).

Site #14: Office of Publisher Henry Holt
Henry Holt quoted from his *On the Cosmic Relations*, 2 vols. (Boston: Houghton Mifflin, 1914).

Site #15: Carnegie Hall
The site description here is drawn from my *Across the Great Border Fault: The Naturalist Myth in America* (New Brunswick, NJ: Rutgers University Press, 2000); and Robert Powell and Kevin Dann, *The Astrological Revolution: Unveiling the Science of the Stars as a Science of Reincarnation and Karma* (Great Barrington, MA: Steiner Books, 2010). Also see Rudolf Steiner, *The Inner Nature of Man: And Our Life between Death and Rebirth* (London: Rudolf Steiner Press, 2013). Rudolf Steiner's teachings constitute a modern "path of the Grail"—both an inner path of self-development and an outer path of investigation and cooperation with the beings of

nature. As such, they offer the safest and most reliable avenue across the threshold of the physical world, *in place of magic.*

CHAPTER 5. FORTEAN MANHATTAN

Fort to *New York Times* quoted in Jim Steinmeyer, *Charles Fort: The Man Who Invented the Supernatural* (New York: Penguin, 2008), 210.

Site #1: Egyptian Hall

See *Magic, Unity, Might* 9, no. 12 (May 1920): 80.

Site #2: Broadway across from City Hall

See the *New York Times* articles "Einstein Explains His New Discoveries," February 3, 1921; and "Einstein Sure He Is Right," April 4, 1922.

Site #3: American Museum of Natural History

Quotations from Charles Benedict Davenport, *Report of the Second International Congress of Eugenics, American Museum of Natural History, New York, September 1 to 28, 1921: Membership, Organization, General Program and Business Proceedings* (New York: Williams and Wilkins, 1923); and Henry Fairfield Osborn, *Men of the Old Stone Age, Their Environment, Life and Art* (New York: Charles Scribner's Sons, 1915), 360. See chapter 4 of my *Across the Great Border Fault: The Naturalist Myth in America* (New Brunswick, NJ: Rutgers University Press, 2000). Though I refrain from extensive commentary here, I consider eugenics to be a form of black magic, since it willfully invades a realm of Nature that belongs to much higher beings, without the proper knowledge or moral development to do so at this time.

Site #4: Hugo Gernsback

See Frank Paul, "10,000 Years Hence," *Science and Invention*, February 1922. A wonderfully rich set of Gernsback's publications can be found at the University of Minnesota's "Perversity of Things" online archive at https://manifold.umn.edu.

Manhattan as Site of Magical Destruction

For Hugo Gernsback's full story, see his *The Perversity of Things: Hugo Gernsback on Media, Tinkering, and Scientifiction*, ed. Grant Wythoff (Minneapolis: University of Minnesota Press, 2016).

Site #5: New York Public Library

Charles Fort quoted from *New Lands* (New York: Boni and Liveright, 1923); and *Lo!* (New York: Claude Kendall, 1931). For a wonderful biographical study of Fort, see Steinmeyer, *Charles Fort*; and for a Fortean-style study of Fort, see Colin Bennett, *Politics of the Imagination: The Life, Work and Ideas of Charles Fort* (New York: Cosimo, 2009). In the notes for "Manhattan's First UFOs" in chapter 4, I suggested as helpful resources the work of Charles Upton and Father Seraphim Rose; these are also helpful in solving the mystery of "disappearances," such as the ones that drew Fort's attention. Rachel Aviv narrates a modern example in "How a Young Woman Lost Her Identity," *New Yorker*, April 2, 2018. Considered in light of the ability of elemental beings to invade our psychic and soul world, such mysteries become understood as another form of "magical" episode, in the sense that the human being is crossing the threshold into the subsensible (and sometimes supersensible) world, accompanied—or, more often, possessed—by elemental beings.

Site #6: Manly Palmer Hall at New York Public Library

See Manly Palmer Hall, *The Secret Teachings of All Ages: An Encyclopedic Outline of Masonic, Hermetic, Qabbalistic, and Rosicrucian Symbolical Philosophy: Being an Interpretation of the Secret Teachings Concealed within the Rituals, Allegeries, and Mysteries of All Ages* (Los Angeles: Philosophical Research Society, 1928).

Site #7: Bruce Barton

Quotations from Richard Fried, *The Man Everybody Knew: Bruce Barton and the Making of Modern America* (New York: Ivan Dee, 2005); and James Rorty, *Our Master's Voice: Advertising* (New York: John Day, 1934). See also Bruce Barton, *The Man Who Nobody Knows: A Discovery of the Real Jesus* (New York: Bobbs-Merrill, 1925);

Site #8: H. P. Lovecraft's Night-Gaunts

H. P. Lovecraft, "Night-Gaunts," *Providence Journal* 102, no. 73 (March 26, 1930); Lovecraft, "Beyond the Wall of Sleep," *Pine Cones* 1, no. 6 (October 1919); Lovecraft, "Shadow Out of Time," *Astounding Stories*, June 1936; Lovecraft, "The Shunned House," *Weird Tales* 30, no. 4 (1937); Lovecraft, "He," *Weird Tales* 8, no. 3 (September 1926). Christopher Knowles's Alice Bailey–as–Chtulhu mythos-inspirer notion and his studies of the connections between superheroes and magic, occultism, and the supernatural can be found in his *Our Gods Wear Spandex: The Secret History of Comic Book Heroes* (York, ME: Weiser, 2007). Erick Davis, in his essay "Calling Chtulhu: H. P. Lovecraft's Magical Realism," *Erik Davis' Figments*, accessed February 1, 2020, www.levity.com, says that Lovecraft used a variety of magical techniques—entheogens, glossolalia, shamanic drumming—in his life and work, but it seems that his own preferred magical technique was late-night walking.

Lovecraft's letters quoted from his *Selected Letters*, vol. 1 (Sauk City, WI: Arkham House, 1965), 115; and *Selected Letters*, vol. 3 (Sauk City, WI: Arkham House, 1971), 243.

It is either symptomatic or just plain Lovecraftian or Fortean that the Trine Day publisher Peter Levenda—a member of the Chelsea Magickal Childe bookshop circle in the 1970s who cooked up the *Necronomicon*—should be a major contemporary researcher and inspirer of research at the intersection of conspiracy theory, occult politics, and magic. For more on this chapter of late twentieth-century American "magical" history—one that I completely omit from *Enchanted New York*, despite Manhattan's seminal role in it—see Daniel Harms and John Wisdom

Gonce, *Necronomicon Files: The Truth behind Lovecraft's Legend* (York, ME: Weiser Books, 2003). A short review of this same microhistory is "The Doom That Came to Chelsea," Straus Media, November 11, 2014, www.nypress.com. Peter Levenda's website is also a rich resource for both biographical and philosophical reflections on these themes and issues; see, for example, this farewell to occult book collector/seller Donald Weiser: Levenda, "Donald Weiser," *Peter Levenda's Journal* (blog), April 13, 2017, http://peterlevenda.com. A perennial pitfall of magically based communities is something that I call "symbolic overdrive"—the tendency to overinterpret the world as a place of *gnomons*—signs, symbols, and arcana. Although the adept magical practitioner can effect transformations through sensitivity to and manipulation of symbols and images, there is always a risk of draining magical potency—and, even worse, the creation of "eighth sphere"–type falsehoods—by the twin errors of the "minimization of mystery" (collapsing or confusing categories of meaning) and "multiplication of mystery" (generating a thicket of partial truths that obscure the transcendent or metahistorical meaning of events). Surrealism—and all "art magic" endeavors—was plagued by these errors; one can see a host of modern "art magicians" (Allen Ginsberg, Ken Kesey, Timothy Leary, Terence McKenna, Jose Arguelles, William Irwin Thompson, Daniel Pinchbeck) as bound by the same limitations.

Site #9: Elks Club

New York Times quoted from the Drama section, February, 15, 1925, 5. Lynn Thorndike quoted from his *A History of Magic and Experimental Science during the First Thirteen Centuries of Our Era* (New York: Columbia University Press, 1923), 7:590, 2:974. See also Carl Murchison, ed., *The Case for and against Psychical Belief* (Worcester, MA: Clark University, 1927); Harry Houdini, *A Magician among the Spirits* (New York: Arno, 1924); Montague Summers, *The History of Witchcraft and Demonology* (London: Kegan, Paul, Trubner, 1926); Arthur Conan Doyle, *A History of Spiritualism*, vol. 1 (London: Cassell, 1926); Doyle, *Pheneas Speaks: Direct Communications in the Family Circle* (London: Psychic Press and Bookshop, 1927); Lynn Thorndike, *Science and Thought in the Fifteenth Century: Studies in the History of Medicine and Surgery, Natural and Mathematical Science, Philosophy and Politics* (New York: Columbia University Press, 1929). A complete and compelling account of both the conflict between Conan Doyle and Houdini and Houdini's demise can be found in William Kalush and Larry Sloman, *The Secret Life of Houdini: The Making of America's First Superhero* (New York: Atria Books, 2006). Though there is a vast contemporary literature in science studies, no critical study has yet been made of Lynn Thorndike's life and work. For a marvelous portrait of the sacralization of select modern scientific projects, see Lisa Sideris, *Consecrating Science: Wonder, Knowledge, and the Natural World* (Berkeley: University of California Press, 2017).

CHAPTER 6. APOCALYPTIC MANHATTAN

Site #1: Headquarters of the Anthroposophical Society

This essay again draws on my *Across the Great Border Fault: The Naturalist Myth in America* (New Brunswick, NJ: Rutgers University Press, 2000) and also my essay "The Rhythms of Spiritual Research at Threefold Farm," *Catalog of the 2010 Threefold Educational Center's Symposium on Anthroposophical Research*, 2010. On the Christ rhythm, see Robert Powell and Kevin Dann, *Christ and the Maya Calendar: 2012 and the Coming of the Antichrist* (Great Barrington, MA: Steiner Books, 2009); and my essays "Contemplating America's Camelot at Fifty: The JFK Years and the Christ Rhythm," in *Journal for Star Wisdom 2013* (Great Barrington, MA: Lindisfarne, 2012); and "Henry David Thoreau and the Christ Rhythm," in *Journal for Star Wisdom 2011* (Great Barrington, MA: Lindisfarne, 2010). (Both are available at my website: www.drdann.com.) For Rudolf Steiner's teachings on the reappearance of Christ in the etheric realm, see his *The Reappearance of Christ in the Etheric* (Great Barrington, MA: Steiner Books, 2003); and also a superb recent essay by Paul Levy, "The Greatest Spiritual Event of Our Time," *Stillness in the Storm*, April 18, 2018, https://stillnessinthestorm.com. On technology and Rosicrucianism, see Paul Eugen Schiller, *The Schiller File: Supplements to the Collected Works of Rudolf Steiner* (Great Barrington, MA: Steiner Books, 2010); and Ehrenfried Pfeiffer, *The Chymical Wedding of Christian Rosenkreutz: A Commentary* (Spring Valley, NY: Mercury, 1984).

Site #2: Salmon Tower Building

Bailey/DK quoted from *A Treatise on White Magic; or, The Way of the Disciple* (1934); *Externalization of the Hierarchy* (1957); *The Next Three Years (1934–1935–1936)* (1934); *Esoteric Psychology*, vol. 1 (1936); and *Education in the New Age* (1954). Almost all of Bailey's channeled texts can be found online; see "The Books of Alice Bailey," Lucis Trust, accessed February 1, 2020, www.lucistrust.org. Sergei O. Prokofieff's *The East in the Light of the West: Two Eastern Streams of the Twentieth Century in the Light of Christian Esotericism: Part II: The Teachings of Alice Bailey in the Light of Christian Esotericism* (London: Temple Lodge, 1993) is both a thorough analysis of Bailey's work and a superb metahistorical narrative of its relationship both to the Roerich's Agni Yoga and to Blavatsky's later inspirers. The last paragraph of this site description points in a direction that *Enchanted New York* perhaps surprisingly leaves completely unexplored: the 1960s "Occult Revival." Other authors have (though again, almost all without a spiritual scientific perspective) exhaustively described this terrain: Gary Lachman's *Turn Off Your Mind: The Mystic Sixties and the Dark Side of the Age of Aquarius* (New York: Disinformation Co., 2001) and *Aleister Crowley: Magick, Rock and Roll, and the Wickedest Man in the World* (New York: Penguin, 2014); Chas Clifton, *Her Hidden Children: The Rise of Wicca and Paganism in America* (Walnut Creek, CA: Rowman Altamira, 2006). Richard Leviton's *The Imagination of Pentecost: Rudolf Steiner and Contemporary*

Spirituality (Great Barrington, MA: Steiner Books, 1994) touches on some of this history and is especially useful because Leviton both writes out of personal experience with some of these "magical" currents and is able to see them objectively from a spiritual scientific perspective.

Site #3: The Master Building

Corbett quoted from *New Yorker*, April 11, 1936, 11. Roerich quoted from his *Fiery World: Book 2* (New York: Agni Yoga Society, 1934), 251; diary entry quoted in Alexandre Andreyev, *The Myth of the Masters Revealed: The Occult Lives of Nikolai and Elena Roerich* (Leiden: Brill, 2014), 124. A comprehensive collection of both published writings and archival documents (and also Nicholas Roerich's paintings) can be found online at Nicholas Roerich Museum, "Museum's Archive," accessed February 1, 2020, www.roerich.org. For superb spiritual contextualization of the Roerichs, see Sergei O. Prokofieff, *The East in the Light of the West: Two Eastern Streams of the Twentieth Century in the Light of Christian Esotericism*, part 1, *Agni Yoga* (London: Temple Lodge, 1993); and Andreyev, *Myth of the Masters*.

Site #4: New Amsterdam Theater

Walter Gibson's remark about *The Shadow* is quoted in Axel Nissen's *Agnes Moorehead on Radio, Stage and Television* (Jefferson City, NC: McFarland, 2017), 7. The "Death House Rescue" episode can be heard at "Orson Welles in The Shadow—Death House Rescue—Sept. 26, 1937," *Heirloom Radio*, Player FM, 2017, https://player.fm. Martin Grams's *The Shadow: The History and Mystery of the Radio Program, 1930–1954* (Churchville, MD: OTR, 2011) and Thomas J. Shimeld's *Walter B. Gibson and The Shadow* (Jefferson, NC: McFarland, 2005) flesh out in full the nexus of cultural currents that made this radio show so popular.

Site #5: Offices of Detective Comics

From an esoteric/magical perspective, imaginary characters from literature, film, and other media are more than strictly *imaginary*; they actually are living beings in the spiritual world. Called by some esoteric traditions *egregores* (Greek for "watcher"), they have a powerful hold upon culture from generation to generation. See *Meditations on the Tarot: A Journey into Christian Hermeticism* (New York: Penguin, 2005), 405–407; and Daniel Andreev, *The Rose of the World* (Great Barrington, MA: Steiner Books, 1997). These two books are perhaps more important for any contemporary investigation into magic, esotericism, and the apocalyptic aspects of "the New Age" than any other source. On superheroes and modern disenchantment, see Jeffrey Kripal, *Mutants and Mystics: Science Fiction, Superhero Comics, and the Paranormal* (Chicago: University of Chicago Press: 2011).

Site #6: Childhood Home of J. Robert Oppenheimer

Kai Bird and Martin J. Sherwin quoted from their *American Prometheus: The Triumph and Tragedy of J. Robert Oppenheimer* (New York: Doubleday, 2007), 15.

"Straight" accountings of the local historico-geographic imprint left by the Manhattan Project can be found in Cynthia C. Kelly and Robert S. Norris, *A Guide to the Manhattan Project in Manhattan* (New York: Atomic Heritage Foundation, 2012); and Catherine Falzone, "The Manhattan Project," Nuclear New York (New York University's Archives and Public History MA program), accessed February 1, 2020, https://sites.google.com. For a wild window into the esoteric aspects of Hiroshima and the bomb, see Bradford Riley's "Fukushima Dai-ichi and the Karma of Japan," *Rileybrad's Blog*, April 26, 2011, https://rileybrad.wordpress.com.

Site #7: Beaux Arts Studios Building

Wedeck quoted from *New York Times Book Review*, May 23, 1948, 19. Maya Deren's films can be seen on YouTube and a number of other sites; for *Ritual in Transfigured Time*, see hada benedito, "Maya Deren—Ritual in Transfigured Time," YouTube, July 20, 2011, www.youtube.com/watch?v=0IG5K65gkTU. There is a vast literature on Surrealism, a smaller subset of which investigates the magical impulses of the movement and an even smaller section that focuses on New York City's Surrealist era. See Judith Noble's "Clear Dreaming: Maya Deren, Surrealism and Magic," Grazina Subelyte's "Kurt Seligmann, Surrealism, and the Occult," and Daniel Zamani's "Melusina Triumphant: Matriarchy and the Politics of Anti-Fascist Mythmaking in André Breton's *Arcane 17* (1945)," all in *Surrealism, Occultism and Politics: In Search of the Marvellous*, ed. Tessel M. Bauduin, Victoria Ferentinou, and Daniel Zamani (New York: Routledge, 2018); and the chapter "Possessed by Rhythm," in Jamie James's *The Glamour of Strangeness: Artists and the Last Age of the Exotic* (New York: Farrar, Straus and Giroux, 2017). Cornell's Johnson Museum of Art mounted a wonderful *Surrealism and Magic* exhibition in 2014; the superb online catalogue is at Cornell University Library, "Surrealism and Magic," accessed February 1, 2020, http://rmc.library.cornell.edu.

Site #8: Bell Laboratories Building

Quotations from *New York Times*, June 30, 1948; *New York Times*, July 1, 1948, 46; and Claude Shannon, "A Mathematical Theory of Communication," *Bell System Technical Journal*, July–October 1948. The New-York Historical Society's 2016 exhibition *Silicon City: Computer History Made in New York* was a comprehensive exploration of the New York City roots of the digital age; see New-York Historical Society, "Exhibitions: Silicon City: Computer History Made in New York," accessed February 1, 2020, www.nyhistory.org.

CHAPTER 7. SINISTER MANHATTAN

René Guénon quoted from his *The Reign of Quantity and the Signs of the Times* (London: Luzac, 1953), 118.

Site #1: Residence of Eileen Garrett

Hereward Carrington quoted from his *The Case for Psychic Survival* (New York: Citadel, 1957), 30. See also Eileen J. Garrett, *Many Voices: The Autobiography of a Medium* (New York: Putnam, 1968). Glimpses of Garrett's paranormal salon occur in Brion Gysin, *Back in No Time: The Brion Gysin Reader* (Middletown, CT: Wesleyan University Press, 2015); and Howard Pollack, *The Ballad of John Latouche: An American Lyricist's Life and Work* (Oxford: Oxford University Press, 2017).

Site #2: Statler Hotel

Peter Levenda's *Sinister Forces—The Nine: A Grimoire of American Political Witchcraft* (Walterville, OR: Trine Day, 2011) provides superb context for the Olson murder and the intrigues of MK-ULTRA. In *A Terrible Mistake: The Murder of Frank Olson and the CIA's Secret Cold War Experiments* (Walterville, OR: Trine Day, 2009), H. P. Albarelli patiently peels away the decades of deception to narrate the details of Frank Olson's murder; he identifies Pierre Lafitte and Francois Spirito as the CIA's hired executioners. Stephen Kinzer's recent biography, *Sidney Gottlieb, Poisoner in Chief: Sidney Gottlieb and the CIA Search for Mind Control* (New York: Holt, 2019), fails to name the killers.

Site # 3: The WOR Building

Gleason quoted in Donald Bain, *Long John Nebel: Radio Talk King, Master Salesman, Magnificent Charlatan* (New York: Macmillan, 1974), 1. See also Bain, *The Control of Candy Jones* (Chicago: Playboy Press, 1976). The 1957 recording is available at tomwsmf, "The Long John Nebel Collection," Internet Archive, accessed February 1, 2020, https://archive.org.

Site #4: CBS Broadcast Center

Walter Cronkite's *CBS Reports* documentary can be viewed at weirdlectures, "UFO: Friend, Foe or Fantasy 'CBS Reports' (1966)," YouTube, February 14, 2016, www.youtube.com/watch?v=yqLCNmaHEww.

Site #5: Residence of John Keel

John Keel quoted from his *UFOs: Operation Trojan Horse* (New York: Putnam, 1970). The book tells the story of the events leading up to the Silver Bridge collapse, along with offering his "ultraterrestrial" hypothesis for the first time. A wealth of primary documents—including the letters quoted in this site description—relating to the 1966–1967 events can be found at the *John Keel: Not an Authority on Anything* blog, accessed February 2, 2020, www.johnkeel.com.

Site #6: Offices of the American Society for Psychical Research

Quotation from Paul Smith, *Reading the Enemy's Mind: Inside Star Gate: America's Psychic Espionage Program* (New York: Macmillan, 2005), 56. Ingo Swann's autobiography, *Remote Viewing: The Real Story: An Autobiographical Memoir* (New York:

American Prophecy Project, 1996), is available online at https://img1.wsimg.com. The *Advance!* interview, "A Scientology OT in Action in the World: An Interview with Ingo Swann," *Advance!* 21 (October–November 1973), is online at *The Wise Old Goat* (personal website of Michel Snoeck), accessed February 1, 2020, www.wiseold-goat.com. In this interview, Swann states, "My greatest win on the OT Levels I think was the ability to separate myself with great conviction from matter, energy, space and time. To have gained the ability to hold my viewpoint without quivering. To have gained the ability to be appreciative of the need for an ethical, philosophic philosophy and to want to help produce towards its fullest use. And to have the great pleasure of being at home in the universe, in which I used to be very uncomfortable. I would like, of course, to express my appreciation to L. Ron Hubbard for making all this possible." See also Harry L. Snyder and Arlene G. Snyder, "Summary and Critical Evaluation of Research in Remote Viewing," June 1979, accessed February 1, 2020, www.cia.gov; Hugh Urban, "The Occult Roots of Scientology? L. Ron Hubbard, Aleister Crowley, and the Origins of a Controversial New Religion," in *Aleister Crowley and Western Esotericism*, ed. Henrik Bogdan and Martin P. Starr (Oxford: Oxford University Press, 2012); and Hugh B. Urban, *The Church of Scientology: A History of a New Religion* (Princeton, NJ: Princeton University Press, 2011).

Site # 7: The Beresford

Helen Schucman quoted from the most recent edition of her *A Course in Miracles: Text, Workbook for Students, Manual for Teachers* (New York: Ixia, 2019). Father Groeschel's experience with Helen Schucman is told in Randall Sullivan's *The Miracle Detective: An Investigation of Holy Visions* (New York: Atlantic Monthly Press, 2004), 430. Superb historical context and analysis for both the *ACIM* story and many other American mediumistic productions can be found in Cathy Gutierrez, ed., *Handbook of Spiritualism and Channeling* (Leiden: Brill, 2015). Ann Taves's *Revelatory Events: Three Case Studies of the Emergence of New Spiritual Paths* (Princeton, NJ: Princeton University Press, 2016) examines the *ACIM* in a comparative context (including Joseph Smith's *Book of Mormon*). For a detailed metaphysical critique of *A Course in Miracles*, see Charles Upton's *The System of Antichrist: Truth and Falsehood in Postmodernism and the New Age* (San Rafael, CA: Sophia Perennis, 2005). Upton's *Vectors of the Counter-Initiation: The Course and Destiny of Inverted Spirituality* (San Rafael, CA: Sophia Perennis, 2012) is virtually the only other work of which I am aware that widely treats the topics and events of this chapter as episodes of magic, interpreted within a Guénonian historical and meta-historical analysis.

Upton's assessment includes a summary statement that can perhaps serve as explanation why *Enchanted New York*'s chronicle ends around 1980 rather than carrying forward to the present: "Whether as Neo-Paganism, as the drive to develop psychic powers according to the New Age model, as the attraction to shamanism, or as the infinitely darker attraction to Satanic practices, magic had effectively replaced enlightenment as the dominant paradigm of the world of alternative spiritualities by the beginning of the 1980s" (*System of Antichrist*, 123).

CONCLUSION

Loren Eiseley quoted from his *The Immense Journey* (New York: Vintage, 1946), 15. Saint Guilhem (755–812) is both the subject of Wolfram von Eschenbach's *Willehalm* and the *source*—as the one called "Kyot"—of Wolfram's *Parzival*. Extraordinary new revelations—both historical and prophetic—about Kyot and other members of the Grail family are given in two works by Estelle Isaacson: *The Grail Bearer: Tellings from the Ever Primal Story: Through the Eyes of Repanse de Schoye*, ed. James R. Wetmore (Peterborough, NH: Logosophia, 2016); and *The Younger Kyot: Tellings of Mages and Maidens: Shimmering through the Grail Land of Grace*, ed. James R. Wetmore (Peterborough, NH: Logosophia, 2017). In 1995, the Cloisters staff member Daniel Kletke published his identification of the Saint Guilhem sculpture in "A New Reading of a Pilaster Capital from St.-Guilhem-le-Désert at the Cloisters," *Metropolitan Museum Journal* 30 (1995): 19–28. The full repository of photographs and field notes for James Reuel Smith's *Springs and Wells of Manhattan and the Bronx, New York City, at the End of the Nineteenth Century* (New York: New-York Historical Society, 1938) are housed at the New-York Historical Society; the photographs can be viewed at the society's website: http://digitalcollections.nyhistory.org. Smith's remarks on the Isham Spring are in his manuscript notes accompanying the photographs. His study of ancient Greek riparia is *Springs and Wells in Greek and Roman Literature: Their Legends and Locations* (New York: G. P. Putnam, 1922).

INDEX

ABOUT THE AUTHOR

Author of a dozen books, including *Expect Great Things: The Life and Search of Henry David Thoreau*, the historian and naturalist Kevin Dann is Director of the Embryonic Arcade. He received his PhD in American environmental history from Rutgers University and has taught at Rutgers, the University of Vermont, and State University of New York.